Advance Praise for *Systemic Collapse and Renewal*

"Gregory Tanaka's piercingly personal account of the slow burn of racism, coupled with his incisive analysis of how greed has choked American democracy, renders his book as timely as it is heartbreaking. Yet Tanaka also manages to inspire with his deep conviction that out of the wreckage a new kind of collective human spirit—a true democracy of the people—might arise. A gorgeous blend of autobiographical reflection and sociopolitical critique."

Mari Ruti, Distinguished Professor of Critical Theory and
Gender and Sexuality Studies, University of Toronto

"Gregory Tanaka's moving and illuminative text is equal parts memoir and analysis of the ethno-cultural predicament as it has evolved from his 1950s childhood to the present. It covers a wide range of experiences and tropes, yet all of them significantly American—business competition, baseball, public education, participatory democracy, the immigrant experience, and so on. In its most concerning moments, the book is, as Tanaka would say, 'an anthropology of collapse.' But then again, as it moves forward, it is also 'an anthropology of renewal.' I read in it promise. I read in it disappointment. I read in it possibility. This book feels like America. And I loved it."

Kevin Michael Foster, President of the Council on Anthropology and Education,
Founder of *Blackademics Television* on PBS TV,
and Associate Professor, The University of Texas at Austin

"In this remarkable book, Gregory Tanaka—education researcher, legal scholar, social scientist, and activist—traces the causes of democratic collapse to the loss of 'shared cultural meanings' whereby relentless individualism eclipses the values of mutuality and responsibility to community. Part autoethnography, part shared storytelling, and part cultural, historical, and economic analysis, this compelling narrative takes readers into the halls of corporate and academic power, interrogating the role of race and capital in the seizure of democracy, and asks 'what it means to be an American.' But Tanaka's narrative is more than a critique of democratic collapse—it is most importantly a humanizing proposal for democratic renewal through collective action and uplift. This is a highly accessible book for an interdisciplinary readership of scholars and educators. Even more, it is vital reading for emerging generations of change makers, and for policymakers and the diverse publics they serve."

Teresa L. McCarty, G.F. Kneller Chair in Education and Anthropology and
Faculty in American Indian Studies, University of California, Los Angeles

"Gregory Tanaka has written a powerful treatise that not only explains the causes and effects of the 2008 global financial crisis but also presents a thorough and convincing argument on why the United States—and its entire socio-economic-political system—must be drastically reformed now to avert extended systemic collapse. A must-read for bankers on Wall Street!"

Allen T. Cheng, Contributing Editor, Euromoney Institutional Investor PLC

Systemic Collapse and Renewal

This book is part of the Peter Lang Education list.
Every volume is peer reviewed and meets
the highest quality standards for content and production.

PETER LANG
New York • Bern • Berlin
Brussels • Vienna • Oxford • Warsaw

Gregory K. Tanaka

Systemic Collapse and Renewal

How Race and Capital Came to Destroy Meaning and Civility in America and Foreshadow the Coming Economic Depression

PETER LANG
New York • Bern • Berlin
Brussels • Vienna • Oxford • Warsaw

Library of Congress Cataloging-in-Publication Data

Names: Tanaka, Gregory Kazuo, editor.
Title: Systemic collapse and renewal: how race and capital came to destroy meaning and
civility in America and foreshadow the coming economic depression / Gregory K. Tanaka.
Description: New York: Peter Lang, 2018.
Includes bibliographical references and index.
Identifiers: LCCN 2018012792 | ISBN 978-1-4331-4740-1 (hardback: alk. paper)
ISBN 978-1-4331-4826-2 (paperback: alk. paper) | ISBN 978-1-4331-4745-6 (ebook pdf)
ISBN 978-1-4331-4746-3 (epub) | ISBN 978-1-4331-4747-0 (mobi)
Subjects: LCSH: United States—Race relations.
Racism—United States—History. | Capital—United States. | Courtesy—United States.
Classification: LCC E185.615.S97 2018 | DDC 305.800973—dc23
LC record available at https://lccn.loc.gov/2018012792
DOI 10.3726/b11627

Bibliographic information published by **Die Deutsche Nationalbibliothek.**
Die Deutsche Nationalbibliothek lists this publication in the "Deutsche
Nationalbibliografie"; detailed bibliographic data are available
on the Internet at http://dnb.d-nb.de/.

In Memory of Mom and Dad
who gave us joy, hope, and a belief in all that is good.

Figures and Tables

FIGURES

TABLES

Acknowledgments

Parts of Chapter 3 "Baseball and the Decline of Myth" appeared in *LA Weekly* March 31–April 6, 1995, under the title "The Myth of Baseball." Copyright Gregory K. Tanaka.

Chapter 4 "The End of Democracy as We Knew It" was published under the title "U.S. Education in a Post-9/11 World: The Deeper Implications of the Current Systemic Collapse of the Neoliberal Regime" in *Schooling and the Politics of Disaster*, edited by Kenneth J. Saltman (2007), Routledge, Taylor & Francis Group, New York, NY. Copyright Gregory K. Tanaka.

Chapter 5 "On Collapse and the Next U.S. Democracy" was published in *Anthropology & Education Quarterly* in December 2015, under the same title. Permission to reprint from *Anthropology & Education Quarterly*.

Foreword

PETER L. MCLAREN

Greg Tanaka is one of the country's last remaining decent men. Although he is acutely aware that we are teetering on the precipice of another crisis of capitalism that bodes ill for all of humanity, a crisis likely to be devastatingly worse than the last, he still believes in the power of goodness, human decency, and dignity. Having faced decades of racism and exclusion from his white compatriots, he manages to channel his anger and despair for the greater cause of political harmony and community. To Tanaka, the ichor of goodness circumfuses the globe, nourishing the human heart.

In no way does this mean he is naïve, as his new book presents a blistering critique of the world devastated by global capitalism and the complex restructuring needed to build a true democracy (where I differ from Tanaka is on the question of the extent to which democracy has ever existed in the United States). Tanaka is more than a fastidious dilettante when it comes to the topic of democracy, he is a true believer who wants to make the dream come true. It is his true belief in democracy that propels him forward in his powerful and extremely engaging narrative account of how to strive for a genuine democracy that will enable the United States, shamed and humbled by imperialist wars and austerity, to join the international community of nations, respected by all sectors.

To achieve those outcomes, he argues the people of the United States will need to learn something about human conduct—that it must be governed by the "shared meanings" of culture—where duties and obligations are passed on from one generation to the next, advising people how to treat each other with dignity, compassion, and respect. As it stands, the United States parades itself as a peacekeeper and guardian of human rights, not unlike a handsome peacock, when in fact, it is, and always has been, one of the world's greatest vultures, purveyors of violence and terror, preying on the dead flesh of its victims. John Pilger (2016) writes:

> This is the country where toddlers shoot their mothers and the police wage a murderous war against black Americans. This is the country that has attacked and sought to overthrow more than 50 governments, many of them democracies, and bombed from Asia to the Middle East, causing the deaths and dispossession of millions of people. No country can equal this systemic record of violence. Most of America's wars (almost all of them against defenseless countries) have been launched not by Republican presidents but by liberal Democrats: Truman, Kennedy, Johnson, Carter, Clinton, Obama. In 1947, a series of National Security Council directives described the paramount aim of American foreign policy as "a world substantially made over in [America's] own image." The ideology was messianic Americanism. We were all Americans. Or else. Heretics would be converted, subverted, bribed, smeared or crushed.

If this description seems extreme, we need to remember that Noam Chomsky (1990) has observed: "If the Nuremberg laws were applied, then every post-war American president would have been hanged." Not to be outdone, Sam Smith (cited in Blum, 2016) writes:

> We need a trial to judge all those who bear significant responsibility for the past century—the most murderous and ecologically destructive in human history. We could call it the war, air and fiscal crimes tribunal and we could put politicians and CEOs and major media owners in the dock with earphones like Eichmann and make them listen to the evidence of how they killed millions of people and almost murdered the planet and made most of us far more miserable than we needed to be. Of course, we wouldn't have time to go after them one by one. We'd have to lump Wall Street investment bankers in one trial, the Council on Foreign Relations in another, and any remaining Harvard Business School or Yale Law graduates in a third. We don't need this for retribution, only for edification. So there would be no capital punishment, but rather banishment to an overseas Nike factory with a vow of perpetual silence. (cited in Blum, 2016)

If we are to act on Smith's advice, we would have to banish Tanaka to an overseas Nike factory for graduating from Harvard with an MBA (note that Tanaka holds a BA, MAT, MBA, JD, and two Ph.D.s and has an impressive research and teaching career at illustrious U.S. universities). Yet Tanaka decided early in his career that his impressive skills would be used in the service of helping people, and not institutions. There are few scholars today that are more committed to a social justice agenda than Greg Tanaka. Tanaka writes with a clarity born of a firm connection to his past, a grounding in time and place, a passionate accessibility to ideas, and a resulting capacity to honor all struggles for justice that have marked our history as a nation and community. With that grounding also comes the confidence to treat others with civility and respect. The core set of values that Tanaka has used to forge his own life are precisely those that *delineate how we should treat each other as part of a larger democratic commons.*

This book is divided into two parts. The first chronicles Dr. Tanaka's journey through time, beginning with his childhood days in the late 1950s—when the United States was feeling its oats, every family could realistically hope to own a house free and clear of debt, and the democracy itself appeared to be in the ascendency forever. From there, his narrative takes us into the 1980s where, as a Harvard graduate, he gained appointment as acting law school dean and then acting president of a small bank. While troubling, under-the-surface issues of inequality and asymmetry continued to plague the nation in that era, it also seemed to Tanaka that matters like race and economic inequality could one day be confronted and resolved out of a commitment to fairness and decency.

But where there had existed a deep well of optimism in the 1970s and 1980s, by the 1990s the seeds had already been sewn for a continued dismantling of U.S. democracy and all the hope it had once contained. In the final chapters of Part I, Tanaka traces the manner in which racism—and a new "culture" of unbridled individualism with its voracious pursuit of capital—came to dominate the lives of Americans. Gone were time-honored duties about how to treat others with respect and gone was the sense of community underscored by the ethic of putting the needs of suffering of others before oneself. Gone also was the opportunity for the next generation of children to feel confident that they could achieve their own dreams. Was this history ever real or only a myth hallucinated out of previous myths, after ingesting poisoned apple pie?

Worse, it was by the late 1990s that the inner workings of the U.S. democracy itself had fallen terminally prey to this new "culture" of deceit and self-aggrandizement—and with that, all the progress achieved in 200 years of democratic history seemed to slip away in the blink of an eye. What happened during this time? And how had events as monumental as the theft of a democracy slipped by an unsuspecting and trusting American public? As Tanaka shows in Chapters 4 and 5, it was through the well-disguised and highly purposeful work of deeply funded think tanks—and the policies of a secret cabal of international bankers—that the legislative and executive functions of the U.S. democracy were silently hijacked and the corrective function of the U.S. judiciary branch eroded. A former judicial intern in the Office of the Chief Justice of the U.S. Supreme Court, it pains Tanaka to know that the cultural practice of democracy *and law* he had known in his life could be so effortlessly relinquished.

But if his own storytelling would be the vehicle by which he would reveal the stealing away of the democracy that had treated him so well in his life, it is through the exchange of storytelling *with others*—and their dreams about how to build a better world—that this democracy will once again be imagined and reclaimed. In Part II, Tanaka engages in a running dialogue with younger scholars about how the U.S. democracy might one day be revisioned—so that it truly becomes "by, for and of the people" and not just a set of dependent hierarchies servicing the interests of wealthy landowners, where there is room for everyone in the country to thrive, prosper, and grow. In place of today's false culture of selfishness, fear, and thievery, there is the promise once again of a healthy economy that supports all members of human society and gives all citizens a chance to better their own lives and the lives of their children. In place of the chimera of "quantitative easing," GMO foods, and manufactured disease, there is the bottom-up policymaking of a new democracy— direct democracy and participative democracy—that gives its own citizens a chance to generate ideas and take action together to protect the people.

Of course, the transnational capitalist class steered by international bankers and their military security interests will not go quietly into the night. We will not awake one day with the air made suddenly tremulous by a chorus of America the Beautiful playing on a cosmic church organ, with bankers in straw Boaters riding high-wheelers handing out free loans to all those attending the county fair. Very likely we will awaken not to the inspired effusion of generosity but to the stridulous sounds of teeth gnashing at the drumbeat of jackboots on their way to arrest another undocumented immigrant. The good news is that the riot, pandemonium, and fear they have been striving fiendishly to sew in the minds and hearts of a trusting public can now be countered by the broad, widespread, and aquifer-like effect of new ideas generated by the people themselves. Out of every community and hamlet, every urban intersection, and every suburb in America, there can be a wellspring of goodwill and creativity—and with that event, the politics of fear of the banker and hedge fund elites instantly turns ineffectual and small.

The many voices of Part II depict and demonstrate just how a percolation of ideas will occur—and how a democracy that is "by, for and of the people" is given birth. This time, the foundation for democracy will be made permanent in the reinstated and foundational cultural patterns, norms, and beliefs of the people. I readily admit that I do not share Tanaka's optimism about the global economy, since as a Marxist I do not believe the planet can survive without a socialist alternative to capitalism, yet at the same time I respect Tanaka's efforts. He and I make vigils at different shrines—mine for the fallen martyrs of socialism, his for the enduring soldiers of jurisprudence. For me, new emerging forms of revolutionary subjectivity emerging from the antagonisms to capitalism and the crisis of value—in the participation of students, professors, domestic workers, the unemployed, migrant workers, etc.—can make a difference in challenging the repressive forms of everyday capitalist life. For Tanaka, it is a culture of optimism, trust, and compassion that will lead the way. Truth be told, we need both.

What is most striking to me about this important new book by Tanaka is that his vision of democracy is artfully patterned in the very structure of the book itself, where the loss of culture that he feels is responsible for the decline of democracy shown to be superseded by the work of young scholars showing us exactly how meaning can be created and shared with an engaging public. The timing of this book couldn't be better: with more and more nations falling into the darkness of economic collapse, overwhelming starvation, and governmental failure, it is time we engage in possible solutions.

I highly recommend this book for use by colleges, universities, and high school programs whose teachers believe in the future of democracy.

REFERENCES

Blum, W. (2016, February 5). *The anti-empire report #143*. Retrieved from http://williamblum.org/aer/read/143

Chomsky, N. (1990). *If the Nuremburg laws were applied*. Retrieved from https://chomsky.info/1990/2

Pilger, J. (2016, March 20). A world war has begun. Break the silence. JohnPilger.com. Retrieved from http://johnpilger.com/articles/a-world-war-has-begun-break-the-silence.

PART I

Sources of Collapse

GREGORY K. TANAKA

The greatest crisis at hand remains the risk of systemic collapse.

John Williams (2017)[1]

---

1 Williams, J. (2017, January 8). *Special commentary, year-end, year-ahead economic review and preview.* Shadowstats.com

CHAPTER 1

After the Rage

It is what one remembers from the past and how one remembers it that determines how one sees the future.

Said (2000)

It was 4:15 in the morning and pitch dark. Upon entering the large fishbowl-shaped mountain on a little used government road, I could hear no sound. Steering my car on to a dirt lot, I parked it and descended to the clearing below. I was standing deep inside Hawaii's famous Diamond Head crater. My skin crawled at the eerie feeling. "Chicken skin," the locals called it. Goose bumps. Here I was, a red-blooded American living in an American city—and waiting for a secret Japanese "*dojo*" to open its doors.

I listened as others began to arrive. In the stillness I could hear them shuffling along a low wooden porch that ran the length of the building and rushed to join them. All were young businessmen and legislators, all here to be trained like modern day "*ninjas*." It gave me a feeling of power to be included, a promise of new things to come. But mixed in with these emotions was a small knot in my stomach, a foreboding about a kind of violence I could already sense.

I had just been granted the MBA holder's dream—the chance to run a company. The state's sixth largest bank, Asia Pacific Bank and Trust, had been founded three generations before by a prominent Japanese American and had 11 branches dotting the major Hawaiian Islands. I was to be its newest president. I recalled how quickly I had accepted the bank chairman's invitation to undergo martial arts training. After all, this *dojo* only took newcomers from an approved list of corporate and government sponsors. It was rumored the master teacher here, the *sensei*, had come to Hawai'i from Japan with a mysterious past. They say he had been hand-picked along with 29 other 12-year-olds in postwar Japan to live at a dojo at the Imperial Palace.

It was with tacit approval from General McArthur that this *dojo* had trained these adolescents in the philosophy and skills of military *zen*, a philosophy devoid of spirit but tailored to win. Unknown to McArthur, the boys were part of a 200-year plan to restore Japan to world power through economic control of a new "global" society. How Japanese, I thought, to plan for world domination at a time when they were climbing out of the rubble of defeat of World War II! And this dojo in Hawaii was to be one of the outposts for that project.

The lure of this "secret *dojo*"—and its untold meanings—had been irresistible.

* * *

But that was two months ago. Since my first day on the job, the rush to learn the structure and personalities of the banking business in Honolulu had been diz-zying. Understanding local ways had been the most difficult. Born and raised in California, I was a "*kotonk*." When I first came to Hawai'i, I heard the story of how Japanese Americans from "the mainland" were arrogant and always getting into fights with Hawaiian Japanese. Losing to the locals, the visitors would fall to the ground, their heads going "*kotonk, kotonk*" on the hard pavement. All I knew was that I was not instantly familiar with the culture of the place—that it would take some getting used to.

But now, as I began the hike up the steep interior slope of Diamond Head to return to my car, my body still trembling from the violence below, I knew it had been for the last time. I still recall how I felt the first time I entered this *dojo*. The novitiates had filed into a chamber that was even darker inside than outside. No one spoke and once inside, no one moved. Having left my slippers on the steps below the low front porch, I was barefoot. I could feel the coolness of the firm mat beneath my feet. Like the mats I used in tumbling class in junior high, I thought, searching for a way to orient myself.

After a long silence, I saw a tiny candle being lit along the far wall. I could now make out the vague outlines of 8 or 10 other figures moving to take their places in two rows facing each other. I hurried to join them. They sat cross-legged, their knees and lower legs resting on the mat and their rear-ends perched on large, square pillows that had been placed on the floor awaiting their arrival. I couldn't quite make it out, but the room appeared to be spacious, perhaps a hundred and twenty feet long and sixty feet wide.

It was then that I smelled the incense. Pungent and delicate, it drifted across the room. I was not sure where it had come from, perhaps from somewhere near the candle to my left. In the semidarkness I strained to see. Had the light come from an incense stick and not a candle? With that thought a faint shadow stirred and the incense, or candle, was snuffed out. I sat in total darkness, unsure of myself or what to do. In the stillness I could not be sure what the future would bring, the last remaining sensation the lingering smell of incense.

* * *

I broke from my recollections about the past several months and continued quickly up the winding path to leave this place. Why had I taken this risky job—where competition was vicious and backstabbing incidents in my own bank were on the rise? I recalled my earlier days at Harvard and knew the answer lay there. As an MBA student, I had felt the early sting of exclusion in that last bastion of capitalism—and whiteness. I remembered the deep pain when I learned in January that my professors had been treating elected student leaders to lunch once a month since September—and leaving me out. Quite innocently, one of the other student leaders asked me if I would finally be joining them since I had been elected to the highest position of Section Representative. I recalled the small pleasure I felt when one day I appeared for lunch—and watched with glee as shocked looks appeared on my professors' faces. Awkwardly, they rushed to receive me but could not hide their shame. I was not surprised when they decided after that day to end the lunch ritual altogether. Years later, the recollection of this experience still hurt. It was that rejection in New England that drove me to seek my "Japanese-ness" now.

* * *

I sensed a thick, shadowy figure moving slowly down the row of participants seated to my left. I stared down at a spot 18 inches in front of my knees, just as I had been instructed to do by a coworker the day before. I closed my eyes until they were slits—and awaited my turn. Soon enough I felt rough hands grabbing my hands brusquely and placing them one on top of the other with fingers curled into a hand-lock I never knew existed. Just when I thought I had passed the ordeal, I felt a sharp thrust into my lower back, forcing me to sit even more upright. Like some distant piano lesson in another life, I thought to myself without amusement.

The room had grown still, and long moments passed until a tiny, clear bell tinkled. My senses phosphoresced at this sound which seemed in the wet stillness unwilling to go away, unwilling to die. Another long moment passed and there was a loud clap, like two pieces of flat wood being slammed together. Several long seconds later, there was another clap, this one softer. And so it went. WHAP, whap. WHAP, whap. LOUD, soft. LOUD, soft. The claps grew softer until I realized I was hearing only the sound of my own breathing, which had adjusted long before to the rhythm of the wooden blocks. INHALE, exhale. INHALE, exhale.

When the clapping stopped, I seemed to know nothing. My mind had simply shut down. With no thoughts and no feelings, I drifted into a timeless void.

* * *

Continuing up the hill, I recalled another "Harvard experience." During the summer between MBA years, a classmate from the Philippines and I were taking a long walk near Wall Street. Noticing that my friend kept bumping into pedestrians who were walking toward us on the sidewalk, I asked what was up. My friend's response caught me by surprise. "They don't move over for me because I'm Asian. They all think I will move for them. But I tell you, I refuse to play their game anymore. So I walk straight ahead and now they have to move over for me. If they don't, I bump them." At six feet and well over two hundred pounds, my friend continued to smack into oncoming pedestrians, some of them much smaller women.

I now realized I had been caught between cultures all my life, not knowing whether I was White or Asian. I, too, smarted at the way some White men apparently expected me to move over for them on the sidewalk. And with my Japanese American upbringing, I was the one always moving over. Putting politeness first, I had been the fool.

I shivered that afternoon in New York when I fantasized that one day all people of color would collectively decide to walk straight down the sidewalk, making all Whites step aside for them! The image of hundreds of Whites getting bumped became surreal, like some Hieronymus Bosch landscape or the strewn carnage of an American "Guernica." Now in Hawai'i, many years later, I saw how this destruction might yet come to pass in a country confused by frenzied buying of condominiums and BMWs, rising immigration and feelings of American exceptionalism.

* * *

Suddenly the lights came on, bright florescent ones overhead, forcing me to squint from the harsh glare. The others were getting up and rushing to take their pillows into a far corner. Attempting to stand and bend down for my pillow, I immediately crumpled to my knees, wobbling from the pain of severe leg cramps. It seemed that much time had elapsed in the *za-zen* meditation, how much I did not know. I hurried to get up again, as I did not want to hold back the others. In the bright light, I noticed the thick, shadowy figure was gone.

Standing now at the center of the room was Kojiro, Vice Chairman of Asia Pacific—and my nemesis. Standing over six feet, Sanford Kojiro stood ramrod straight as he directed a haughty gaze about the room. Make no mistake about it, this was his class.

Kojiro began to lead the small group through calisthenics. Like in high school gym but not quite, I thought, still struggling to orient myself. I noticed the room was indeed large and elongated. The entire floor was matted. Along the far wall were several dozen *bo-ken*, or heavy wooden practice swords, mounted horizontally on four long racks. In the center of the far wall stood a small shrine, where I guessed the incense had been burned.

After calisthenics, Kojiro turned the group over to an assistant and motioned to me to follow. In the far corner, Kojiro showed me in a one-on-one session how to hold the *shinai*, a bamboo practice sword. It was almost like holding a baseball bat but with hands spread farther apart, I thought. In the ready position, I held the *shinai* with hands down low and the end of the sword pointed at the eyes of the enemy. I stood with right foot in front of left and slightly off to the side. My eyes were directed ahead in a steady gaze.

Forward, backward. Side, side. With each quick practice step, I conducted a full sword stroke. While striding, I lifted the *shinai* high above my head and pulled it down swiftly as if slicing an imaginary foe. In front of a full length mirror, I watched myself being transported in time and space to a medieval Japan. At this moment could I now be, finally, Japanese?

* * *

It was also at Harvard that I realized I had been pretending citizenship. An American by birth, I had always been denied a firm connection to place. This rang clear before my first day of class at "the B School" when I went to use a bathroom in Aldrich Hall. Standing at 5'6", I discovered the urinals were too high for me. Embarrassed, I looked out of the corners of my eyes to see if anyone would see me backing up to reach the target. My face burned, but it was inside me that I registered a shame I could not then comprehend, a "put down" to my identity as a man and a person. I had a sinking feeling of doubt about why I was even there in the first place.

* * *

Halfway through the practice session, Kojiro returned to take me into a corner for more one-on-one instruction. "Here, face the mirror. Remember, you must have no thoughts when you do a sword stroke. Four things, especially, must never appear in your mind. *Anger. Fear. Uncertainty. Arrogance.* Four things. Wipe them from your mind!"

Silly from the newness, I silently repeated those words for my amusement as Kojiro strode away. *Four things. Wipe them from your mind.* I smiled at the mock seriousness of the whole experience—but then noticed in the mirror that Kojiro was coming back one more time.

Kojiro had hesitated before returning to show me one more "advanced technique." Observing a small smirk on Kojiro's face, I heard his words.

> You won't be needing this 'til much later, but I'll show you anyway. Here, hold your *shinai* vertically, close to your chest like this. Then move with force into your opponent, shoving your hands into his sword and body. In this way you push back your opponent. It's defensive and it's good to use if you feel temporarily overwhelmed.

I was sure Kojiro was laughing at me as he turned and walked away.

As I continued my strokes in front of the mirror, I thought I detected a flickering movement out of the corner of my eye. I turned quickly to look at the corner window but saw nothing. Had a person been watching me? A wisp, a shadow? The fabled *sensei*?

* * *

As I continued my climb up the steep interior slope of Diamond Head, other memories of Harvard came flooding back. The first residential house mixer across the river had been a disaster. Going with my roommate's friend from Yale, I had been flattened. Every woman I approached had turned away from me. Some were haughty but most had simply shown fear in their eyes. *You're not white*, those eyes said. There were few people of color at the party. A lone moment of hope also turned illusory. A petite Asian woman came up and asked with a pretty smile and accent, "Are you Chinese?" Returning the smile, I shook my head and said, "No, I'm Japanese American," then watched as she, too, turned on her heels and walked away.

The feeling of hollow did not end at the mixer. Later that night my roommate's bouncy friend from Yale, an Italian American, announced that he had met the girl of his dreams and then asked me if as a Californian I had enjoyed the mixer's Beach Boys music. Already in a dulled state of misery, I felt the air go completely out of me. The mixer had stripped me of my identity not only as an American, but also as a Californian. Initially denied membership because of skin color, I now felt as if I had lost all connection to place—to California, to home.

Still other memories came rushing back. One incident had lasted just seconds. I had gathered with five other MBA students, all White males, to play pick-up basketball at the old Harvard gym. Formerly a captain of my high school C-basketball team in California, I felt I could now be in my element. But as we negotiated how to divide the group into fair teams, one student from Alabama halted the process and asked how we could play "with only five players." Confused, the rest of us counted again and saw six guys waiting to play, three against three. I recalled how the fellow repeated his words, this time staring hard at me. After a long moment of tension, a tall, strapping kid from Iowa stepped in and divided the group into two teams.

I remembered how relieved I was that the Iowan had defused the situation, and how disappointed I was in myself for not coming to my own defense. A familiar blaming mechanism had quickly kicked in that led me to blame myself for causing trouble for the others. While the American in me had registered a put-down to my ego, the Asian side was recording the full weight of shame brought to the group. A double dose. Forgotten until now, the memory had gone into my old, heavy bag of jangled, raw experiences that seethed there in a quiet rage, shielded from the public eye.

Later in the year I recalled being invited to attend a school-wide faculty meeting where, amazingly, I was to be introduced as the newly elected president of the B-School student government. I recalled coming into the large bowl-shaped classroom almost cringing from the accumulated power of 100 famous professors all gathered together in one place. There, to my further amazement, several men in dark suits were waving at me and calling out my name. The same professors who had barred me from coming to their unannounced, exclusive lunches—my own section professors—were now calling out to me to sit next to them! The nerve.

But the crowning blow came on a different day from the dean of the Business School himself. At a meeting of the MBA Policy Committee held to discuss admissions policies, there had been discussion about the inexplicably high number of applicants from India with GMAT scores in the 99th percentile. The committee decided the scores coming out of India must be rigged. The dean's words? "Let's put a stop to this. These sleezy Orientals can't even find their way to the front of Baker Library!"

Realizing that I, as the lone student representative to this committee and an Asian, had been sitting quietly in the group, the dean looked at me and quickly apologized. But the damage had already been done. Trying to save face for the dean, my own response had been just as shameful: "That's okay, we don't really count India as part of Asia anyway." I knew then the price of being at this place was too high; it strained my own sense of decency just to participate.

* * *

When class was over, the senior *kendo* practitioners asked me to join them for tea. Feeling honored, I exited the sliding *shoji* screen doors to encounter a brilliant sunshine—and a Japanese garden complete with manicured shrubbery. Having arrived earlier in darkness, I had not been able to see the garden, only a narrow pathway. Proceeding now along a long wooden walkway, I turned right just before the locker room and entered a small but neat dining area.

I had to smile. Along the length of the room ran a long, low table with people sitting on both sides and "cross-legged." Growing up in suburbs in southern California, I had not had occasion to sit Japanese-style except once at a trendy *teppan-yaki* restaurant. The quaint image of *kendo* practitioners sitting before a low table overwhelmed my sense of who I was—and I smiled again, partly out of embarrassment and partly from the momentary disorientation.

Quietly, I took the last available seat at the far end and turned to survey the room. A bay window ran the length of the wall facing out on to the long wooden porch outside. Anyone passing from the *dojo* sparring room to the locker room would have to walk past this dining area in plain view of all seated here. Outside in the distance, I saw a tall tower made of four long heavy poles in a Japanese village style. The whole place seemed like a different world, perhaps a distant memory long forgotten, partly illusion, partly real.

It was then that a soft but powerful voice drew my attention. There seated, at the far end and closest to the window, was a man I had never seen before. Thick and well-muscled, the man appeared to be in his fifties. His face was both intense and calm—a man of paradoxes it seemed. But there could be no doubt who he was. Feeling the pull of some long ago command, I realized this was the *sensei* and promptly cast my eyes down at my bowl of soup, listening politely.

"*Karate* is for thugs," this man was telling Kojiro. "So we don't do that here. And *Judo* is bland. We teach it here but it is a mish-mash of different styles and so it stands for nothing. *Judo* is okay if you want to be a middle manager. *Aikido*? *Aikido* is only for weak people. It is purely defensive and so it imparts no energy of its own." The thick, well-muscled man paused before continuing. "But *kendo*. Ah, *kendo* is different. *Kendo* is swift. Emotionless. Remorseless. *Kendo* teaches whole action, balance, flexibility, centeredness—all at once. In business *kendo* is the superior martial art. Look at the top bankers in Japan. They all practice *kendo*."

The room had grown silent. Even the colorless women who had been quietly serving fish, pickled vegetables, rice, and *miso* bean soup had stopped to listen. For a reason known only to myself, I suddenly felt my cheeks redden. Not three months before, at my final job interview for the bank president job, the chairman had asked me which martial art I liked best and I had quickly answered "*aikido*." Hearing the *sensei* announce publicly that *aikido* was for weak people, I wondered if the sensei's words were now being directed at me.

When breakfast was over, I felt invigorated. My body was clean and racing. It was 7:30 am and time to go to work. I wondered then about the words of the mysterious *sensei*, the man with a calm exterior and piercing eyes, a man rumored capable of reading people's auras. I also wondered if the *sensei* was thinking of me.

* * *

But if I learned at Harvard that I wasn't White, I also learned I wasn't Japanese. At least not one from Japan. That lesson came from a waiter at a Chinese restaurant located just off Harvard Square. I went there often to get away from the pressure and pretense of Harvard. One day the waiter asked me why I looked so downcast. To this I answered there was too much racism at Harvard, too much in Boston, too much in America. After listening politely to a few choice anecdotes, the waiter shrugged his shoulders and smiled: "Well, what are you going to do, go back to Japan? You're not even from there. You have to go on. *You have to go on.*"

I smiled and my step became lighter as I recalled one last Harvard experience. It was after his last exam and I was walking down the sidewalk toward Kresge Hall sharing a feeling of relief with a classmate from Japan. The fellow was very brilliant—and very Japanese. Suddenly, the student pushed off my shoulder and ran directly at a tree. Fearing for my friend, I stopped in my tracks and watched in horror as the Japanese classmate screamed and literally ran up the tree, his momentum carrying him far up the trunk. Landing back on earth with a light plop, the "Japan" Japanese flashed a crazed smile and looked at me with wide, electric eyes. Only a Japanese, I thought as I looked around in embarrassment. Only a Japanese.

* * *

Halfway up the slope now, I stopped and shook my head gently. I recalled how unnerved I had been by my second visit to the *dojo*. I should have known then, I thought.

After *za-zen* breathing and warm-up exercises, the beginners spent the next hour running and hopping down the length of the hall. On each lap, Kojiro admonished the group for one failure or another. Nothing it seemed was good enough for him. Go again! Do it right this time!

Kojiro then ordered everyone to grab a heavy wooden *bo-ken* and form a long line facing the wall. High overhead, then down. High, then down. After ten minutes my arms felt like lead. Dropping my *bo-ken* to the floor by mistake, I was verbally assailed by Kojiro who seemed to revel at each opportunity to diminish me before the eyes of the others: "Go to the front of the class. We were finished but since you were clumsy, we will all practice a little longer! You will lead because you made the mistake. Always honor your sword. Never, never drop it!"

Later, exhausted and dripping with sweat, I followed the others out the front door after class had ended. Unthinking, my body numb, I reached down to the steps and put on my slippers. Walking past the bay window, I continued to the men's locker room where I entered and took off my drenched t-shirt. There my thoughts were broken by someone yelling to me, "Hey, what are you doing! Never, *never* wear your slippers on the deck. Go back and put your slippers on the steps!"

Out I ran, past the big bay window and toward the front steps. But before I could reach the steps, someone else yelled, "Hey you, what are you doing! Get back inside and put your t-shirt on. Never, *never* go outside the *dojo* without a shirt on!"

Confused, humiliated, and bowed, I ran back down the walkway to the locker room to put on my wet t-shirt. Once my t-shirt was on, I went out one more time to the walkway and put the slippers by the front steps. Finished at last, I started again toward the locker room.

That was when I noticed the eyes of all the people in the dining room. They had been watching as the whole circus unfolded! My face burning, I gathered my things from the locker room and walked quickly past the bay window, not bothering this time to stay for breakfast.

* * *

At Harvard I felt betrayed. The school I loved had admitted but not accepted me. Ever since receiving my letter of admission I had dreamed of the time I could finally look in the mirror and see myself as worthy. But I quickly discovered that my quiet, nonaggressive manner, my preference for team advancement over individual success, the giving of nonverbal cues, staying out of the limelight were not valued here. In this Western capitalist place, these old-fashioned norms—imported from a Meiji-era Japan and taught to me by my mother and father—were *dys*functional.

At the B-School, I learned I had to act in exactly the opposite way from how I had been raised. I learned to be direct, outspoken, and most difficult of all, a smooth talker. To invent answers and give clarity, even when such clarity did not exist. To pat myself on the back. To look professors in the eye and put forward belief as if it were fixed truth—even when everyone in the fishbowl-shaped classroom knew I was only mouthing a part in a play.

It was like being held captive in a glass box, visible to all to see. Even my writing and speech patterns were all wrong: wonderfully emotional and contextual back home, they were too herky-jerky, pained, and constipated for this place. At the B-School, survival dictated that I be blunt, linear, and passion-less. Studying 800 cases over a two-year period, I watched my classmates and professors mold a kind of certainty out of a world that did not truly admit of such finality. Was it a false religion? I did not know. But one thing was clear, at the B-School the urinals were too high and the glass ceiling was too low!

Yes, it was becoming clear why I had to come to Hawai'i—and why I had taken this risky job. Growing up in a traditional Japanese American family, I had been told over and over again I would have to do better next time, that what I did wasn't good enough. *Kaizen*—the positive social norm that drove Japanese people always to do better the next time—had for me reached a dead end at Harvard where this "meritocracy" was for Whites only. With nowhere to go, the pull of *kaizen* now turned inward and generated a kind of self-hate. Propelled by a norm of "not good enough this time," I was hearing from Harvard that I would *never* be good enough.

A moment of *chiaoscuro* in junior high school then came into view. Sitting with legs spread, palms on the floor at each side, I was ready to pounce up the rope dangling in front of my face. It was the finals in the eighth grade rope climb. Six of us were sitting in front of a packed audience ready to spring up and climb our ropes on command. I had just broken the junior high school record in the semi-finals and learned later that kids were betting nickels on me to win. When the command to climb was issued, however, I froze in place. With the others a full body length ahead of me, I finally sprang into action. Too late to win, I won third place and a nice bronze medal. But I would always wonder why I had in effect "sabotaged" my own efforts.

How many Americans of Japanese descent had agonized over the same dilemma—of *kaizen* from distant past and glass ceiling today? How many had sabotaged their own efforts? Could this be the result of a deep, suppressed self-hate? In fact, was my country creating a monster by "granting admission" to so many African-Americans, Latinos, Native Americans, and Asian Americans—and then denying us full membership? Was there a collective anger ready to blow—or would the anger simply be passed on from one damaged generation to the next?

At another time, when I was in law school, I would comment to a Japanese American classmate from the Big Island about how difficult it was to feel equal to Whites on the east coast. My friend from Hawai'i responded with quiet confidence: "What do you mean equal? We're superior!" That was the day I decided to move to Hawai'i.

* * *

I paused before walking the final yards to my car. Looking out over the wide, barren interior of Diamond Head, I noticed the sunlight creeping down its steep interior walls. I remembered the *sensei* denying the *dojo* had any special ties to Asia. There was no grand plan to take over the world, the *sensei* had said. But I had suspected otherwise. I could picture the *sensei* leaving on a red-eye flight for Nagasaki or Seoul—and returning late at night a few days later. Darkness on the outside, darkness on the inside. I wondered if any of that darkness had already rubbed off on me. Or was evil copresent all along with the good in each of us, merely waiting for the right triggering event to emerge?

I wondered, too, about Hawai'i. Was this really paradise, the land of harmony? I had experienced in Honolulu what tourists would never see—a different kind of social pyramid. In Boston, the White Anglo-Saxon Protestants had clearly been on top of the social pyramid, with Irish and Italians a few rungs down, and African-Americans on the bottom. Asians were seemingly just below the level of poor Whites, and Latinos were barely visible and suspect.

But when I came to Hawai'i, I found a different social hierarchy, this time "flipped." Now *Whites were on the bottom*, and Asians were on top. In fact, here local Asians and Hawaiians controlled the government by dominating the Democratic Party machinery. The chief justice of the Supreme Court was Chinese, the former one Hawaiian. The state's legislature and public school system were both run by local Japanese Americans. Just as there had been gradations among Whites in Boston, in Hawaii there were gradations among the Asians and other "locals." The Japanese were ranked highest, Chinese coming a close second, and Hawaiians and part-Hawaiians next on the social pyramid. Filipinos and Samoans were after that. And at the bottom were the Whites, or "*haoles*," as they were called in the pejorative. Even though they still controlled much of the economic power in the state, Whites were treated disparagingly in many social circles.

I had also encountered an unspoken political rule in Hawai'i—that you had to "marry a local Japanese" if you wanted to get anywhere in this state. Indeed, several of the governor's cabinet members were Whites married to local Japanese American women. The governor himself, a part-Hawaiian, was married to a local Japanese. Same for the mayor.

I recalled how just last weekend a local friend was telling me, "Who wants to be White? Whites smell. Whites don't wash their hands. They're loud. Nah, it's better to have some skin color here. If you're too white it's not good." Referring to the White legs of a tourist wearing shorts, he added, "Haven't you heard the local expression, 'shark bait?' Too white isn't good."

I thought back whimsically to the previous month. I had been racing down the off-ramp from H-1 toward Vineyard Boulevard. At the bottom of the hill two police officers, both "locals," were aiming a speed gun at me. Caught going 20 mph over the speed limit, I slowed and prepared to pull over. To my surprise, the officers peered at me, smiled, and waved me on. Chastened and confused, I wondered if it might have turned out differently had I been *haole*.

It got worse. Registered as a lawyer in Hawai'i, I had once defended a youth in Juvenile Court. The kid, a Hawaiian, had been arrested for slugging a White boy in intermediate school. The story? The 15-year-old had thought it was okay to beat up the White boy since it was "Kill *Haole* Day." As an outsider, I had to ask the probation officer if such a day in fact existed. To my horror I was told that ever since the plantation days, it had been a tradition to beat up White boys on a certain day using what was called "a false crack," or blindside sucker punch.

It was then that I realized something important. This was *the same* kind of ritual I had sought to escape in leaving Boston—where I had been told by a perfect stranger on the street, "Go back to China, you chink!" And now here, in Hawai'i there was a "Kill *Haole* Day." Only the sides had changed; it was still wrong.

Recently, a professor at the University of Hawaii, a part-Hawaiian, had been forced to write an editorial responding to a White student from the mainland who complained in class about being treated rudely in Hawai'i. Noting he had not bothered to learn the ways of Hawai'i, she wrote, "Go back to the mainland, you *Haole*. You're not wanted here. *Haole*, go home!" Her story was in the newspapers for days. But on seeing this, I realized my own complicity. Having been near the bottom in Boston, I had thoroughly enjoyed being on top in Hawai'i. By simply moving to Hawai'i, I had gone from rage to a false sense of superiority over Whites—*and Hawai'ians*. Shamefully, I realized I had become a willing participant in this charade.

I also realized my feelings of adequacy might not be valid if they derived from a race-based hierarchy that placed me artificially on top in Hawai'i. In Hawai'i, it was as futile for the "*haole*" to wait for full membership just as it had been for me to do so in Boston. But maybe, just maybe, Whites *were* "good enough" to be fully accepted in Hawai'i—and maybe they, too, could begin by accepting their own complicity. In a similar way, I thought I might begin to see myself as "good enough."

* * *

As I trudged up the final yards toward my car, my body still tingled from that early morning session. This had been my last *kendo* class—a flurry of violent, passionless violence had ended in a wholly unexpected purity of spirit. I noticed then that the inner cavity of the volcano was almost a mile across, and steeper than I had before thought. Except for the dojo complex, the place was arid and almost without vegetation. These brown slopes did not even yield a perceptible smell. In this eerie morning silence, not even birds could be heard and the bright sun had not quite begun its march across the crater floor. During mid-day, the heat from the sun would be intense. I felt I had to escape now—to break free from this suffocating place, this place with no center, no spirit, no meaning.

The last class had started, like all others, with *za-zen* exercises at 4:30 am and then warm-up exercises. But this time Kojiro informed the class that on this day there would be full contact *kendo*. This would be my first chance to fight. In my excitement I rushed to mimic my classmates who were already donning breastplates, heavy facemasks, and thick gloves.

The students were separated into three groups. My group, the beginners, went over to the "Makai" or west end of the *dojo*. There we were told to stand in line, with the first person stepping away to face the others. The challenger took each person on, one at a time, for 60 seconds—and then went to the back of the line so that the next challenger could step forward. When we had fought through three such rounds, our sparring had grown quite ragged. The lightweight bamboo *shinai's* had suddenly felt like iron bars. When Kojiro finally ordered all combatants to stop, the members of my group breathed a collective sigh of relief.

But for me there would be no rest. "Hey you!" I heard a voice calling out to me with a deep and menacing tone. I turned to look.

There, in the middle of the hall, stood Kojiro waving the tip of his *shinai* in tiny circles and looking directly at me. Like he was penciling in his target, I could barely discern his features as he peered at me through the heavy mesh mask. I was being mocked.

It is said that everyone has at least one moment of stillness in his or her life, when everything seems to come to a halt and nothing that had occurred before that time held any meaning. In such stillness—and now with the whole class watching—I felt my heart sink to my bare feet. "Now me," Kojiro said, this time softly and for effect. With his mouth turned down at the corners, Kojiro appeared almost sinister. In the last two weeks, he had made my life at work miserable. The vice chairman of the bank had disrupted my schedule time and again with one false alarm after another, finally dumping a portfolio of failing commercial loans at my feet.

And now this. With Kojiro standing tall and confidently in the center of the room, I keenly felt the presence of other bank officers—some from my own bank—waiting to see what I would do. In fact, everyone was waiting to see how I would answer Kojiro. I knew Kojiro had practiced *kendo* for ten years—and was good enough to be the *dojo's* lead instructor. Not having even sparred this morning, he was fresh and strong. And after sparring so aggressively with other novitiates for the first time in my life, I knew that I was too tired even to have a chance. What to do?

Taking a deep breath and grabbing the cool mat tentatively with my toes, I inched cautiously toward the haughty class leader. Kojiro was clearly taunting me now, sneering and waving the tip of his *shinai* at me in even tinier circles. With my own *shinai* pointed at Kojiro's face mask, I realized there was no hope and let go of all thought and emotion. I stood there, already vanquished.

But it was precisely at this moment of nothingness that there came a millisecond of unexpected clarity. In Kojiro's own sneer lay the answer to all of the questions of today, yesterday, and possibly many tomorrows to come. In Kojiro's sneer was an opening.

Without thinking I moved. Raising my *shinai* high above my head, I let out an uncharacteristically loud growl and quickly closed ground on Kojiro. But just as we were about to clash, I lowered my wrists to my chest and thrust my hands, *shinai*, and body out at Kojiro's torso, using the same "advanced" technique he had shown me a few weeks earlier. Making hard contact and feeling the weight of Kojiro's body give way, I saw his eyes widen in surprise—and in that instant I raised and lowered the boom on Kojiro's forehead. Whump! The class leader had been felled! It did not matter thereafter that Kojiro rained blow after blow upon my head. I knew I had already gotten in the first blow. In a real fight he would be dead. In front of the whole class Kojiro, the master, had been felled—by his own arrogance. What was it? *Four things, wipe them from your mind*, he had once told me?

I also knew that in some sense I had accomplished all I had come to Hawai'i to accomplish. Quietly and without fanfare, I glided to the entrance of the hall where I removed my facemask, breastplate, and gloves. At the door I turned and bowed politely to the little shrine in back. Calmly, I strode down the wooden walkway to the locker room and gathered my things. Back at the front steps I paused to put on my slippers, straightened, and walked out to the pathway. Out of the corner of my eye, I thought I saw the image of a man following my departure with his eyes. A thick, well-muscled man.

* * *

Reaching my car door, I looked back one last time at the temple and its clump of trees below. I knew I was right to leave that place and its dark religion. This mountain, which had once harbored explosive rage, had given up that force by venting its top. And out of that violence had come a certain beauty—Diamond Head's famous silhouette. I felt like I had done the same.

I also suspected I had taken a big step in my own journey of self-discovery. I did not need to learn who I was by "returning to Japanese roots" at some radical martial arts *dojo*. I did not need to become a bank president, or bury myself in status and money, to find meaning and feel worthy. I was "good enough" the way I was.

But I also realized that the next step in my journey would be to learn how to value myself, on my own terms. I did not know yet how I would do this—find my own meaning—but knew I had to find a way.

And for the first time I noticed there had long been a whirring sound in my head, when it ceased.

NOTES

1. This autobiographical writing, perhaps one day reflective of what might be called "A New Anthropology," is inspired by my college professor, Nicolas Fersen, and by my early exposure to the deeply humanistic work of the authors listed below.
2. I will also note that all events presented in this chapter were as portrayed. Only the location of this secret dojo has been disguised to protect the anonymity of this place of learning.
3. In the 1990s, this novelistic nonfiction piece was selected as the winner of the James Clarell Literary Award.

BIBLIOGRAPHY

Dostoyevsky, M. (1968). *Crime and punishment*. New York, NY: Signet Classics.

Kondo, D. (1990). *Crafting selves: Power, gender and discourses of identity in a Japanese workplace*. Chicago, IL: University of Chicago Press.

Rosaldo, R. (1989). *Culture & truth: The remaking of social analysis*. Boston, MA: Beacon Press.

Said, E. R. (2000) *Reflections on exile and other essays* (p. xxxv). Cambridge, MA: Harvard University Press.

Schama, S. (1991). *Dead certainties: Unwarranted speculations*. New York, NY: Knopf.

CHAPTER 2

Losing Culture, Losing Soul

(C)ivilizations begin to die when they lose the moral passion that brought them into being in the first place.

Jonathan Sachs, acceptance speech for 2016 Templeton Prize

April 29, 1992. Did you see the guy throw a brick, hit the other guy on the head? Gray hollow-tile brick—you know, the ones they use for building cheap homes? Smoke was all around. Fires. People were running madly in the streets. L.A. was on fire. Following the acquittal of four L.A. city police officers for beating motorist Rodney King and captured live on videotape, the Rodney King riots were now underway.

May 2, 1992. Institutions—business, law, government, education—continue to flounder and in stark contrast, a crowd of several hundred gathers at one mini-mall in L.A. to clean up following the torching of the city, and with no elected leader, no organization chart, and no public financing, an unmistakably *ordered* experience occurs wherein people rush to help people, charred structures are stripped, asphalt is washed clean—and child and elder and student and professional of all color and belief pause from their work to watch as a pack of eight police squad cars each jammed with dark blue uniforms roar by as if afraid certainly not of us, maybe of themselves, and for a moment in time, humanity proceeds not because of, but in spite of, its institutions.

I had come home to L.A. in 1991 looking for a way to connect with community after ten wonderful years in Hawaii. I did not expect that the city of my childhood would descend within the year into the darkness of complete racial fragmentation and civil anarchy. Oddly, it was also then that unexpected flashes of memory connected to my days in Hawaii would appear and further color my vision of a world in the throes of riot.

* * *

Buster Piikoi walked into the elevator by the first floor courtyard. He had spent the week trimming and weeding the large interior garden at the Pearl City Makai Vista. There were split-leaf philodendrons, yellow hibiscus bushes, anthuriums and stately red torch ginger—all distinguishable from each other yet dependent on each other for their beauty. It made him feel good—like he was helping to re-create paradise every month. He had finished one six-pack. The second was dangling from his right hand.

Buster pressed the button for the eighth floor where he lived without charge in exchange for doing maintenance and gardening. He waited for the door to close and lifted his gaze to watch the numbers light up. But before the elevator could begin to climb, a large hand shot into the closing doors just inches from his head. The doors re-opened.

* * *

My memories from Hawaii tugged at me as I tried to make sense of my present sense impressions and the emotions of L.A. And soon it would be as a graduate student at UCLA that I would witness a number of acts of racial and cultural hegemony—and resistance—driving parties into ever-wider conflict. It was also in those failed attempts, however, that I began to discern a path to race harmony:

> Thirteen motorcycle officers, all white males, were standing in front of Murphy Hall. They were collectively eying a small group of Mexicans dancing on the corner and dressed in Native American garb. Every now and then one of the officers would tell a snide joke about the dancers and the snickering of the officers would overwhelm the steady rhythm of a hollow drum. Off in the distance a lone figure sat on a motorcycle, his head hunched down. When the sergeant yelled over to him, the officer shrugged but did not speak. Upon closer examination, I saw that he was very possibly Mexican-American.

What had led to this show of force? Since Chicanos (from "me-xicano") made up almost half the population of L.A., the protesting students were insisting that a public university like UCLA would better serve its city by establishing a Chicana/o Studies Department on campus. The students held a demonstration. City Council members came. Congressmen, too. A famous actor asked for nonviolence, and student posters joyously proclaimed a new unity:

> *Afro American Students Support Chicana/o Studies!*
> *Asian American Studies Supports Chicana/o Studies!*

And with humor, a poster held by an Asian American student:

> *Bruce Lee Supports Chicana/o Studies Now!*

Behind the facade of coolness at Murphy Hall, one could sense a growing unease. When the UCLA faculty rejected a formal proposal for a department in which Chicanos could study their own cultural stories, the students held a sit-in at the Faculty Center. Glass was broken, works of art were damaged, and several students were injured; 87 Chicano, black, Asian, and white students were rounded up, arrested, and held overnight at a downtown police cell.

Hunger Strike!

Students responded by pitching tents in a park directly in front of Murphy Hall. As the days passed, both sides postured through the student newspaper. It was only when doctors announced that strikers would soon inflict permanent damage to their bodies that the administration finally relented. The Chicana/o Studies Center would receive more faculty positions and make its own tenure decisions—but still be denied the full status of an academic department.

* * *

Startled, Buster's eyes widened as three tall haoles entered the elevator one by one. They were all wearing t-shirts and long pants and had short haircuts. Buster guessed they were military grunts. 19 or 20 years old. From their well-muscled physiques, he suspected they were lifters.

Buster backed up subconsciously and dropped his gaze to the floor. When the door closed, he realized he was breathing heavily. Maybe he had too much to drink already. A few beads of sweat began to drip down the sides of his face.

The three soldiers were smiling at each other, their eyebrows raised in the "high sign." This wasn't good, Buster thought. They're up to something. These buggahs are all over six feet. At 61, Buster wasn't quite the 5'6" he had stood in high school—when for Kamehameha he placed second in 120 pound wrestling at the state finals on the Big Island. That was a long time ago.

"Hey, Haw-wai-yun," the middle grunt was saying to him.

"You're sure drunk, aren'tcha?" the one on the right added.

"Hey, 'li-ke, li-ke,'" the one on the left said, "can you hula for us?"

Buster blinked his eyes. Sweat was pouring down the sides of his face now. He backed further into the elevator—until he felt the wall against his back. He prayed the elevator would reach the eighth floor before anything could happen.

As he looked from one soldier to another, he realized they were all facing him, swinging their arms and swaying their hips. He didn't know which one jabbed a fist first. Soon all three were flicking their fists at his face. He ducked as they shadow-boxed him. None of the punches were landing but they were coming close. The elevator was still moving.

Buster did not know what this was. Fists kept coming at him from multiple angles. As he ducked first one way, then the other, he felt someone touch his shoulder. Without thinking, he dropped the six-pack and reached into his back pocket.

* * *

It also struck me that UCLA was experiencing a dissonance—from 64% of its entering freshmen class now being of color and the faculty and administration remaining predominantly white. The Kafka-esque image of 87 students being hauled off from a Chicana/o Studies protest by West LA's white police unit now hinted (in flashing neon lights) at a larger confrontation to come: the breakdown, perhaps, in shared meaning about the norms and duties of this city and what counts? Was this the end of common culture? There was more…

Looking straight at the audience, the young man is tall, athletic-looking, and clean cut. He is standing under a spotlight.

FRATERNITY LEADER

We didn't mean it personally. It was only in fun.

The spotlight on the man goes out and a second spotlight goes on. It highlights a woman who is slender with long, straight, dark brown hair. Her face speaks of passion and commitment.

CHICANA SPOKESPERSON

It was wrong of them to sing songs about a 10-year old Mexican girl losing her virginity to fraternity men.

The spotlights again switch. This pattern continues—with neither person aware of the existence of the other.

FRATERNITY LEADER

We never really knew any Mexican-Americans where we grew up—except maybe the ones that worked for our fathers. So this song wasn't anything personal.

As the spotlight now highlights the woman, she appears agitated.

CHICANA SPOKESPERSON

I know why white leaders can't deal with race difference. It's because the only identity they have is based on superiority!

FRATERNITY LEADER

This song is just our way of knowing we have become men. It's not meant to be taken personally.

CHICANA SPOKESPERSON

There's a real violence here. To Chicano culture. To women. To young girls.

But most of all, to white men. By using young girls' bodies to define themselves, these men taint their own identities.

FRATERNITY LEADER

The real loss here is the loss of tradition. If we can't tell our stories, how will frat brothers celebrate manhood?

CHICANA SPOKESPERSON

These same "Lupe" song sheets were thrown out in the Sixties. What does it take?

* * *

In interpreting the sexually and racially offensive language of the "Lupe Songsheets," one larger question needs to be asked: Why do white male fraternity brothers even need to demean women and girls of color in order to establish their own positive meaning and sense of self? This would turn out to be the question that, in my case, drove an entire career inquiry. And with the indecency of this conduct finally made visible for all to see, what specifically is missing in the lives of these young men that would propel such a desperate ritual in the first place?

* * *

The Office of the Public Defender was located on the fourth floor of the United Way Building on Vineyard Boulevard in downtown Honolulu. Downstairs the lobby direc-

tory described a broad range of services—the Seniors Kokua Project, the Honolulu Child Abuse and Neglect Center, The River Street Disability Center, and others.

In a small office on the fourth floor, I was a young attorney who sat in a room with smudged cream-colored walls with nail holes and peeling wallpaper. Looking up from the Mokuleia appeals file, I saw that a smallish, weather-beaten man was standing in the hallway and nervously rolling a piece of paper in his hands. The man seemed mild-mannered, almost timid. He looked to be in his mid-60's. He was not comfortable in an office setting. The knot in his tie was off to one side. Not a likely candidate for Terroristic Threatening II—with a knife no less.

I listened as my client began to tell his story.

* * *

It was when I was a graduate student at UCLA in the early 1990s that I completed a study that provided a hint at how we might end racial conflict on U.S. college and universities campuses. Using data from questionnaire responses from faculty and students at 159 colleges and universities in the early 1990s, this correlation analysis revealed that as a campus gets increasingly racially diverse, the overall sense of community reported by students will decline—unless the faculty include race and gender diversity in their course content and own research. With the inclusion of race and gender content in courses and faculty research, any increases in racial diversity of the student body will tend to switch from −0.09 to +0.11 and become *positively* correlated with "sense of community" reported by white students:

Table 2.1: Correlations (r) Between Four Dummy Variables and "Sense of Community," Demographic Diversity

Demographic Diversity (race diversity in student admissions, faculty hiring, and hiring and events on campus)	Correlations (r) Between Four Dummy Variables and "Sense of Community" (N = 10,159)	
	Race and Gender Diversity in Courses and Research	
	Low	High
Low	−0.06**	0.03**
High	−0.09**	0.11**

** Indicates significant at 0.01 level.

Source: Gregory K Tanaka

Nb. The dependent variable in the national study cited here was the "priority a campus places on building sense of community among students and faculty," as reported by students. After controlling for over 80 input variables including race, gender, and socioeconomic status, a stepwise multiple regression analysis was performed. To test for interaction effects, significant variables were then paired and tested, as shown in the data above, for correlations with "sense of community." Original data came from student follow-up and faculty surveys administered at 159 U.S. colleges and universities as part of the Cooperative Institutional Research Program in 1991 and 1989, courtesy of Alexander Astin and the Higher Education Research Institute at UCLA. While the individual correlation coefficients in these matrices are low, what is important is their directionality.

What this means is that as a campus becomes more racially heterogeneous, *the failure of its faculty to change their course content and their own research topics to reflect the race and gender diversity of the students (and, thus, amend the prevailing campus narrative) will be associated with a decline in sense of community for white students.*

In light of this, I wondered *if there might exist a particular way to enhance the transition to greater race and gender diversity* through a college's course content and research. The data from this study provided a compelling solution. It showed that a diverse campus will be *more* likely to have a positive sense of community while increasing diversity in course content and research *if it also has a high "humanities emphasis" (r = + 0.17):*

Table 2.2: Correlations (r) Between Four Dummy Variables and "Sense of Community," Faculty Humanities Orientation

		Correlations (r) Between Four Dummy Variables and "Sense of Community" (N = 10,159)	
		Race and Gender Diversity in Courses and Research	
		Low	High
Faculty Humanities Orientation	Low	−0.17*	0.06*
	High	−0.06*	0.17*

*Significant at the 0.05 level.
Source: Gregory K. Tanaka

What does this mean in terms of educational policy? *It means that one key to building harmony at racially heterogeneous campuses lies in diversifying the stories or narratives told in the humanities.* The above table demonstrates there is clear benefit from *combining* a high "humanities emphasis" *with* high diversity content "in courses and faculty research."

* * *

"State of Hawaii vs. Ezra 'Buster' Pi'ikoi!" Having announced the next case, the young, female court clerk looked out into the audience and caught my eye.

My client and I were already rising. We passed through the swinging gate that segregated the judge and parties from the pews that held multiple sets of defendants and an anxious public.

I liked this judge. Tough on the outside, a sweetheart on the inside, Judge Malolo was from Nanakuli and had come up the hard way. You never knew exactly how he would rule, and you certainly didn't want to catch him on a bad day. With broad, wrinkled features, he looked like a bulldog.

"Counsel, I understand your client has a change of plea."

* * *

The data from my study was also confirming a long-standing thesis that a college or university campus would have a lower sense of community on campus if it placed too great an emphasis on "status and money" (Astin, 1991; Kerr, 1964). In other words—*just like experiencing an increase in the racial diversity of the student body without increasing the race and gender content in the courses and faculty research*—an emphasis on "status and money" is associated with a decline in sense of community.

Is there a way to address this? It turns out that a campus that has a status and money orientation but also manages to achieve *greater humanities emphasis* will tend to be associated with a higher "sense of community" felt by white students (with the correlation switching dramatically from −0.24 to + 0.09):

Table 2.3: Correlations (r) Between Four Dummy Variables and "Sense of Community," Emphasis on Status and Money

	Correlations (r) Between Four Dummy Variables and "Sense of Community" (N = 10,159)	
	Emphasis on Status and Money	
	Low	High
Faculty Humanities Orientation		
Low	−0.00	−0.24**
High	−0.15**	0.09**

** Indicates significant at the 0.01 level.
Source: Gregory K. Tanaka

In other words, with a greater humanities emphasis, *the harsh effects of a college or university's overemphasis on "status and money" on sense of community are reversed.* Thus, the negative associations of *both* (1) increased emphasis on status and money *and* (2) increases in student body race diversity with the "sense of community" on campus are likely to be reversed when there is greater emphasis placed on the humanities.

So here is the dilemma. What if a large number of students, staff, and faculty at one university like UCLA—its white campus members—are unable to trace their allegiance to the shared meanings (norms, duties, obligations, beliefs, behaviors) of a particular ethnic culture in Europe? Would this mean that some of them have *no* sources of positive meanings from which to draw—other than race or money? The pronouncement by a white emeritus professor in the student newspaper at the completion of this study proved both timely and instructive. Addressing the student demands for a new Chicano Studies Department at UCLA, he concluded it should not be permitted because, "Chicanos don't have a culture."

In his railings against the wishes of the Latino students, the plaintive white UCLA professor *made no reference to the shared meanings, or culture, of the European country or countries of his* own *ancestors*. Did he even know what culture was? Or was he merely projecting his own sense of inadequacy (from not having a designated ethnic culture of his own) on to the Mexican-American students and faculty? If he had no ethnic culture of his own, then the fact that the Mexican-American students were trying to do something constructive to retrieve, study, and perform the elements of their current and historical cultural identities—through the establishment of a Chicana/o Studies Department—made the words of this professor all the more ironic.

The comment by the emeritus professor also demonstrates in clear terms how whiteness works its insidious magic. By operating as the "naturalized" standard of superiority because it is already "the norm" against which all other identities and meaning systems must compare and always fall short, (1) his whiteness does not ever have to be announced and (2) the so-called "cultures" of people of other races will never be allowed to count. If this professor did not in fact have an ethnic culture to tell him his norms, duties, and other meanings, then the naturalization of his "superior" white identity and the apparent absence of an ethnic culture of his own would seem to be codependent operations in that each operation supports the existence of the other.

And how about the UCLA fraternity's persistent use of Lupe Songsheets: "If we can't tell our story, how will frat brothers celebrate manhood?" And the uncivil treatment of a senior Hawaiian in an elevator by three young, well-muscled white Marines? These acts do not reflect the affirmation of an ethnic culture, but rather its absence. It also struck me that all these incidents were reflecting a lack of meaning— and these lacunae were beginning to add up. *Might they constitute early indicia of the possibility that the United States was fast becoming a nation without soul?* We would do well to remember the words of Mari Ruti (2006, p. xv) who in contemplating the importance of soul, urged thinkers to find "ways in which human beings relate to the world in active rather than merely passive ways—*as creators of meaning* rather than as helpless dupes of disciplinary power."

So, is it not then possible that many white college students—just like this emeritus professor—also lack the reassuring meanings, duties, and norms of a clearly defined ethnic narrative (e.g., from France or England or Germany) to call their own? Had centuries of intermarriage between descendants of immigrants from many different countries in Europe all but destroyed the *ethnic* cultural meanings of 65% of the U.S. population, as Alba (1990), Steinberg (1981), and Waters (1990) would contend: See also Abu-Lughod (1991), Astin (1984), Pritchard (1940), Geertz

(1973), hooks (1992), Kondo (1990), Levin-Strauss (1975), Radcliffe-Brown (1955), Rosaldo (1989), Sachs (2016), Tanaka (1991), Tanaka (2003), West (1993)?

If so, then this suggests to me that *before the practice of "racism" and spiritually empty "money-based greed" could ever be reduced if not eliminated, there would have to be a resurgence of ethnic cultural identity*—and the norms and duties that come with that—for white Americans. But is this even possible? Could schools teach to this? One has only to look at the growing number of positive studies of "language and culture revitalization" to see that this is not only possible—it is something that tends to lead to other gains in school performance. One can go all the way back to the 1970s study of the Kamehameha Early Education Program ("KEEP") in Hawaii by Tharp (1982), where it was found that the overall learning success of native Hawaiian youth increased significantly when the methods of teaching in that school reflected the values and meanings of Hawaiian culture and language.

Closer to today, one can look to the work of Dementi-Leonard and Gilmore (1999) who studied "language and culture regenesis" among the Athabascan children in Alaska; the telling of "geo-ethnic family histories" in racially mixed groups urged by Vigil and Roseman (1998); and the Social and Public Art Resource Center's (e.g., Tanaka, 1993) proposed intercultural visuality in which different ethnic groups' public art was to be rotated as "cultural explainers" in an attempt to build race harmony in the years following the Rodney King riots.

One might also find persuasive the call for a new narrative for African-Americans not based on race (Johnson, 2008) and a parallel call by ReGena Booze (2006) for the construction of an Afro-Centric theory of human development not shackled or delimited by race; a scholarly wish expressed by Viego (2007) for new subject formation among U.S. Latinos that departs from the victimology of racialization; and the push for new identity formation for European descendents living in New Zealand that would no longer be linked to trauma, as urged by White and Epston (1990).

At some point, one would think, these calls for new identity formation and meaning reclamation that are truly "postracial" and "culture regenerative" are bound to reach some policymaker who decides to make a real difference. It is not such a great stretch to imagine white K-12 students in one school performing the work of storytelling and relishing the "language and culture revitalization" that those stories will evoke.

The continuing refrain—indeed, the "elephant in the living room" that no one seems to want to talk about—is this growing possibility *that the United States has already become a nation without culture (Gonzalez, 1999; Tanaka, 2009)—and that without the shared meanings that derive from culture, there can be no clear norms and duties to bind the people together, help them know right from wrong, and tell them how to treat others in a more participatory democracy.* In other words, the wish for a far larger humanities emphasis—and the fresh storytelling that it would bring—may well constitute a pathway not only for achieving social cohesion in a diverse population, but for remaking the democracy itself.

These were my thoughts as I reflected back on the Rodney King riots, the "Lupe Songsheets," and the Chicano Studies movement of the 1990s.

* * *

"Your honor, my client is a good man." I told the judge. "He is employed and he goes to church every Sunday. He is well-liked in the community and before this incident, he had never violated the law. In this particular case, your honor, no one was actually hurt."

I continued my request for a "Deferred Acceptance of Guilty Plea" or "DAG." On my advice, Buster had decided to change his plea two weeks earlier. It was a calcu-lated risk. The hope was that the judge would later dismiss the charges as long as Buster did not run afoul of the law for one year.

While the judge read the court files, I thought back to my first day in law school. It had been Property Law I with Professor Mienski. The case was about "seisin," the old British rule that held a parcel of land must always rest in the hands of one named owner or another—or the system would fail. It struck me that this law had come from the days of serfs. Raising my hand, I asked the professor whether there weren't in fact two kinds of property law—one that protected elite landowners and another that gave minimal rights to renters. Professor Mienski grew livid. In front of the whole class he lectured me sternly about the fact that there was only one law.

Who, I now asked myself, was served by this one law, and have we reached the limits of what the law—perhaps relied upon too much in the absence of culture— can do for humanity?

As the judge continued reading, I turned and scanned the rows of pews behind me. There in the back row, by the door, sat three tall, young, white men. Short hair. Well muscled.

BIBLIOGRAPHY

Abu-Lughod, L. (1991). Writing against culture. In R. Fox (Ed.), *Recapturing anthropology: Writing in the present*. Santa Fe, NM: School of American Research.

Alba, R. (1990). *Ethnic identity: The transformation of white America*. New Haven, CT: Yale University Press.

Astin, A. (1984). Student involvement: A developmental theory for higher education. *Journal of College Student Development, 25*, 297–308.

Astin, A. (1991). *Assessment for excellence*. New York, NY: Macmillan.

Booze, R. (2006). *Teaching Kujichagulia: Mentoring strategies for African American females in predom-inantly white colleges and universities*. Paper presented at the annual meeting of the National Conference on Race and Ethnicity.

Dementi-Leonard, B., & Gilmore, P. (1999). Language revitalization and identity in social context: A community-based Athabascan language preservation project in Western Interior Alaska. *Anthropology & Education Quarterly, 30*(1), 37–55.

Evans-Pritchard, E. (1940/1968). *The* Nuer. Oxford: Oxford University Press.

Fox, R. (Ed.) (1991). *Recapturing anthropology: Writing in the present.* Santa Fe, NM: School of American Research Press.

Geertz, C. (1973). *The interpretation of cultures.* New York, NY: Basic Books.

Gonzalez, N. (1999). What do we do if culture does not exist anymore? *Anthropology & Education Quarterly, 30*(4), 431–435.

hooks, b. (1992). Representing whiteness in the black imagination. In L. Grossberg, C. Nelson, & P. Treichler (Eds.), *Cultural studies* (pp. 338–346). New York, NY: Routledge.

Johnson, C. (2008). The end of the black American narrative. *American Scholar, 77*(3), 32–42.

Kerr, C. (1964). *The uses of the university.* New York, NY: Harper.

Kondo, D. (1990). *Crafting selves: Power, gender and discourses of identity in a Japanese Workplace.* Chicago, IL: University of Chicago Press.

Levin-Strauss, C. (1975). *Tristes tropiques.* New York, NY: Atheneum.

Morrison, T. (1992). *Playing in the dark: Whiteness and the literary imagination.* Cambridge, MA: Harvard University Press.

Radcliffe-Brown, A. R. (1955). *Structure and function in primitive society.* New York, NY: Free Press.

Rosaldo, R. (1989). *Culture & truth: The remaking of social analysis.* Boston, MA: Beacon Press.

Ruti, M. (2006). *Reinventing the soul: Posthumanist theory and psychic life.* New York, NY: Other Press.

Sachs, J. (2016). Acceptance speech for receipt of the 2016 Templeton Prize, cited by Simon Black, *Sovereign Man,* and reprinted in *SilverDoctors.com,* July 20, 2016.

Steinberg, S. (1981). *The ethnic myth: Race, ethnicity and class in America.* Boston, MA: Beacon Press.

Tanaka, G. (1991). Is this the end of common culture? *Wall Street Journal.* August 19, 1991.

Tanaka, G. (1993). Toward unity and difference: The traveling art of cultural explainers. In G. LeClerc & A. Moctezuma (Eds.), *Cultural explainers: Portals, bridges and gateways.* Los Angeles, CA: Social and Public Art Resource Center, pp. 7–8.

Tanaka, G. (2003). *The intercultural campus: Transcending culture and power in American higher education.* New York, NY: Peter Lang Publishing.

Tanaka, G. (2009). The elephant in the living room that no one wants to talk about: Why anthropologists are unable to acknowledge the end of culture. *Anthropology & Education Quarterly, 40*(1), 82–95.

Tharp, R. (1982). The effective instruction of comprehension: Results and description of the Kamehameha Early Education Program. *Reading Research Quarterly* (1(1): 503–527.

Viego, A. (2007). *Dead subjects: Toward a politics of loss in Latino studies.* Durham, NC: Duke University Press.

Vigil, J. D., & Roseman C. (1998, December 2–6). *Ethnicity and place.* Paper presented at annual meeting of the American Anthropological Association, Philadelphia.

Waters, M. C. (1990). *Ethnic options: Choosing identity in America.* Berkeley, CA: University of California Press.

West, C. (1993). *Race matters.* Boston, MA: Beacon.

CHAPTER 3

Baseball and the Decline of Myth

In baseball, everyone wants to arrive at the place where they started (home).
Baseball Commissioner A. Bartlett Giamatti (1989)

In a quick, snaking column two nearly identical Japanese boys closely followed a white boy who was darting behind the last of eight tightly packed rows of chairs on the front steps of City Hall. A large crowd had gathered to pay tribute to professional baseball, and people were beginning to turn their attention toward the stage. As the two slid to a stop beside the first boy they heard him say, "...got three pens. Let's give 'em with these papers to the guys in back."

With a deep feeling of "*enryo*," a self-abasement and reserve, the two Japanese boys froze before finally nodding in agreement. Soon the first boy was pressing three sets of papers and pens upon the left thigh of a man-like-god seated in the very last row, nearest the bandstand. As he turned to look down into a boy's steel blue eyes, the man-like-god shattered a convention of all gods asked to suspend their gift of motion, who sit with some difficulty staring forward, caught in time and place. A large hand deftly snatched the papers and pens.

Bobbing now between large shoulders and under metal chairs the boys strained to see what would happen next. "If we fail," they all thought, "we will know it right away." Slips of paper—dreams and hopes—would flutter and fall to the hot cement where evening would come and sweep them away as it already had the summer.

But there were no falling papers. Nothing could be seen except for an occasional turning of one demi-god to his left and then his right—a welcome break from the monotony after all. The ceremony ran for nearly half an hour before the boys saw what their eyes could not accept. A demi-god in the front row was twisting to look back, searching for the owners of…he was holding up papers and pens! Too afraid to move, the two Japanese boys watched as their friend ran quickly to the front of the stage to claim the rewards for all three. Real baseball autographs! He was stooping as he ran.

I was 11 when the Dodgers brought the first World Championship home to Los Angeles. That was in 1959.

BASEBALL AND RACE

Where Is Joy?

In the decades since, there has been a more sobering trend. It came to a head for me with the 1994 suspension and fining of Cincinnati Reds owner Marge Schott for racial slurs. "That goddamned nigger," among others. Not long after that, it was again Marge Schott who said in reference to certain ballplayers, "Only fruits wear earrings."

The trend seemed to call for outbursts like this to occur at least once a year. Before Mrs. Schott it was Al Campanis, the Dodger executive who said on "Nightline" that blacks don't have "the necessities" to manage. And then it was media personality Jimmy "the Greek" Snyder who said that blacks are "bred" to be athletes. During those years, Robin Yount who was white was named American League MVP despite very good numbers by Ruben Sierra who was black, prompting at least one writer to quip, "when it's close, give it to the white guy." Later, it was Houston Astros executive Drayton McLane who allegedly told two Latino managers from Houston Channel 48 that Hispanics don't understand baseball, don't read the newspapers, and when they do attend games, only sit in the cheap $2 seats.

It takes its toll. The fond memory of sneaking behind rows of seats to get player autographs is stripped away and one begins to tire of looking at white people as white people—which is what happens every time you see there are no announcers of color in the broadcast booth. Know what happens next? You start not liking yourself. You start not liking the mounting resentment and the thought of incipient hatred toward others. The hurt is magnified, then displaced on to yourself.

In the end there is only one baseball, this baseball, and so the hurt steals the emptiness inside you and rips it into shreds and tosses even that away, leaving you with less than before, like having less than nothing.

How bad is it? It's so bad the deed itself no longer matters; it's waiting for the next shoe to drop that squeezes out all the joy. It makes you wonder if baseball by its stubborn inability to accommodate race difference isn't finally signaling the end of all binding spirit in America.

But baseball has a higher duty, as noted by A. Bartlett Giamatti (1989):

> *When those running a sport do not believe their own conventions, then the essential convention of a sport as a meritocracy in every sense will be undermined…. For instance, when baseball desegregated itself in 1947 on the field, the first American institution to do so voluntarily…baseball changed America. (But) baseball thereby made a tremendous promise—to play the game of America by the rules of the Constitution and the American Dream—and when it failed to deliver completely, it cheated itself and the country by not entirely fulfilling the very promise it had voluntarily made.*
>
> Bartlett Giamatti, former baseball commissioner, in *Take Time for Paradise.*

Where Is Mystery?

Recently I realized why baseball has always had its allure—in different ways each day it combines the certain with the unknown. Nine innings, three outs, three strikes and four balls, a confined area of play—all tell us that our world is ordered in at least this contrived way. At the same time baseball reminds us there is "mystery" each time a starting pitcher takes the mound or a pinch hitter comes to the plate—or heaven forbid, another grounder is hit to that rookie at short!

In this way baseball acknowledges for us that our existence lies somewhere between two worlds, the world of reality, perhaps itself an illusion, and the world of mystery. Baseball therefore means something very large: that if there are things we cannot control in life, it is enough for us to try our best. Baseball used to remind us that it is very American "to be brave."

Not all that many years ago I asked a baseball magazine writer how many of their editors and correspondents were persons of color. "There are several minorities on our production staff but we can't control who is assigned to us as correspondents," he said.

In fact, 38 of 39 domestic correspondents for this magazine were then white. All 19 editors and columnists were white. This is not mystery. It is a lie: it is in complicity with all those schoolbooks that promised there would be equality because this is America. It is in cahoots with a dying myth of Horatio Alger that said anyone can make it if they only try. The telling of untruths—or hiding of truth—literally crowds out mystery.

In that same year, none of the 26 Major League baseball teams had a single African or Latino announcer in their English speaking broadcaster booths. None. It meant that all of baseball let the 1992 Los Angeles riots come and go without making any changes in these highly symbolic positions. It was as if the riots had never occurred.

By what right then did those writers and broadcasters deign to cast calumny on a misguided Marge Schott? By what jurisdiction is the privilege to describe public ritual conferred upon one class of citizen in America—and denied others?

The crowning blow came some years back when Major League Baseball—the same owners who touted "free market capitalism" and then blocked the sale of the Seattle Mariners to a Japanese national living in Seattle because he was a "foreigner"—*approved* the sale of the Dodgers to a *white* Australian entrepreneur who owned Fox News. It hurts. The dual imbrication of race and capital would wound the soul of a nation and one more missed opportunity to unite a diverse populace would leave a society, for one more year, without new dreams for the future.

Take a look next spring. See who sits in the broadcast booth and see who writes the stories then. You will likely see that baseball which can be so large has again left itself small.

Where Is Myth?

In the years when boys discover girls but do not wish to let go of a childhood that holds few cares or concerns, my best friend and brothers and I would go down to the Lincoln Elementary School courtyard in South Pasadena to play Whiffle ball.

Standing on thick grass and surrounded on all four sides by two-story buildings, it was not a far fetch for us to imagine being in a baseball stadium. We played with an intensity to match—owing as much to the times. In those years we simply "lost ourselves" in whole summers chasing dream and desire: *we* were Wally Moon, Sandy Koufax, Jim Gilliam, Charlie Neal. That was many decades ago and I was foolish enough to believe that youth would never end—and that there would always be the Dodgers.

This, I think, is what constitutes myth. It is a way of connecting past and place to the self—in Milton's (1667, p. 21) words, that "dark, illimitable ocean, without bound, without dimension, where length, breadth and height, and Time and place are lost." Myth is our way of seeing, not in rational terms, or even by the accumulation of knowledge, but by positive feeling and sentiment.

I am quite fearful for our social institutions. The world is changing too fast and they are ill-equipped to fathom the new requirements of myth. But in this epoch we are also being told something new—that far from wishing to bury mystery the people want to reengage it. To reencounter myth, but not in denigration of science. And this is why the spiritual health of baseball is so crucial to us now: simply put, it is the American institution best suited for creating new and unifying myth. What will hold this diverse country of ours together if not baseball?

BASEBALL AND CAPITALISM

Today there are teams with payrolls over $200 million playing against teams that have total team salaries *under* $60 million. I can think of no quicker way to end the deeper meaning produced by sport than to have a money structure like this. It is no contest for the New York Yankees with its $200 million plus team salary to play against teams like the Minnesota Twins or Tampa Bay Rays that have sub-$60 million team salaries.

And why not? U.S. corporate behavior in the global economy operates in the very same way. Like the Yankees of baseball (and yes, the Dodgers too), large "Yankee corporations" with massive amounts of money to spend abroad, greater economies of scale—and a foreign policy that indebts foreign local economies to U.S. banks and the IMF—used the mantra of free market capitalism to destroy the social cohesion and domestic economies of other countries around the globe.

With this disparity in power, asking Brazil or Mali or Bolivia to fairly negotiate trade policies with the United States is like asking the Minnesota Twins to win three of four from the New York Yankees. No mystery there. This is not myth. It is not ritual. This is not the epitome of fair play and it is certainly far removed from the Elysian connection to past and place of the long ago Dodgers of 1959.

I remember vividly the day the façade of American fair play would fall away, even if for just an instant, and thus revealed for all to see what would be the true colors of capitalism at the end of the century. On this day, the sentiment of the people would come to prevail and thousands of baseball fans would register their frustration at the deeper failings of baseball. On this extraordinarily clear night, I was at Dodger Stadium with 11 friends and family members sitting in the Loge level. We were about halfway down the left field line and it was a night I would never forget. On this warm evening in August 1995, there was not one baseball thrown on to the field but *hundreds, even thousands.*

Baseball had just ended its strike. While the greedy owners with their legal monopoly—and players with their $10 million salaries—had finally settled their dispute, members of the baseball public were still holding a bitter taste in their mouths. Many in attendance knew the public that would one day again be called upon to pay for this monopoly and its runaway salaries in the form of higher ticket prices and higher cable TV monthly rates. *This public also suspected that this form of capitalism was no longer for the benefit of the larger public but for a small group of stakeholders, the richest few.*

On this evening, the umpires would botch a call so badly that every person in the stadium could see it was the wrong call. No one could anticipate what would happen next. This one small mistake by an umpiring crew would become *the flashpoint* for a massive, spontaneous yet peaceful and highly symbolic display of public disapproval and discontent for baseball and all that it had come to stand for. It was also the last time that Dodger owners would ever again hold a "Ball Night" in which everyone in attendance received a free baseball when entering through the turnstiles!

Like moths drawn to a bright light, first one, then three more, then finally hundreds of tiny, protesting white specs came cascading down on to the field, bouncing and flitting from one spot of grass to another. The umpires had lost control of the game. But there was more to the moment than that. When the umpires shut down the game and ruled it forfeited to the visiting team, the bigger event was that the fans didn't care. Sitting among the jeering/cheering fans, I joined in this feeling of release. *The merriment in the stands that night was so powerful it was like being part of a public display of carnivale*—a suspension of hierarchy and in its place, a new ideology of interconnection with each other and solidarity no matter what one's station (e.g., Bakhtin, 1929, p. 123). What was being celebrated here was not the loss of a game by the home team but rather the upending, for one brief instant, of an unfair form of owner greed and hierarchy that had come to violate the very sport's historic connection to past and place.

With hierarchy brushed aside for a moment in this evening of laughter and community cohesion, the viewing public had also made fun of the sport's failure to fulfill its sacred duty to protect and sustain mystery and myth. In dreamlike *chiaoscuro*, the tiny white flecks flitting on to the field may even have constituted an early premonition of a larger revolution to come, one that would bring with it hundreds of thousands of small promises—and very large demands—for a better time and place.

MY LIFE AFTER VIN SCULLY

On the surface, my dad had been a capitalist through and through. The first Asian American to become a registered stockbroker in the United States, he had always straddled two worlds and paid for that dissonance dearly. Ripped out of his student days at UCLA by the World War II policy of "relocating" Japanese Americans to U.S. concentration camps after Japan attacked Pearl Harbor, he entered the U.S. Army as one way to avoid the camps. And when the war was over, my dad entered New York University where he began his life on weekdays toiling as a student of high finance in the MBA program and reserving the weekends for his passion as a watercolor artist in Greenwich Village. As time went by, this tension between head and heart would always be resolved the same way, in favor of the practical need to protect his family and generate the income to guarantee his family the security he had been denied as a youth.

So when my father passed away in November of 1996, his life had come to an end a little sooner than he anticipated. He had lived the quiet life of sacrifice—shunning the limelight but pushing himself daily to win at the game of stock market investing for clients and family. Despite earning among the highest annual commissions for stockbrokers in the city, he was still prevented from gaining membership in the posh Jonathan Club and California Club in downtown Los Angeles—because he was not white. Distrusting of politics, he also turned down a chance to become a member of the LA Harbor Commission.

Too scarred and too Japanese to open up and tell us his stories, my father succumbed to stomach cancer in all too common "Japanese style"—having held all that suppressed pain and rage inside in his stomach, his *hara*, for so many decades. But like Vin Scully, I like to think, my father in his own way had also lived his life in search of myth, in search of that time and place that was utopian and only just beyond our immediate reach. Through stories *not* told—and by a dropped word or raised eyebrow—my father would tell my four siblings and me not just what life was about, but what it could *or should* be like in the future.

So if Vin Scully's storytelling about "the origin of the American hot dog"—or the strange behavior of this 1950s catcher or that 1960s manager—became an un- bending thread that ran through my youth and well into my adulthood, it was my father's terse exhortations to achieve, succeed, and bring honor to the family (*"You have to do better next time"*) that brought an equally unbending sense of purpose, meaning and hope into my life. Now into my sixties, I find a certain clarity at last in my father's own struggle. Born of missionaries who helped to found the Iao Congregational Church in Wailuku, Maui, a century ago (Urata, 2005), he forged his own successes and willed himself forward into that better future.

This also means that when my father departed this world, he left without telling us much about the difficulties he had encountered in World War II and later, as the first licensed Asian American stockbroker. Born an American in East Los Angeles, he settled early into a patterned life of Japanese stoicism and quiet suffering. It was only after he died that a friend of his from World War II days told me that my father had stood up and protested the Army's decision to prevent him and 21 other Intelligence Corps trainees from visiting their families during Christmas vacation just like the white soldiers were allowed to do. (His younger sister and mother were still in the internment camp at Gila Bend in Arizona and his father in a separate camp in Rowher, Arkansas.) For this respectful protest he was dismissed from the highly prestigious Intelligence Corps and placed in the dental technician unit of the Army—where as a corporal he went on to train sergeant after sergeant and was himself never granted further promotion in rank.

While my father never said it in so many words, I have to think "the long lost watercolor artist of Greenwich Village" must have suffered internally from that nose-to-the-grindstone existence and his life of quiet sacrifice and uncele- brated achievement in the financial world. For him, the Japanese norm of *enryo*, or self-abasement, that I even studied with a sense of desperation for my college thesis (Tanaka, 1970) had likely become more firmly internalized with each new oppression that he faced.

* * *

Now as I look back, I am convinced that every time Vin Scully spoke, it was as if my father was finally expressing to me his own deeply repressed human passion for all that is good and possible. With each accounting of a Dodger victory, Vin Scully was telling me about my father's special joy in being a Bohemian watercolorist in Greenwich Village, New York—or his quiet satisfaction from finding greater financial success than his parents might have imagined possible from the clapboard shelters of the Gila Bend and Rowher relocation camps. And each time Vin Scully described a bright blue sky under which the Dodgers took the field, the imprisoned artist was set free—and new myth was again possible.

* * *

WHAT IT MEANS TO BE AN AMERICAN

So when baseball fails to give us joy, I know with a certainty that it can only offer bare statistics—and we know that baseball can be much more than that. When baseball is without mystery, we are left with the material and predictable—runaway player salaries, rampant owner greed, and teams unequally positioned because of unequal resources. When baseball fails as ritual to produce new myth, it leaves us most vulnerable since we are now holding on to the thin reed of "fixed truth." In this era there will be no more "Willie Mays basket catches," "Maury Wills stolen bases," or "Bobby Thompson home runs"—because even if the dramatic were to occur we wouldn't be able to recognize it as such, the process for myth-making having long since shut down.

Yes, there have been glimmers of hope. Each time a local boy returned home to play for his home team, the Dodgers, we are reminded of our own connection to past and place. It happened years ago when Eric Davis and Darryl Strawberry asked to be traded home in the 1990s and again when southern Californians Tim Wallach, Todd Worrell, and Shawn Green followed suit. More recently, it was local boy wonder Nomar Garciaparra who briefly joined the Dodgers and brought with him his new wife, soccer star Mia Hamm. Whether the decisions to "come home" from all these players presaged a resurgence of baseball's mythic potential remained unclear. Absent a larger pattern, the mythic nature of baseball remains eclipsed by the twin U.S. psychoses of race and capital.

So what is it we ultimately lose when there is no joy, mystery, or myth? We lose our ability to connect with each other. We lose our ability to be rooted in time and space—that clear sense of where we came from, where we belong. We lose our positive spirit. And of course we lose baseball. In such times, one merely has to look at what's been lost to know what it means to be American.

Former commissioner Bart Giamatti (1989) once said, "In baseball everyone wants to arrive at the same place, which is where they started," home. Well I can't go back to being 11 and the old grass courtyard at Lincoln School has long since been covered over with asphalt. But I can retreat into that quiet place deep inside me where I hold my childhood joys. I can stare at those 17 autographs of the 1959 Championship Dodgers now framed on my bedroom wall—and know there's a story that comes with it. I can wait and hope for baseball to return to its own source, this time bigger and more spirited than ever, this time a celebration of what we hold dear in our adulthood *and* our youth, where grass and sky and mystery collide, this time a baseball that aspires to myth.

NOTES

1. Much of this essay appeared originally in *The LA Weekly* in shorter form on March 3–April 6, 1995, under the title "The Myth of Baseball." It is reprinted here with its permission.
2. In very recent times, it should be noted that the Dodgers hired a team manager, Dave Roberts, who is half black and half Japanese. What this tells me is that in baseball—as in life—things can always "come full circle" and present you with new opportunities to make the world a better place and perceive it that way, too. It also means to me that we should never give up in our efforts to build that better world.

REFERENCES

Bakhtin, M. (1929/1984). *Problems of Dostoyevsky's poetics*. Minneapolis: University of Minnesota Press.

Giamatti, B. (1989/2011). *Take time for paradise: Americans and their games*. New York, NY: Summit Books; Bloomfield Publishing.

Milton, J. (1667). *Paradise lost; A poem written in ten books*. London: Samuel Simmons.

Tanaka, G. K. (1970). *"Enryo" and the changing personality needs of Japanese Americans* (Honors thesis). Williams College, Williamstown, MA.

Urata, B. (Ed.). (2005). *The crucible of trials and tribulations: Memories of a Meiji missionary, Gi'ichi Tanaka*. Los Angeles, CA: Creative Continuum.

CHAPTER 4

The End of Democracy as We Knew It

The U.S. judicial system was poisoned by rightwing foundations underwriting law and economics courses taught to judges that, in effect, leave all rights in the hands of the capitalists.
Paul Craig Roberts, former U.S. Assistant Secretary of the Treasury and father of
Reaganomics (April 29, 2018)

When the men from Think Tank X began passing out bright Kelly green baseball caps, we laughed and put them on. It was only two years after the Rodney King riots, or L.A. Rebellion of 1992, and we had come to attend a day-long retreat at the all-new Sunset Canyon Recreation Center atop a hill overlooking UCLA. I felt honored as the lone graduate student sitting among assistant police chiefs, assistant school superintendents, fire department commanders, Parks & Recreation and Health Department officials, and leaders from other agencies in Los Angeles to engage in a simulation to learn how a local government might better respond to crisis.

"Your mission, should you accept it, is to create a model city government that responds in better ways to crisis than in the past." The smiling convener in his 50's added, "The goal of this exercise is to build a more harmonious community. Should you accept your mission...."

WORLD SYSTEMS ANALYSIS

In this story I inquire into the limitations of systems analysis as a tool for U.S. democratic governance deployed by think tanks today. In this analysis I argue the current democracy has been cut off from the "meanings" of the people it was intended to serve—their norms, duties, beliefs, passions, and dreams. Without those meanings, there can be no impedance to the selfish individualism and unregulated profiteering that gave us our financial crisis today. It is this loss of meaning, I suggest, that is the underlying cause of collapse not only of the prevailing economic model, free market capitalism, but also of the U.S. democracy and its education policy "No Child Left Behind."

"World systems" theorists were among the earliest to foresee in free market capitalism a recipe for disaster. Wallerstein (2004, p. 156) warned of the danger of reversal of three trends that had given structural advantage to free market capitalism and generated profits for U.S. elites: low labor costs, low materials costs, and low rates of taxation. With this "unstable structure," Wallerstein (2005, p. 331) predicted an epic battle between democracies promoting economic hierarchy (like the U.S. democracy) and the onset of a new democratic system that is egalitarian. "We can call this a battle between the spirit of Davos and the spirit of Porto Alegre," he wrote, referring to a place in Switzerland where global capitalists plan the coming year and a second place, in Brazil, where democracy is controlled by the people themselves (p. 160).

Arrighi (2005, p. 26) added America's growing reliance on foreign debt to fund its highly leveraged economic growth was "without precedent in world history," giving a clear advantage to China (p. 23). One reviewer argued, however, that Arrighi and Silver (1999) exhibited "little or no problematization of whether the current era may be witnessing an ongoing systems reorganization that might change the logic of systems functioning" (Chew, 2001). In other words, the usefulness of world systems analysis may well be confined to the era of free market capitalism already coming to an end.

A capital markets overview shows the U.S. economy is in the middle of a comprehensive economic collapse that is the natural outcome of the core traits of neoliberalism, including

- Neoliberalism's promise that *"free markets"* will bring cheaper goods to U.S. consumers from countries opened to U.S. producers (hence "free"), a promise that indeed came true but at the long-term costs of exporting millions of jobs out of the United States, trampling local businesses abroad, and growing reckless levels of U.S. debt (Ferguson, 2008).
- The *"deregulation"* of U.S. businesses, a second core trait of neoliberalism, that brought higher U.S. corporate profits and a proliferation of fast-return investment platforms like hedge funds, derivatives trading, and private equity buy-outs—but also scandals demonstrating that markets cannot regulate themselves and a condition of frenzy feeding last seen before the 1929 Crash (Ferguson, 2008).

- A shift in the U.S. economy from one based on manufacturing to *overfinan-cialization* with layers of financial instruments stacked one on top of another was like a house of cards ready to fall. With a proliferation of leveraged buy-outs and razzle-dazzle investment vehicles, it was "a mountain of debt" (*Monthly Review*, 2002).

One result of this economic model has been a widening gap between rich and poor. Through altered tax schemes, the net worth of 90% of U.S. households *failed to grow* between 1950 and 2000, while the upper 1% experienced *a forty-fold increase* (Tabb, 2006). With the wealthiest paying a tax of 70% in the 1950s to 1970s and the middle class paying 25% or 30%, by the 2000s the wealthiest were *only paying a 15% capital gains rate* on massive investment income with the average citizen continuing to pay 25% to 35%. Supported by *both* political parties, this tax scheme reversal marked one of the greatest wealth transfers in world history.

With the average U.S. taxpayer paying for three Middle East wars—and billionaire Warren Buffett paying less in taxes than his secretary—the U.S. household was bled dry. With 70% of the spending base—the U.S. household—having lost its purchasing power, U.S. markets could "only stimulate demand through the creation of debt, both personal and public" (Tabb, 2006, p. 12). With inflated mortgage debt, high credit card debt, job downsizing, and lost health and pension support, the U.S. consumer was by 2008 already "tapped out."

But in the face of this massive dislocation, the "systems" way of knowing of Wallerstein and Arrighi did not position them to offer fresh alternatives. Wallerstein came closest to moving off a systems epistemology but in the end only romanticized the Porto Alegre democracy as a generalized "spirit" he did not develop further.

* * *

"In this simulation, you will have a mayor, form policy, and respond to events that arise. This simulation will therefore test..."With words to this effect, the three facilitators at the Sunset Canyon Recreation Center all smiled as they stood with their backs to a long picture window that ran along the far end of the conference style meeting room. The 35 or so of us who served as guinea pigs sat along two long rows of tables, eagerly awaiting the rest of our instructions.

In a city that had experienced the pain and dislocation of the L.A. Rebellion of 1992, we were hopeful that our participation in this exercise would contribute to a new model of civic governance and better race relations in a city whose population was now 70% of color.

A middle-aged African American woman with a highly professional demeanor was picked by the conveners to be our "mayor." While almost three-quarters of us were of color, we noticed that all three facilitators from Think Tank X were over 50, white, and male.

We also saw that the organizers had donned different colored baseball caps from the bright green ones we were wearing. Theirs were white.

THREE TICKING TIME BOMBS

Like multiple, rolling earthquakes, the 2000s brought with them a "Cascade Effect" of economic crises—beginning with the dot.com bubble of 2000 and continuing to the World Trade Center bombing and financial panic of 2001, subprime mortgage crisis of 2008, and sovereign debt crises of 2010–2011. At each turn, the U.S. government took "desperate measures" to right the ship. First, it suspended the sale of 30-year treasury bonds—but this meant the United States could only bring them back at a time when their reinstatement would place massive upward pressure on mortgage interest rates. Then the Federal Reserve began printing billions of dollars without underlying basis or worth—cheapening the dollar and making hyperinflation more likely down the road. When arcane "credit default swaps" led to the subprime mortgage market failure in 2008, the U.S. government gave trillions of dollars in "corporate welfare" to bail out the auto industry, financial institutions, and largest U.S. insurance firms. The Federal Reserve then bought $1.2 trillion of toxic (failing) debt from the largest banks—paying for this *at face value*.

And with further rounds of money printing since 2009 and the addition of a zero interest rate policy—all designed to keep their member banks afloat while damaging the average citizen—the Fed reduced the value of the average American's accumulated savings and in millions of tiny cuts, destroyed the "comfortable retirement income" that seniors were counting on and had been promised to them much earlier, when they had much more energy and the physical capability to work. With these desperate measures by the Fed—and a Congress that continued to "look the other way"—the leaders of a once proud nation and who had held the public trust now ensured that many Americans who lack the minimum funds with which to live would die from starvation and disease. To top this off, these measure would set in motion the "three ticking time bombs" (or "three D's") that would collectively constitute the greatest threat to national security in U.S. history:

- **Debt in U.S. in Excess of $150 Trillion (an amount that is simply too large to ever pay back).** This includes the accumulated debt and obligations in all U.S. capital markets, agencies, and consumers, U.S. corporate debt, state and local government shortfalls; underfunding of corporate and government pension funds, the massive underfunding and theft in Social Security and Medicare accounts, the accumulated credit, grants, loans, and guarantees for the Federal Reserve backed by U.S. taxpayers, and the ever-rising federal government debt;

- **Derivatives Globally in Excess of $1.5 Quadrillion (von Greyerz, 2018).** These unregulated razzle-dazzle instruments created with the consent of President Clinton in the 1990s and then Federal Reserve chairman Alan Greenspan in the 2000s include massive interest rate plays, bets on packaged debt, and other forms of high stakes gambling. These tiered instruments are not publicly traded, are not protected by pubic accounting, plagued by counter-party risk, and accordingly have underlying true worth that simply cannot be known. With the subprime crisis caused by weakness in just 2% of all derivatives in 2007–2008 (Farrell, May 12, 2010), the effects of a weakness in 20% of all derivatives would be beyond comprehension.
- **Disintermediation—Where Foreign Investors Dump All U.S. Stocks, Bonds, Real Estate, and Treasury Bonds.** A wholesale departure of foreign investors and sovereign banks from the U.S. capital markets would be the "final act" and lead to skyrocketing interest rates on U.S. bonds, mortgages, and corporate debt—the onset of unimaginable hyperinflation—and the end of today's de-regulated capitalist economy. The recent dumping of U.S. treasury bonds by Russia, China, and Japan—and formation of international trade pacts between Russia and China and Saudi Arabia—are explicit rejections of the U.S. dollar as the "global reserve currency," meaning that the days when more U.S. dollars can be printed to further the illusion of wealth and well-being will have already come to an end.

So in masking the true condition of the economy and permitting the gross devaluation of the U.S. dollar, the actions of a "free" market (neoliberal) U.S. government and its complicit official media are merely exacerbating the broader "economic snap" to come—one that will visit horrific terror upon U.S. children and families, lead to enormous psychological dislocation and death, and demonstrate the ultimate folly in letting markets govern the state. With the global *"interconnectedness of capital markets,"* the collapse of one sector like the Eurozone or China—and the original culprit, the "U.S. derivatives market"—would trigger a worldwide "systemic collapse" of mind-boggling proportions. A collapse of this magnitude would cast epochal doubt not only on the idea of representative democracy but a narrow-minded and self-destructive neoliberal national education policy (e.g. No Child Left Behind) that leaves its citizens without the awareness to know when they are being cheated and the skills to rebuild their nation's damaged social infrastructure.

* * *

The White Hats had told us we would be divided into four teams, each meeting in a different side room of this conference center. One group had become the mayor's office, another had become the Police Department, a third became the L.A. Unified School District, etc. The day was divided into three modules with each module giving us a chance to react to a different event by discussing and then forming new policy. From their words we could tell the White Hats had been very concerned despite their broad smiles.

The first crisis was a 15% cut back in the overall city budget. We were asked to devise a strategy to respond to the crisis in a way that maintained our mission but led to the reductions needed. We were also told that we could send an emissary once during each module to any of the other groups to ask questions or relay a request. From my participation in my group's response to crisis in the three modules, I learned much about how negotiation between government agencies can proceed during unforeseen events visited upon a city government.

Following the budget crisis came two more modules in which (a) a 13-year-old black teenager was shot by the police and (b) segments of the city were beginning to riot in response to the shooting. It was beginning to feel like the LA riots all over again.

* * *

FUNGIBILITY AND "NO CHILD LEFT BEHIND"

With all the current economic weakness in the United States, I suggest there is a deeper source of collapse of a U.S. neoliberal regime seen in the simulation—its concept of "fungibility" and the resulting inability of a society to create and share the social and cultural meanings that would bind a people together.

- "Fungibility," in reference to capital, means having a common, homogeneous and interchangeable medium of exchange (e.g., the U.S. dollar) between different traders. To prosper, a free market mentality must therefore *diminish* all forms of individual or shared group meaning (i.e., culture) that would threaten the fungibility that undergirds the free market regime. By enforcing sameness, fungibility is inherently destructive of culture, forecloses the creation of new shared meaning, and ironically deprives a country of the capacity to build other forms of cohesion across difference.
- The national education law "No Child Left Behind" (NCLB) enacts this very same mentality: it treats all students as if they were "fungible." Under a standardized test-driven mentality, children are seen as interchangeable as if they all learn in the same way. Teachers are prevailed upon *to teach to that presumed homogeneity*, assess outcomes as if all students could one day perform at the same level, and refrain from teaching children how to create new meaning or become independent, critical thinkers.
- Reduced to "fungible" units like any other commodity, students and teachers alike must now perform to a common standard—*or be labeled "underperforming."* In this regard, educational anthropologist Norma Gonzalez (2004, p. 17) asks, "Is our notion of quality tied up with global economic practices

and texts that define educational achievement and success in an atomized fashion, conflating education with discrete skills and market performance?" Yet reports show NCLB's emphasis on testing leads some states to lower standards for teachers (Southwest Center for Teacher Quality, 2004), does not benefit families constrained by economic and political disadvantage (Mickelson & Southworth, 2005) or rural geography (Jimerson, 2005), pushes lower performing students out the backdoor (Orfield, Losen, & Wald, 2004), puts racially diverse schools at greater risk of failing (Kim & Sunderman, 2005, p. 12), and falls short on promised practical outcomes (Mintrop & Sunderman, 2009).

In promising to uplift *all* children, NCLB thus appears to *magnify* existing inequities. In an uncanny parallel to this, David Harvey (2005, pp. 64–65) once defined a "neoliberal" state as one that is governed by free trade and individual property rights and holds each individual "responsible for his or her own actions and well-being (so that) individual success or failure are interpreted in terms of entrepreneurial virtues *or personal failings*" (emphasis added). Like its education policy, the current U.S. democracy reflects an unmistakable chimera in its "declared public aims… *the well-being of all*" that conflict with the "actual consequences—*the restoration of class*"*-based inequity* (p. 79, emphasis added).

In valorizing individualism and competition, Harvey concludes "the anarchy of the market (might) even lead to a breakdown of all bonds of solidarity and a condition verging on social anarchy and nihilism" (p. 82). Instantiating fungible units in place of the richness and particularity of different student perspectives, histories, and imaginations, the greatest weakness in a neoliberal democracy might now be seen as a *cumulative loss of meaning* deriving from its homogenizing effects that render a people fearful, without anchor, without compass.

I note the above to underscore that "construction of the self," as one antithesis to fungibility, is likely to be where the project of democratic renewal must begin. With the collapse of free market capitalism comes a fresh opportunity to replace the empty, soul-less quality of a standardized "neoliberal student" and standardized "neoliberal teacher" with the richness that derives from having learners develop their own notions of self in relation to others (i.e., *meaning*) while helping others do the same—and teachers who teach to that mutuality. This schooling would enact the exact opposite of the controlled, atomizing, artificial democracy of Think Tank X. One wonders, is that already a different democracy?

* * *

It was around 2:00 PM when the facilitators told us the modules portion of the simulation was over and we would now have a chance to deliberate as a whole.

"Let's hear your group's recommendations for how municipal units can work together to solve a crisis, shall we?" the senior white hat said to the gathered officials. "Mayor, would you like to facilitate this?"

Reaching the podium, the stately mayor looked out at the participants who sat in two long rows of seats and tables and asked if we had any questions or wished to make any comments. A slender, athletic male in his early sixties was first to raise his hand and when called upon, he spoke tentatively. The only man I had known before this day, this high ranking official from the Los Angeles Police Department spoke softly but quickly touched a chord in us all.

"Here's what I think," he began, "I love all the chance for dialogue in this simulation and so I want to thank the facilitators for this. But at the same time, I feel a little bit manipulated. We've been doing this exercise obediently for about four hours now but there is one tiny group making all the rules. And it isn't us."

With these words, the senior White Hat seemed to freeze and he struggled to maintain his ready smile.

"You wanted us to model how a democratic city government responds to crisis," the police official continued, "but it doesn't feel like we have any power. Instead of making our own policy and moving the city forward as we'd like, we spend all our time reacting to one crisis after another that you present to us." He paused briefly before finishing. "It doesn't feel right."

One by one, other invited participants began to chime in, adding to what had spontaneously become an open criticism of the simulation exercise itself. While each individual had a point to make, the collective feeling was unmistakable. An exercise that had been conceived and funded to study how to improve civic response to urban crisis was itself beginning to spin out of control for the White Hats.

"But we have to keep the simulation going!" interjected another White Hat, unable to hold back the strain in his voice. He rushed to add that this was all part of the exercise, to see how officials feel and then make the city work even through a crisis.

When he saw that the audience was staring back at him, unmoved, the White Hat looked to the mayor in desperation and asked her if she wouldn't mind steering the group back to completing the exercise.

Pausing for an instant, the "mayor" turned to her leaders and began to speak.

* * *

ALTERNATIVE DEMOCRACIES?

In contrast to the current top-down, think tank democracy of the United States today, alternatives democracies exist that bring great promise and treat schooling as the primary vehicle by which future citizens are prepared for direct participation. One such model is the *"autonomous community"* of Chiapas, Mexico, where hamlets, towns, and cities in the entire southern one-third of Mexico have become self-functioning democracies with citizens deliberating and making decisions from the bottom-up—instead of ceding that duty to a neoliberal federal democracy (McLaren, Flores, & Tanaka, 2001). In Chiapas the pre-K to 12 schooling, directed by women elders, gives every child voice and meaning-making capacity and teaches them the intersubjective skills they would need to be good listeners and nurturing of others.

A second model of participatory democracy lies in the region surrounding Porto Alegre, Brazil—mentioned by Wallerstein—where dialogue-based Freirean schooling teaches local publics the duties and responsibilities of *"participatory public budgeting,"* or "PPB" (Baiocchi, 2003; Deantoni, 2004). This model shows that a participatory democracy can deal with budgets, work across a large region, and be sustained by Freirean pedagogy that is designed to foreground the meanings of a local community.

A third model can be found in the town of Reggio Emilia, Italy, where decision-making for the school budget is conducted by the community. With children taught from a very young age to identify questions and address them in groups (Malaguzzi, 1993), this emergent form of schooling instills a sense of *"complementarity"* in which all children grow and find personal meaning as a part of a process of helping other children also to grow and find meaning—patterning the behavioral expression "I am me through you."

Fourth, a culturally based practice of participatory democracy can be found in the *Kaupapa Maori model* of New Zealand, where Smith (1999/2005, p. 156) reports an "indigenous agenda focuses strategically on the goal of self-determination." Unlike the Western concept of "collaboration" between individuals, Maori participants affirm *a deeper sense of "connectedness"* that links one's personal identity and meanings to the overall well-being of the Maori community.

In a fifth project, I am involved with a group of applied education researchers seeking to take scholarly research assessing NCLB to volunteers from the U.S. public who will be placed in *"citizens panels"* (e.g., Guston, 1999), undergo training, and propose "the next" U.S. education policy. Convened in such places as a small Midwest town, a metropolitan New York, a Latino-based community in south Texas, a suburb in central California, and an Indian reservation in Arizona, these panels would be made up of citizens from all walks including labor, the elderly, businesspersons, former teachers, parents, and teenagers. While nonbinding, the idea is to let local public consensus and meaning-making percolate upward to federal policymakers, thus potentially modeling "participatory democracy" on a nationwide scale.

Yet other variants of direct civic engagement can be seen in the *decentralized government* of Kerala, India (Isaac & Heller, 2003), the Calpulli *autonomous commu-*

nity in San Bernadino, California (Rodriguez, 1998), Eastside Café's *performance-based autonomous community* in East Los Angeles (Flores, 2002), a schooling approach in Sweden that views *children as future agents of social change* (Lancy, 2006), the ethnically diverse MollyOlga *community-based arts project* of New York (Fine Weiss, Centrie, & Roberts, 2000), and the communities in Chicago that still have the power to govern their own public schools through *Local School Councils*, or LSCs (Fung, 2003, p. 113; Hursch, 2006, p. 21; Lipman, 2003, p. 54).

What all the above models have in common—in direct contrast to this simulation held at UCLA—is a trait of getting local publics directly involved in both meaning and policy making, from the bottom-up. The belief is that a local-to-national flow of meaning in a participatory democracy offers each citizen an opportunity to feel a direct connection to her or his government—*and be personally involved in a meaning-making process that culminates in policymaking*. With its potential for humility and soul-construction, the practice of participatory democracy ushers in new ways of knowing, being, and interrelating that "make small" the cold logic of capital, fungibility, and systems analysis.

* * *

"I have listened to the group," the mayor began, as she stood behind the podium and looked back and forth between the White Hats at her side and the participants who sat before her.

"I have to say that I agree with what everyone has said," she continued. "All of us participants never had any real say in what decisions would be made."

Hearing this, the three White Hats of Think Tank X stood as if caught in a kind of camera snapshot, frozen in time. On their faces could be seen a conflicted state of continuing hope and mounting anxiety about a world that wasn't the one they intended.

Facing her people, the mayor said, "I know the organizers want us to finish this day with some group decision-making but I can't do this anymore...I quit!"

* * *

DUTY TO PROMOTE RECONSTITUTION DURING SYSTEMIC COLLAPSE

As an education researcher and applied anthropologist, I feel we have a special duty to help the public during times of systemic collapse. During moments like this, we can use our skills to test new models that might reclaim and renew the democracy while minimizing the chances of neoliberal recrudescence. Such incursions would have to resolve a number of deeper concerns.

The first concern was evident in the simulation itself: an unmistakable *absence of humanism* in a systems approach to running the world. The failure of this think tank simulation approach to civic governance demonstrates that blind adherence to an epistemology that hopes to solve all human problems through linear, compartmentalized thinking can overlook much—and even be the cause of a collapse. In a similar way, NCLB with its cold fungibility might now be seen as a kind of "poster child" for neoliberalism and a desperate attempt by a small, elite group to turn a far larger population of people (who are middle class, working class, rural, of color and all looking for meaning) into automatons who are easily manipulated because they are denied meaning and subjected to the alienation that begins with standardization in school. If the United States aims to build security, its next education policy will need to *re*create meaning and culture.

A second concern revealed itself as a chasm in ways of knowing and assigning meaning between the White Hats and the green hats. While one might see humor in a spontaneous "uprising" by public officials convened in order to study the very opposite—how to promote order during crisis—the larger concern revealed here is that the systems way of knowing of the White Hats holds a peculiar *inability* to adapt itself to populations that are racially diverse; *systems analysis is "inapposite" diversity*. With U.S. diversity growing, the subtle, stubborn racism/sexism/classism of this chasm was shamelessly encoded in the coloring of hats worn that day, signaling "whose democracy" this was and whose it wasn't. Where the participants were overwhelmingly of color, diverse in gender, class, and professional training—and wore green hats—the think tank leaders were all male, systems thinkers, racialized as white, and culturally nonspecific. The symbolism in having Think Tank X leaders wear white hats was inescapable: television westerns had told us the ones wearing white hats were "the heroes." It grated.

One implication for the next democracy, then, is that it will have to bridge across cultures more effectively than in this simulation. If a diverse democracy is ever to be participatory, its citizens will likely benefit from *preK-16 education that is intercultural* (Touraine, 2000, p. 269). I have found in field research that "intercultural storytelling" can show diverse groups of students how to create and share meaning across difference (Tanaka, 2003, p. 135; 2009, p. 89), affirming that there are schooling-based alternatives to neoliberalism and its anomie.

Third, revealed in this exercise was the larger possibility that *a systems approach to running the world is simply too binary and confrontational* to be a palimpsest for global human society. Indeed, as seen here, it may be *the cause* of revolt. Here the participants refused the status of "atomized" citizens in a preplanned, systems-managed democracy and demanded instead to be "subjects" and agents who can have voice, govern their own democracy, and, importantly, help each other along the way. Missing from this think tank's emphasis on order, pathways, and decision nodes was any examination of the importance of having shared approaches to human agency and "subject" making—*mutuality*—demanded by the participants at UCLA (see, e.g., Couldry, 2004, p. 8; Ricoeur, 1992, p. 183; Tanaka, 2002, p. 283, 2009, p. 90). If the United States is to become a better global citizen, its future education will need to teach to this, too.

Fourth, the very notion of *systems analysis may be incompatible with democracy, especially when controlled by rich men.* In fact, the breakdown of this simulation reveals that a larger tension exists between its function as a neoliberal tool to control a compliant, consuming public—and the opposing belief that democracy should and can be intrinsically "by, for, and of the people." Tocqueville (1835, p. 322) had expressed early concern about a U.S. democracy in which citizens do not have the skills and norms for the direct participation he saw in New England town meetings. In the absence of direct, informed citizen participation in local civic decision-making (id at 95), he feared the U.S. democracy would turn into an "aristocratic government" controlled by "rich men" (id at 225; compare Ober, 1989, p. 334).

As seen in this simulation, systems analysis from think tanks funded by rich men—like the American Enterprise Institute, the Heritage Foundation, and the RAND Corporation—can too easily become a ready instrumentality to delimit and even undermine the core precept in a democracy that requires elected officials and top level bureaucrats (here, officials from the city of Los Angeles) to fulfill their duty to look out for the interests of the people first and foremost.

But at this simulation—where the study of an uprising itself led to an uprising—the notion of "a neoliberal democracy" was finally seen as an illusion, a misnomer, not a democracy at all. So when the mayor of this imagined city said "I quit," it spelled more than an end to a preplanned simulation: the White Hats could do nothing, the exercise was over, *and so was their pretense to democracy.* In the current economic collapse, the United States as a nation of people could find it is without a lasting economic model *and* a democracy that is by, for, and of the people.

At the same time, a resolution of this simulated crisis in favor of "the people" did not solve the larger problem of how to engage members of future publics in their democracy without the anarchy seen in this Sunset Canyon exercise. While not intended by the White Hats, however, *the actions of these participants may already have adumbrated something akin to a new and more "organic democracy"* where meaning is established on an "as you go" basis by the people themselves—rather than falling back on a "managed" system or structure. But how do we teach this? In this context, U.S. educators might turn to the kind of personal and social agency that Touraine (2000, p. 284) envisions in what would be "schools for the subject":

> The fate of modern democracy, defined as a politics of the Subject, will be decided mainly in our schools and cities. In educational terms, we have to construct a school for the Subject and for inter-cultural communication, or in other words recognize that the goal of education is not to train and prepare young people…for their future economic roles. Its goal is to train and educate them to be themselves.

In light of Touraine's words, I will now suggest the simulation at Sunset Canyon did not fail at all but rather served to demonstrate what might be wrong with a democracy informed and controlled by private think tank researchers who are predisposed to a system that, much like NCLB, looks for and rewards preconceived, measurable results rather than vesting power in the public it serves. So if we are to avoid a return of the twin free market evils of fungibility and full democratic unraveling, U.S. citizens will soon want to discover the meanings that come from a sense of mutuality—*the interconnectedness of humans*—in a more participatory democracy. In other words, the most lasting ramification of today's neoliberal collapse may well be the rare opportunity it now presents to remake the democracy along the lines of more participatory "deep" democracies and seen around the world.

Fifth, *the peaking and decline of this neoliberal system begs the question what precautions might be taken to minimize the possibility of recrudescence of a belligerent, greed-based, free market mentality in the future.* After all, the same impulse had taken root before, culminating in the crash of 1893, Panic of 1907, Stock Market Crash of 1929, and cascading "Waterfall of Free Market Collapses" of today. To prevent that return, progressive educators may want to consider closely what the simulation participants at UCLA wished for most: a democracy that gives people a capacity to remake that democracy each day, as "subjects," rather than function as fungible "objects" in a simulated exercise controlled by private think tanks—by finally teaching agency to all U.S. schoolchildren and on a nationwide scale.

So for urban leaders who had come to UCLA with such curiosity and high hopes, a true democracy was never encountered, only the illusion of a democracy that had been shrewdly concocted and controlled in a thinly veiled way by the facilitators of Think Tank X. But in their revolt, the brave participants at Sunset Recreation Center revealed precisely what is wrong with the U.S. democracy today. On this day, the actions of one conservative think tank to "model democracy" had been exposed for what it truly was—serving as a synecdoche for the larger reality of the United States today—and signaling that in fact the democracy as originally conceived was already dead.

NOTE

This chapter was originally published in 2007 in an edited volume by Kenneth Saltman entitled *Schooling and the Politics of Disaster*. The original title of the chapter was "U.S. Education in a Post-9/11 world: The Deeper Implications of the Current Systemic Collapse of the Neoliberal Regime." It is reprinted here with the permission of Routledge.

BIBLIOGRAPHY

Arrighi, G. (2005). Hegemony unraveling. *New Left Review, 32*, 23–87.

Arrighi, G., & Silver, B. J. (1999). *Chaos and governance in the modern world system*. Minneapolis, MN: University of Minnesota Press.

Baiocchi, G. (2003). Participation, activism, and politics: The Porto Alegre experiment. In A. Fung & E. O. Wright (Eds.), *Deepening democracy: Institutional innovations in empowered participatory governance*. London: Verso.

Chew, S. C. (2001). Book review: Arrighi and silver, chaos and governance in the modern world system. *Canadian Journal of Sociology Online*, cjsonline.ca/reviews/chaos.html.

Cochran-Smith, M. (2005). No child left behind: 3 years and counting. *Journal of Teacher Education, 56*(2), 99–103.

Couldry, N. (2004). In place of a common culture, what? *The Review of Education, Pedagogy, and Cultural Studies, 26*, 3–21.

Cowen, T. (2006, September 7). China is big trouble for the U.S. balance of trade, right? Well, not so fast. *New York Times*, C3.

Deantoni, N. (2004, April). *The Freirean approach to education and participatory democracy in Porto Alegre, Brazil*. Paper presented at the annual meeting of the American Educational Research Association, San Diego, CA.

Farrell, P. B. (2010). Financial blog. *Marketwatch.com*. May 12, 2010.

Ferguson, N. (2008). *The ascent of money: A financial history of the world*. New York: Penguin Press.

Fine, M., Weiss, L., Centrie, C., & Roberts, R. (2000). Educating beyond the borders of schooling. *Anthropology & Education Quarterly, 31*(2), 131–151.

Flores, R. (2002, May 13). The Eastside Café: Not a place but a state of mind. *In Motion Magazine*. eastsidecafe_2000@yahoo.com.

Fung, A. (2003). Deliberative democracy, Chicago style: Grass-roots governance in policing and public education. In Fung, A., & Wright, E. O. (Eds.), *Deepening democracy: Institutional innovations in empowered participatory governance*. London: Verso.

Gitlin, T. (2006). *The intellectuals and the flag*. New York, NY: Columbia University Press.

Gonzalez, N. (2004). Disciplining the discipline: Anthropology and the pursuit of quality education. *Educational Researcher, 33*(5), 17–25.

Von Greyerz, E. (2018). The 2007–9 crisis will return in 2018—with a vengeance. Goldswitzerland. com (February 16, 2018).

Guston, D. H. (1999). Evaluating the first U.S. consensus conference: The impact of the citizens' panel on telecommunications and the future of democracy. *Science, Technology & Human Values, 24*(4), 451–482.

Harvey, D. (2005). *A brief history of neoliberalism*. Oxford: Oxford University Press.

Hursch, D. (2006). The crisis in urban education: Resisting neoliberal policies and forging democratic possibilities. *Educational Researcher, 35*(4), 19–25.

Isaac, T. M. T., & Heller, P. (2003). Democracy and development: Decentralized planning in Kerala. In A. Fung & E. O. Wright (Eds.), *Deepening democracy: Institutional innovations in empowered participatory governance*. London: Verso. Pp. 77–110.

Jimerson, L. (2005). Placism in NCLB: How rural children are left behind. *Equity & Excellence in Education, 38*(3), 211–219.

Jubak, J. (2006a). Fed kills a key inflation gauge. *Jubak's Journal*, March 31, 2006.

Jubak, J. (2006b). Stagflation: A new peril for stocks. *Jubak's Journal*, July 4, 2006.

Kim, J. S., & Sunderman, G. L. (2005). Measuring academic proficiency under the No Child Left Behind Act: Implications for educational equity. *Educational Researcher, 34*(8), 3–13.

Lancy, D. F. (2006). Review of Eva Poluha. *The Power of Continuity.*

Light, Jay. (1974). *Lecture on capital markets.*, Boston, MA: Harvard Business School, Boston, MA.

Lenkersdorf, C. (1996). *Los hombres verdaderos: Voces y testimonios tojolabales.* Mexico: Siglo Veintiuno Editores.

Light, J. (1974). *Lecture on capital markets.* Boston, MA: Harvard Business School.

Lipman, P. (2003). *High stakes education: Inequality, globalization, and urban school reform.* New York, NY: Routledge.

Malaguzzi, L. (1993). History, ideas, and basic philosophy. In Edwards, C., Gandini, L., & Foreman, G. (Eds.), *The hundred languages of children: The Reggio Emilia approach to early childhood education.* Norwood, NJ: Ablex Publishing, pp. 49–97.

McLaren, P., Flores, R., & Tanaka, G. (2001). Autonomy and participatory democracy: An ongoing discussion on the application of the Zapatista method in the United States. *International Journal of Education Reform, 10*(2), 130–144.

Mickelson, R. A., & Southworth, S. (2005). When opting out is not a choice: Implications for NCLB'S Transfer Option from Charlotte, North Carolina. *Equity & Excellence in Education, 38*(3), 249–263.

Mintrop, H., & Sunderman, G. L. (2009). Predictable failure of federal sanctions-driven accountability for school improvements—And why we may retain it anyway. *Educational Researcher, 38*(5), 353–364.

Monthly Review. (2002). Slow growth, excess capital, & a mountain of debt. *Monthly Review, April, 2002,* 1–14.

Ober, J. (1989). *Mass and elite in democratic Athens: Rhetoric, ideology, and the power of the people.* Princeton, PA: Princeton University Press.

Orfield, G., Losen, D., & Wald, J. (2004). *Losing our future: How minority youth are being left behind by the graduation rate crisis.* Cambridge, MA: Harvard University Civil Rights Project.

Perelman, M. (2006). Some economics of class. *Monthly Review, 58*(3), 18–28.

Pomboy, S. (2006). MacroMavens Report. Cited in Alan Abelson. 2006. Infestation of bugs. *Barron's Financial Weekly, October 2,* 2006, 8.

Ricoeur, P. (1992). *Oneself as another.* Chicago: University of Chicago Press.

Roberts, P. C. (2018, 29, 2018). Capitalism works for capitalists (and the rest of us get exploited). Silver Doctors.com,

Rodriguez, M. (1998). *Mito, identidad y rito: Mexicanos y Chicanos en California.* Mexico: Ciesas.

Smith, L. T. (1999/2005). *Decolonizing methodologies: Research and indigenous peoples.* London: Zed Books.

Southwest Center for Teacher Quality. (2004). Unfulfilled promise: Ensuring high quality teachers for our nation's schools. In *No Child Left Behind: A status report from southeastern schools.* Chapel Hill, NC.

Tabb, W. (2006). The power of the rich. *Monthly Review, 58*(3), 6–17.

Tanaka, G. (2002). Higher education's self-reflexive turn: Toward an intercultural theory of student development. *Journal of Higher Education, 73*(2), 263–296.

Tanaka, G. (2003). *The intercultural campus: Transcending culture and power in American higher education.* New York, NY: Peter Lang Publishing.

Tanaka, G. (2009). The elephant in the living room that no one wants to talk about: Why U.S. anthropologists are unable to acknowledge the absence of culture. *Anthropology & Education Quarterly*, *40*(1), 82–95.

de Tocqueville, A. (1835). *Democracy in American*. New York, NY: Vintage Books.

Touraine, A. (2000). *Can we live together? Equality and Difference*. Stanford, CA: Stanford University Press.

Wallerstein, I. (2004). *Alternatives: The United States confronts the world*. Boulder, CO: Paradigm Publishers.

Wallerstein, I. (2005). After developmentalism and globalization, what? *Social Forces, 83*(3), 321–336.

CHAPTER 5

On Collapse and the Next U.S. Democracy

We've been hoodwinked to allow the theft of our wages, savings and retirements, by (an) unconstitutional substitute currency that steals our labor, twists our language, and even distorts our thinking.

David Morgan (May 1, 2018)

While concern has been growing in recent years about the structural precursors to economic collapse in the United States, and a parallel decline in democracy, few have asked: (1) what moral and cultural foundations might be necessary as building blocks to launch a democratic renewal and (2) whether a different and "deep" democracy might be constructed this time that accords everyday citizens the agency they will need to initiate policy at the national level. The chapter also introduces a research methodology to frame and assess change at this macro, or systemic, register and examines the role that education can play in teaching citizens how to exercise agency in a reconstituted democracy that is more nearly "by, for and of the people."

In my life I have noticed a decline in shared meaning in the U.S. society to which I was born. In place of the binding quality of symbolic meaning representing the "culture" of a people (e.g., Geertz, 1973, p. 89), I have observed a startling rise in selfish individualism (Gitlin, 2006, p. 60; Tocqueville, 1840, p. 102). In my view, it is a particular loss of shared meaning about the beliefs and practices needed to sustain a social contract—and spell out a violation of those norms—that opened the door to the greed, casino capitalism, and abdication of democracy (Gilens & Page, 2014) that plague the United States today. In this regard, former Assistant Treasury Secretary Paul Craig Roberts (2014a) writes the United States is now "facing an extraordinary crisis…massive social instability, starvation…(and the) complete and total failure of the United States government."

But a decline in shared meaning also presents U.S. education with a rare opportunity to take an initializing role in launching a democratic and cultural renewal to come. With crisis occurring at the level of the economy and democracy (e.g., Geryerz, 2014; Roberts, 2014a; Russell, 2014; Stockman, 2014; Willie, 2014a), applied researchers will now need a whole new range of tools that can be deployed at the same systemic register where collapse is taking place. It is here that I draw courage from a thought that Margaret Mead (1955) offered at the end of a seminal event in U.S. educational anthropology: "(V)ery rapid total change…makes it possible to build new patterns extraordinarily rapidly." It is through this door that I wish to enter today.

I will begin by demonstrating through statistics just how misdirected it may now be to insist on assessment-driven education reform while ignoring the larger loss of democracy—and deepening economic inequality—occurring today. Those endeavors overlook the importance of meaning and in particular any agency that future citizens might acquire over it. The immediate challenge then would be to trace that inequality and democratic decline to their root causes with the aim of infusing meaning and agency into what will likely be a social reconstitution. I present one possible avenue for educational anthropologists here by peeling back the layers to discover who benefits most from this democratic and economic disenfranchisement—and then describing how to re-instill the shared norms and values that might lead everyday citizens to remove elites from their hidden seats of power, address their own disenfranchisement, and reclaim democracy.

My wish to see more applied work at the systemic level also stems from a belief that progressive thinkers have in recent decades yielded the terrain at the macro register to financial elites while focusing on the "mid-range" issues of organizational and community-based change (after Roseberry, 1998). At base then, this chapter is about how to evoke social change at the macro or systemic register by outlining an approach to applied research that will: (1) rally broad public support for the rebuilding of America's largest social institutions, (2) initiate the teaching of norms, duties, and obligations (i.e., shared meaning) that ethnically diverse citizens will need if they are to support this work, and (3) operationalize this social transformation by shifting the direction of democratic policymaking from exclusively "top-down" (Uhl-Bien Mason, & McKelvey, 2007, p. 306) and "hierarchical" (Tanaka, 2007a) to, in part, "bottom-up" (Aigrain, 2014), "interactive" (Uhl-Bien *et al.*, 2007, p. 309), and "deep" (Fung & Wright, 2003).

Finally, I will present data from a limited study suggesting the United States already has the wherewithal to enhance if not save its democracy by using such mediating tools as *citizens' panels*—tools that may outline a new scholarship that I will call *applied systemic research*. Again, our research tools will need to match the register (systemic) in which the work is to be performed. By systemic, I refer to change effectuated at the macro level of the nation and suggest this differs from recent usage of the term macro by linguistic anthropologists (e.g., Rymes, 2012; Warriner, 2012) who envision the capacity of an individual (micro) to author meanings that elide a dominant discourse (macro). Here, I will develop the notion that mid-range mechanisms for deep democracy, like a citizens' panel, can be inserted between the individual and the policymaking of a nation state, in effect granting individuals the agency to alter the macro (Bartlett & Vavrus, 2014, p. 142).

EARLY SIGNS OF ECONOMIC COLLAPSE

By 2013, four out of five U.S. adults were struggling with joblessness, near poverty, or had been on welfare at some time in their lives (Zero Hedge, 2013a). Alienation was particularly acute among whites, with 76% having experienced economic insecurity before the age of 60 (ibid). In this weak economy, four Americans were on food stamps for every manufacturing job (Snyder, 2013a) and 76% of all Americans were living paycheck to paycheck (Snyder, 2013b). With three-fourths of new jobs in 2013 only part-time, the average hourly take-home pay, corrected for inflation, had dropped from $20/hour in 1973 to $8/hour by 2013 (ibid). With consumer spending now 60% of the economy, a 1930s style depression is fast approaching (Deninger, 2014).

And the college student? The cost of tuition went from $500/semester in the 1970s to $29,000/year by 2013 (Hudson, 2013). From 2011 to 2013 alone the increase in tuition was 70% (Zero Hedge, 2013b). Many students were graduating with $200,000 to $300,000 in student loan debt, unable to land jobs, and living with their parents (Hudson, 2013). From 2003 to 2013, total student loan debt had increased by 275%, and by 2013 37% of all heads of U.S. households under 30 were living in poverty (Snyder, 2013c). Simply put, there is no opportunity for this generation to make "a fresh start."

As 2013 marched into 2014, the disparity in wealth between the ultra rich and the rest of U.S. society had reached the grotesque: the top 1% in the United States held 65 times the wealth of the bottom 50% combined (Snyder, 2014a). Globally, the richest 85 people in the world held net worth matching that of the bottom 50% of the entire world population (Fuentes-Nieva, 2014). In contrast, 50 million people in the United States were on food stamps.

By 2014, the *true* U.S. unemployment rate (after adding those who had stopped looking for work or were working part time) had risen to 23%, compared to 25% during the 1930s Depression (Williams, 2014a)—and far higher than the federally published rate of 7%. With a higher percentage of Americans going hungry than in all but two of the European countries (Shah, 2014), it could be argued the United

States has already fallen into an economic depression. On top of this, when adding in the increase in food costs (22% year-over-year per Street, 2014) and energy, real household inflation had reached 9.7% and not the published rate of 2% to 3% (Williams, 2014b). And college graduates? As of April, 2014, 83% of college graduates had not had a job lined up (Roberts, 2014b).

By 2014, Thomas Piketty had also determined that capitalism automatically produces inequality in wealth and income. Arguing it is the economic that drives the political, he provided persuasive evidence consistent with Orlov's (2013) "five stages of collapse" (from economic to commercial collapse, then political, social, and finally cultural collapse). But while Piketty and Orlov emphasize the centralized, top-down impact of macro forces on a society, as an applied educational anthropologist I would urge a more interactive interpretation, trace the origin of today's collapse to the surrender of binding cultural values at an earlier point in time, and thus "flip" Orlov's sequence.

In my view, the current economic collapse and democratic decline are the result of an earlier dissipation of shared meaning or values (or culture) that would normally give U.S. citizens a clear sense of what is morally right and wrong and thus the capacity to act on major transgressions by elected officials who fail to represent them. Lacking that moral foundation, there is no impedance to the leaching effects of today's greed-based economics of runaway debt (Mannarino, 2015)), financial derivatives (Willie, 2014b), and disintermediation or dollar flight (Light, 1974; Smith, 2014)—the three D's that are structural determinants of today's economic collapse (Tanaka, 2007b, 2012, 2013).

In fact, the moral collapse of America seems everywhere apparent. According to Snyder (2014b), one in every three children in the United States lives in a home without two-parent support, the United States has the highest divorce rate in the world, and has the highest incarceration rate and the largest total prison population in the entire world by a wide margin. McCoy (2013) recently reported, "Wall Street's future leaders, the young professionals, have lost their moral compass, accept corporate wrongdoing as a necessary evil, and fear reporting this misconduct" (Farrell, 2014, p. 1). It was anthropologist Crapanzano (2000, p. 2, 24) who wrote it is a "loss of values" that leads to "breakdowns in the moral order of a society." The particularly corrosive decline in values on Wall Street has been described by Taibbi (2014) as a total moral surrender, and it is in this context that Bishop and Green (2011) have concluded, capitalism must rediscover its soul, put values back into business, and come to serve the greater good.

But a loss of values also begs the larger question of whether we can improve how we do democracy, and with which new values. It wouldn't hurt to try. A recent poll shows that Americans want change: "Only 4 percent believe it would 'change Congress for the worse' if every member was voted out during the next election" (Snyder, 2014c, p. 1).

THE CITIZENS' PANEL

In October 2005, I was asked to be one of 27 participants in a mock citizens' panel convened at Howard University in Washington, D.C. Coming from across the United States, we were diverse in age, race and occupation but did share one trait: we didn't know anything about nanotechnology. Federal legislation had just authorized $3.7 billion in public funding to jump-start the nanotechnology industry and put the United States in the lead globally. The Loka Institute asked us to come and test whether a citizens' panel could be used to elicit useful feedback from people who knew nothing of this. This is that story.

While the citizens' panel had its genus in the Danish consensus conference (Joss & Durant, 1995, p. 9), Guston (1999, p. 452) notes that citizens' panels function more like a jury and can, for example, "improve decision making about science and technology by expanding access...beyond the traditional elite, increase the public understanding of science and technology...and enhance democracy by fostering civic engagement."

The U.S. Nanotechnology R & D Act of 2003 was the first federal law to call for use of citizens' panels to give the public a say during implementation of a new law. As a participant observer, I entered the weekend with my own doubt and bias—and a larger question, really, of whether the U.S. representative democracy hadn't already been lost and was now controlled by "rich men" (Tocqueville, 1835, p. 225). After studying the United States in the early 1800s, the French political historian cautioned that, "aristocratic governments" controlled by "rich men" could easily turn "despotic" (p. 420).

Would the citizens' panel, I asked myself, make a difference by providing a fresh alternative to what I believed had already become a fiction of representation in the current democracy—and help launch a new democracy that would reach deeper, be more bottom-up, and be more nearly "by, for and of the people" (Gong, 2003; Pateman, 1970; Tocqueville, 1835, p. 61; Touraine, 2000)? Or instead, is today's usurpation too far along and far too entrenched for the democracy to be retaken and revived?

A number of themes appear in my field notes that may shed light on the feasibility of a new U.S. democracy and the role that U.S. education can play. One is that (1) in a citizens' panel, norms of mutuality and interdependence can be realistic outcomes of collaboration where a public sphere is ethnically diverse. Eschewing a politics that pits one group of Americans against another, the citizens' panel demonstrates that when a Latino educator from Inland Valley, California expresses a wish to see "better cures for diseases," his appeal fuels the voices of others: a Latina from an autonomous community in San Bernadino, California, follows by asking that regulations protect the health of workers in nano production, and this leads an African-American high school student from a Washington, D.C. to call upon the U.S. government to act at all times on the public's behalf by "providing the basics of health, welfare, food for every human being."

Here, each participant is able to exercise voice and be listened to—enacting a pattern of intersubjectivity formed out of a double-voicedness where speaker and listener each support the other as a subject and neither is turned into an object of the other's speech (Bakhtin, 1929/1984). In other words, the panel demonstrated that interactive approaches can be useful in democracies serving ethnically diverse publics.

In generating recommendations for federal officials, (2) the participants acquired agency by making their own meanings ("personal agency") and then took action by turning those meanings into suggested steps in the implementation of a new statute ("social agency"). For instance, a young white woman from the Tar Creek Superfund Site in Oklahoma translated concerns she heard raised by others into a wish for a new K-12 curriculum that would teach future users the basics of nanotechnology.

So while some talked of protecting the health of nanotechnology workers, still others asked that those jobs specifically be kept in the United States in the first place. As they exchanged meanings with each other, the participants outlined specific governmental and economic policies they hoped would make life in their communities better. Instead of being objects in a top-down democracy, each arguably became a subject and an agent, or an agental subject after Ruti (2006), in a more bottom-up democracy.

A third theme encountered was that (3) where citizens collaboratively design and put forward new ideas to public officials and thus acquire an obligation to listen to and support others, they model both, a bottom-up or deep democracy (Fung & Wright, 2003) and a shift in human development to an ethics of "mutual immanence" where individuals come into being by helping others also to come into being (Tanaka, 2009, p. 90). So when a female African-American social services director from New England urges that nanotechnology be taught to future citizens in schools, that leads a young Latino researcher from south Texas to ask that community-based research organizations also be consulted. While more research is needed, I now believe learning mutuality-based duties and obligations will enable members of an increasingly diverse nation to deepen their satisfaction from working together in a common public sphere.

In projecting out the dialogical implications of a citizens' panel then, (4) deep democracy and mutual immanence would seem to be interdependent operations, each begetting the other. As each participant articulates a wish for change in policy or practice and then supports the capacity of others to articulate their own wishes, that mutuality becomes both the foundation for and outcome of a deep democracy. This connection between the onset of mutual immanence and the steps one can take to collaboratively improve one's own democracy could also inject fresh momentum into reconstructive work in education reform: a society would not likely sustain either deep democracy or social agency without also teaching mutual immanence in schools.

Further, it appears that (5) the citizen subject in a deep democracy is an inchoate subject—never fully formed, always in formation. The subjects fashioned in this mock panel would leave this shared process, go back home and tell their stories— and hear what still others have to say, again in mutual reliance upon each other.

A final thought regarding themes. This kind of research—focusing on how a local community (or individual participant) can inform policy on the national level— presents an opportunity to expand beyond the field's frequent emphasis on mid- range analytics (of the organization, the school, the local community) to the exclu- sion of individual agency and systemic impact. The citizens' panel thus opens up a fresh dynamic from which to observe and facilitate behavior at the intersection of all three registers, where: both personal meaning and social agency are enjoyed by individuals ("micro"), policy recommendations are made in groups or by com- munities ("mid-range") and the suggested change can have systemic level impact (national, or "macro"). Here, each of the 27 members of the mock panel could look back on this midrange event and view her/himself as an individual who took steps to promote systemic reform (Roseberry, 1998).

THE 1913 CREATION OF THE FEDERAL RESERVE BANK— AND THE ONSET OF TODAY'S COUNTERMAJORITARIAN DEMOCRACY

A second story began a long time ago, in 1911, at an island resort off Georgia. There, a brilliant thinker from London linked to the Rothschild banking family, Paul Warburg, participated in the drafting of new legislation to create what would become the Federal Reserve Bank, a private central bank with vast powers over the United States (Griffin, 1998). When tracing the sources of harm to the democracy today, it is this story that raises a very large red flag.

In his writing, G. Edward Griffin picks up an earlier trail left by Eustace Mullins (1991) who had written with anti-Semitic overtones about a secret meeting held by eight men at the island resort in 1911. These men included representatives from J.P Morgan, National City Bank of New York, and First National Bank of New York, along with U.S. Senator Nelson Aldrich (Senate Banking Chair), Warburg, and others. That work is believed by some to have launched, ultimately, a debt-based scheme to take over the world's resources in two stages: (1) first by lending to the United States and its people—arguably committing the US. democ- racy to serving the interests of New York and London bankers—and (2) then by extending that indebtedness worldwide (ibid).

With the Federal Reserve Bank (the *Fed*) created by the above-mentioned consortium of U.S./London bankers, it has since 1913 drained over 96% of the value of the dollar by printing paper *fiat* dollars (Snyder, 2012). As a result, the savings of average Americans have indeed been replaced by heavy debt they owe to the very banks led by the Rothschild, Rockefeller, and Morgan "troika," and others. And with that debt now a major source of U.S. inequality (Hollenbeck, 2014), *Stage One* of the almost mythical 1911 debt scheme has arguably been achieved.

Today the Federal Reserve sponsoring banks are also using trillions in "taxpayer dollars" given to them in the form of U.S. bailouts and interest free loans (i.e., other people's money) to clean their own books (Hunter, 2014), feather a speculative $1.5 quadrillion derivatives market consisting of under-collateralized synthetic financial and debt packages (Greyerz, 2012), and pawn off those derivatives on other nations worldwide. *Stage Two* also partially achieved.

In fact, these very derivatives are already believed by some to have caused the collapse of such "debt serf" countries as Greece, Cyprus, Italy, Spain, and Portugal (WilliamBanzai7, 2014). In this regard, Former Assistant U.S. Treasury Secretary Roberts (2013) further opines:

> The sovereign debt crisis in Europe…is being used to establish two things. One is that the public must bear the cost of mistakes made by private bankers… And the other…is to take away the sovereignty of the individual countries by turning their budget and tax policies over to the E.U. (Paul Craig Roberts, TheKaiserReport.com, April 13, 2013)

Can the United States be far behind? With a manufactured 2008 economic crisis— arguably created in the first place by those same U.S. mega banks—some argue those very banks have been seizing the opportunity presented by that crisis to replace democratically elected presidents in several countries with senior executives from their own ranks.

In fact, President Obama's *own* three chiefs of staff had previously been on the payroll of: Goldman Sachs (Rahm Emanuel), J.P. Morgan Chase (Bill Daley), and Citigroup (Jacob Lew). It is no wonder that critics of banks believed to be seeking to control democracies around the globe have focused their investigations on these very mega U.S. banks (e.g., Kaye, 2014; Taibbi, 2009; also Segarra, 2013).

The larger pattern is that since the Fed's formation in 1913, there have been major spikes up and precipitous dives down in the U.S. stock market. At each point, the big bank insiders—in symbiotic relationship with the Fed—knew when the markets would be manipulated to skyrocket and when they would be led to crash via induced market panic or war. In other words, the Fed member banks knew when to *go long* and when to *short* the market—and no one was giving the same heads up to the average investor (Prins, 2014).

Worse, the Rothschild cofounded Bank of England and the U.S. Federal Deposit Insurance Corporation FDIC have recently entered into an agreement that will allow large U.S. banks to seize U.S. checking and savings deposit accounts, and in this way save themselves through "bail-*ins*" (Black, 2014). It might not be a surprise, then, that the Fed's "Quantitative Easing" of today is the same policy that hurt Americans in 1928 (Mirhaydari, 2013). That should constitute fair warning of what could very well come next: great harm to the American public via another massive stock market crash.

It was the father of capitalism Adam Smith (1759, p. 198, 203) who once wrote there must always be a "sense of duty" in capitalism that prevents us from "hurting our neighbor." Anthropologists agree, noting a society that loses that sense of duty will one day encounter the end of its social order (Gailey, 1987). Today, the United States seems without this moral sentiment (Smith, 1759), just waiting for the right moment to collapse.

So where does this leave us today? Former Republican brain-trust official David Stockman (2014) suggests that "as we reach the end of this era of massive central bank expansion and domination…the monetary system will break down, the central banks will become totally discredited, and the markets will be in anarchy and dislocation." In an uncanny way, this prognostication recapitulates the very mood and predicament that led President Franklin Delano Roosevelt (1933) after the 1929 crash to issue a call for "strict regulation of all banking…(and) an end to speculation with other people's money."

FDR went on to use his 1933 inaugural speech to exhort Americans to take the moral high ground, reclaim the obligation to help one's fellow man, and work with him to rebuild the U.S. social infrastructure. His words were unambiguous: "(R)estoration lies in the extent to which we apply social values more noble than mere monetary profit"—including "interdependence on each other," a sense of "duty," "honor," "courage," and "honesty." We are, in my view, faced with an identical need for shared meaning today.

A further gloss on the source of collapse can be found in *The Least Dangerous Branch*. There, Bickel (1962) explains how U.S. Supreme Court justices tend to be much older than most Americans and act according to a belief system from a different era than that of the broader public. Termed "the countermajoritarian difficulty," reasoning by an older Court can easily come into conflict with the values of the wider American public.

What I would suggest is that all three branches of the U.S. representative democracy now reflect a *countermajoritarian democracy*—no longer representing the people of America. In recent times: (a) the White House championed a NAFTA law that exported U.S. jobs offshore with 10 million lost jobs from 2000 to 2008 alone, and in this way helped to kill the U.S. manufacturing base (Black, 2014); (b) Congress allowed the Executive Branch to give banks $27 trillion in bank bailouts stolen in part from the Social Security fund (Fitts, 2012); and (c) the Judiciary in *Citizens United* arguably gave the richest Americans an open door to "buy" future U.S. elections, further removing the representative feature from the democracy. Not only has the government caved in to the Fed (a private bank), it has magnified that harm by undermining its own legitimacy.

In the latter regard, economist Jeffrey Sachs (2013) reports, "(T)he financial markets are the number one campaign contributor in the U.S. system (showing) we have a corrupt politics to the core." The U.S. mainstream media also seems unwilling to do its part in sustaining the idea of democracy: it chose not to report the success of a grassroots movement in Iceland that blocked the award of bank bailouts, rejected banker control of national politics—and saved the Icelandic democracy (Sevastio, 2013). In contrast to that, the current U.S. democracy seems to have lost its representative quality altogether.

Have we finally become the democracy of "rich men" that de Tocqueville (1835/1945) cautioned us to avoid? And is the testing of military force on urban citizens like the one in Ferguson, MO, part of a larger plan to induce anarchy as an excuse to usher in a more overt fascism? Upon reflection, a countermajoritarian democracy—no longer representing the majority—does not seem like a democracy at all. President Jimmy Carter (2013) has said as much: "America does not have a functioning democracy at this time."

Perhaps even more shocking, Kim (2014) notes that many assassination attempts on U.S. presidents have come after steps each had taken to either block creation of a private central bank like the Fed (with Presidents Jackson and Harding) or break up the monopoly of an existing central bank's paper currency (with Lincoln, Reagan, and Kennedy). Kennedy was killed not long after asking the U.S. Treasury in E.O. 11110 to print its own silver-backed dollars—an act that would compete and interfere with the Fed's fiat dollar (unbacked paper) monopoly. If true, this would suggest that today's usurpation of democracy has had a longer history and deeper roots than before imagined.

In light of the economic stress faced by FDR in the 1930s, and Obama in the 2010s, this all makes me wonder if there is another hidden layer operating behind the Fed and if so, who is pulling those strings? Behind the veil of central bank secrecy there indeed exists a Bank for International Settlements in Switzerland, also inaccessible by the global public (Hodges, 2014). Who are they? We know they are the coordinating agency for all central banks and facilitate all that antidemocratic power globally. Is this one more extra-democratic policymaking layer controlled by the same Rothschild, Rockefeller, Morgan troika? The Payseurs (Janda, 2018)? Whatever their influence and motives, democratic citizens of the world deserve to know. Otherwise there can be no democracy.

While some might address the above problems through structural change at the federal level, I believe it would be more strategic to take an approach to democratic reform that is initiated in bottom-up fashion through vehicles like citizens' panels—which can elicit the flow of ideas from individuals and communities upwards to the federal government. With a new pattern (after Mead, 1955) in which the public initiates some of the policymaking, my belief is that habits formed in this more local community-based democracy would serve as a deterrent to future attempts by elites to resurrect the top-down, countermajoritarian democracy of today. We are fortunate in that there are several proven vehicles for a bottom-up democracy and all can be taught in schools:

1) *Participatory Public Budgeting (PPB)*. Vallejo, California was the first city in the United States to use participatory budgeting and give its citizens the power to propose ideas for how to spend several million dollars in special tax revenues. The P.B. Project reports unqualified success in helping local citizens in 2013 to translate their ideas into proposals, develop budgets, and then explain those proposals to voters using posters mounted on the interior walls of a special voting site (see P.B. Project, 2013; also Baiocchi, 2003; Wampler, 2007). In the 2014 budget cycle, I assisted in this process and saw racially mixed teams of citizens ranging from age 12 to seniors—and with significant economic diversity—all treating each other with respect. This adds credence to Acemoglu and Robinson's (2012) assertion that political institutions are more likely to succeed and less likely to fail if they are inclusive. This also serves as a rebuttal to any claims that ethnic diversity in the United States will be a bar to a more participatory democracy

2) *Local School Councils (LSCs)*. For a number of years now Chicago has successfully used LSCs, where local citizens make budget and hiring decisions for their local schools (Fung, 2003; Lipman, 2004; Potter, 2013). This vehicle requires citizens to learn what makes for excellent schooling and how to cultivate their own agency as policymakers—and this underscores how education can and should become a leading part of an applied research effort to establish and sustain a deep democracy. Needed next is a way of bridging the gap between the agency seen in grass roots policymaking like this and the actions of decision-makers at the federal level.

3) *Community-Based Research*. Guajardo, Guajardo, and Casaperalta (2008) detail the benefits of teaching youth how to perform research on their own communities and then use their data to secure grants that address the problems they identify. In copublishing their findings, teenage researchers from south Texas were able to describe to other communities nationwide the solutions and models they had designed and tested with professors while evoking micro and mid-range change in their own community.

4) *Art Unbound*. Applied researcher Derek Fenner (2014) has developed yet another model which can now be introduced into local schools and replicated nationwide. Drawing from Deleuze, Guattari, Lacan, Ruti, and others, he proposes the use of art and narration (developed by *each* child) as a means of teaching agency and subject formation. Through self-expression, each child moves into and through her/his own sense of *lack* to become an inchoate subject—no longer stuck in victimology or heavily prescribed tracking. In this way, both art and "the storytelling student," or subject, are "unbound." This is one more project in agency development at the micro level of the individual that can lead to new practice, new theory, and new policy at the mid-range and macro levels.

5) *Autonomous Community Building.* The autonomous community is a form of self-governance in which citizens of a city or village run their own mini-democracy. With success in Chiapas, Mexico (Lenkersdorf, 1996; McLaren, Flores, & Tanaka, 2001), Reggio Emilia, Italy (Malaguzzi, 1998), the Calpulli Project of San Bernadino, CA (Rodriguez, 1998), and the Eastside Café in El Sereno, Los Angeles (Flores, 2018), this form of democracy goes hand-in-hand with intersubjective schooling, where children can learn the skills of mutuality and subject formation and an obligation to serve the community (Flores, 2008). It is also one more model that combines individual agency with a mid-range venue and the macro potential for bottom-up democracy.

To accommodate the above, applied researcher D'Andrea Robinson (2014) urges creation of a new unit within the U.S. Department of Education (DOE) that will have responsibility for providing policymaking support to local communities and school districts (see Appendix). This unit would support citizens' panels (originally from Denmark and London), PPBs (from Porto Alegre, Brazil), LSCs (Chicago), art unbound projects (Massachusetts), and autonomous communities (Mexico) and pass along recommendations generated by them to Congress and the president for use in new federal policymaking. This unit would also address the current problem of having wonderful work done in local communities but no entity at the federal level to receive and forward that work to policymakers.

Stated differently, one can have *both* a bottom-up, deep democracy and a representative democracy that receives and incorporates those recommendations from the people. In other words, the remaking of democracy and an education system to support this can be ongoing U.S. cultural inventions, borrowing from models around the world, and cultivating new shared meaning. Here, Margaret Mead (1955, p. 275) was again prescient: "One of the sources for new cultural invention is what other people have done…(as this) gives us an element that we might be neglecting at the present moment."

LARGER PATTERNS IN THE STUDY: A COPRESENCE OF CYNICISM AND POSSIBILITY, AND THE CRITICAL IMPORTANCE OF TEACHING MUTUAL IMMANENCE

In reviewing the structure and purpose of democracy in a transnational society, two opposing belief systems would seem to come into play. One holds there will always be an incommensurability (e.g., Mouffe, 2000, p. 99; Ober, 1989; Spivak, 1988;) that prevents people who are from different backgrounds and subjectivities from understanding and working with each other with the trust required in a truly deep democracy. This cynicism appears time and again—from India where, under Spivak's

(1988) analysis, British occupier and occupied could never be seen to understand the other's meanings, to places of superficial "interculturalidad" where some indigenous people of South America have come to see interculturality as one more attempt to colonize (Garcia, 2005). That cynicism can be a legitimate response to entrenched, colonizing regimes and it was one of the feelings I had as I entered this experiment.

In contrast to that cynicism, however, there is the countervailing view of possibility that holds a diverse democracy can engage all its citizens equally, no matter their ethnic, racial, and class-based status, or other subjectivities (Couldry, 2004; Mouffe, 2000). What I experienced here was that a racially diverse group of individuals who did not know each other, or the topic, beforehand could come together, quickly attain "cumulative force" (Bucholtz, Barnwell, Skapoulli, & Janie Lee, 2012, p. 170), and make recommendations about how to implement new law in a way that protects the public. The citizens' panel thus functioned as a vehicle to harness and formalize "the power of the micro to transform patterned regularities" (Warriner, 2012, p. 185) operating, here, at the macro register.

Collapse of an elitist democracy thus brings with it a rare opportunity to remake the largest of U.S. social institutions while reducing the economic asymmetry and educational inequities of today. With pressing need to reclaim the democracy and make it more inclusive, educators will want to learn how to teach each child both "mutual immanence" and the language use skills needed in participatory budgeting, local school councils, citizens' panels, art unbound projects, and community-based research. In other words, a democratic public must know how to use its new democracy. Where to start?

An initial step would be to hold a Model Schools Conference to showcase successful, locally run pedagogies and curricula. This way, citizens' panels, LSCs, and community-based research teams will have the future benefit of being able to choose from a number of different success stories in modeling their own schooling regime. Articles describing the best models could later appear as a special theme issue in educational journals (Shaw, 2014). Another step would be to promote, in school districts across the country, the norms of interdependence, duty, honor, courage and honesty that FDR had called for in an earlier era of economic collapse and wished for democratic renewal.

To extend that work, I am also working with others to launch a progressive think tank that will sponsor applied systemic research and promote the duty of U.S. education to teach citizens how to remake their democracy through deep democracy vehicles like the ones discussed here. This work would differ from many current efforts to promote civic engagement in that it will have the goal of reconstituting a broken democracy rather than increasing public engagement in a compromised one.

While I felt lucky to have witnessed the kind of possibility envisioned by Pateman (1970) and Barber (1984), my belief is that the collaboration across difference required for a deep democracy would be more likely to occur if the United States could also take steps to prepare its future citizens for such a role: via "schools for the subject" (urged by Touraine, 2000, p. 158) where children from diverse populations learn the intercultural communication skills to work with each other as subjects and agents (Couldry, 2004); and by teaching the capacity to see "oneself as another" (after Ricoeur, 1992, p. 161) where children focus on the well-being of others as part of their own growth, setting in motion a heuristic for mutual immanence. Thus, a deep democracy does not happen overnight but will need to be scaffolded; its citizens will want to learn the norms and skills to use it well and ultimately, I suspect, the importance of compassion.

So ironically, it is out of the inequalities of today's government of rich men that I believe the impasse between cynicism and possibility will be resolved. In other words, it will be the failure of today's countermajoriatian democracy that leads the public to demand change and with that mood, a heartfelt openness to possibility. In Not for Profit, Nussbaum (2010, p. 25) had asked that schools return to teaching "the ability to have concern for the lives of others." That would be a good place to start.

ELEMENTS OF APPLIED SYSTEMIC RESEARCH

Several tentative conclusions might also be reached about how to cultivate an applied systemic research methodology to support the infrastructure renewal needed today. First, researchers will want to identify a macro systemic issue and peel it back to its root cause or causes. Only then can solutions be advanced that lessen or eliminate the deepest sources of inequity or harm. My inquiry revealed that beyond the counter-democratic hegemony of the Fed, there will need to be more serious research into the workings of a group of international of financiers behind that bank who seek to steal the wealth of a democratic nation, undermine its democracy, and through the remaining shell of governmentality, gain control of the world's resources. This strikes me as a large, blinking, neon sign calling out for fresh interdisciplinary work, and now. I find this terrain especially fertile for the activist researcher (Emihovich, 2005).

Second, it seems apparent that an applied systemic research must test and recommend concrete solutions that move beyond critique (e.g., Kwon, 2008, p. 6, citing Freire, 1996). Finding solutions here meant researching financial bloggers who track economic developments in real time. I was also lucky to learn firsthand how a citizens' panel could elicit, from multiple players, both "unrealized possibility" (Kundera, 1984, p. 221) and "unfinalizability" (Bakhtin, 1929/1984, p. 117) and then model a democracy that creates new meaning. I urge other researchers to broaden their own view of possibility.

Third, because macro systemic change will impact people in their daily lives, work in applied systemic research will need to traverse all three major registers. It did so here by (a) providing opportunities for panelists to share their meanings and dreams (the micro register) (b) in a deep democratic vehicle like a citizens' panel (mid-range) (c) that will forward their suggestions to the federal government about how to implement a new nanotechnology law (systemic, or macro). In granting policy-initiating agency to citizens, the bottom-up (Aigrain, 2014) democratic machinery of a citizens' panel augments the vertical case study of Bartlett and Vavrus (2014, p. 131; see also Niesz & Krishnamurthy, 2014, p. 153) by putting that agency in motion. So rather than waiting for cumulative force to build over time (Bucholtz *et al.*, 2012, p. 170), the citizens' panel accords citizens the immediacy to take their ideas directly to Congress and the president.

Further, an applied systemic research project will ideally put into practice the very power relations that researchers hope to see in the outcomes of their own work. It would not have worked for this mock citizens' panel to deny voice to teenagers—or the inner city organizer—if the larger goal was to harness ideas from all Americans. So in wishing for a democracy that has its population cohere as subjects (e.g., Couldry, 2004; Touraine, 2000), the applied research must itself act out that formation of agency and mutuality. Deployed at the local level, applied systemic research thus patterns, in effect becomes, the systemic outcome desired and prefigures the arrival of deep democracy.

Finally, an applied systemic research protocol will want to put both meaning-making and meaning-sharing in motion so that citizens reproduce and honor shared national norms—like interdependence on each other, duty, honor, courage, and honesty—and acquire the capacity/agency to know and share one's own family's meanings with others. In other words, a deep democracy will facilitate *both* shared meaning *and* meaning shared, in this way covalorizing both "societal and individual meaning-systems" as envisioned by post-humanists (Becker, 1971, pp. 186–187; Rank, 1932).

I also had a strong feeling that experiences like the panel I participated in could jumpstart the return of "moral sentiment" (Smith, 1759, p. 198). I noted how panelists treated each other: there was a warmth of spirit (Crapanzano, 2000) and it felt like we had established a common "community of mutual aid" (Gitlin, 2006, p. 139). But would this kind of work—in three registers—succeed in generating enough "general will" to sustain a "social contract" (Levy, 2008, p. 116, citing Rousseau, 1762? Help a beleaguered nation to replace the "poverty of…Emersonian self-reliance" and "individualism" with an "agentic analysis of subjectivity"—where citizens become "dynamic participants" in their society and thus "reinvent soul" (Ruti, 2006, pp. xvi–xvii)? More applied research is needed.

So, then, what systemic changes might be possible in the ideal? What strikes me after following the trail of money and power here is that educational reform will very much miss the mark if it continues to exclusively foreground student outcomes, school performance, and teacher evaluation—though important—while democracy itself is crashing. To sweep aside and make small the layers of power that I encountered, a number of practical steps come to mind that could have the secondary benefit of funding the building of a new U.S. democracy. Future applied systemic researchers can work to:

a) Reestablish that this democracy is by, for, and of the people by calling for a Constitutional Amendment that readopts and re-alleges the full legal authority and primacy of the Declaration of Independence of 1776, U.S. Constitution of 1789, and 27 U.S. Constitutional Amendments; makes future creation of a private central bank unconstitutional; and promotes the use of deep democratic vehicles like citizens' panels, participatory public budgeting, local school councils, and art unbound projects;

b) Prepare future citizens for democratic renewal—and honor those responsible for preparing young citizens for that work—by urging that new U.S. legislation: (i) provide full federal subsidy of all public preK–12 education, (ii) signal "honored status" for all full-time PreK–12 public school teachers by exempting them from having to pay federal income taxes, and (iii) promote the development by each local school district of schools for the subject, intercultural communication (Touraine, 2000), and most importantly, their own unique ways of teaching values like those recommended by FDR;

c) Seek subsidy of the above by (i) calling for seizure of all tax-dodging offshore bank accounts of U.S. citizens held in Switzerland, the Cayman Islands, the Netherlands Antilles, etc.—estimated by some to be as much as $100 trillion; (ii) appropriating all electronic and paper titles to U.S. stocks, bonds and real estate held on behalf of the City of London Corporation by "the DTCC/Cede & Company" in violation of the U.S. Constitution of 1789 and Declaration of Independence (K/RogueMoney.net, Before Its News, 2014; Weir, 2014); (iii) conducting a full public accounting of U.S.-owned gold and silver including a N.I. 43–101 assay of deposits in the Grand Canyon (*New York Times*, 1912; also Weir, 2012); and (iv) readopting the federal income tax scheme of the 1950s–1960s where the top 1% paid a graduated income tax rate of up to 75% and the middle class thrived;

d) Place all funds in "c" above into a "U.S. Sovereign Wealth Fund" like Norway's, with interest from that account used to fund "a" and "b" above plus full healthcare, women's rights, job training, social security, and art education for all Americans (Tanaka, 2012/2013); and use the interest from gold taken from the Vatican by Prince Rizal and from Japan's General Yamashita—believed by some to be in a Global Debt Facility—to fund health and education for all citizens of the world; and

e) Immediately end the Federal Reserve (Maehrholtz, 2014; Tanaka, 2013) so the United States can (i) extinguish several trillion in Treasury bonds and issue precious metals-backed dollars; (ii) urge states to follow the public bank model of North Dakota and permanently reduce U.S. dependence on private banking (Brown, 2013); (iii) let big banks fail rather than bailing them out again with taxpayer money (unemployment *fell* in Iceland after it let the banks fail in 2008); (iv) return banking to a philosophy of credit for production instead of "paper money" for speculation (Schlanger, 2014); and given that "only 37% of all student loan balances are currently in repayment" with the rest already delinquent (Black, 2015), (v) pave the way for a "debt jubilee" that accords college students a fresh start by forgiving them from having to pay back their student loans.

Could applied systemic researchers help to induce any of the above to happen? Again it was Mead (1964)—who said before coining the name Council on Anthropology and Education (LeCompte, 2013)—"Never doubt that a small group of thoughtful, committed citizens can change the world. Indeed, it is the only thing that ever has."

So while this inquiry was born out of a meeting of 27 brave souls to discuss a nanotechnology they did not before understand, perhaps it signals that a far larger shift may now be possible for the activist researcher to move from making change at the edges, to becoming part of a wider process of resurrecting and strengthening the very idea of democracy. Stated another way, the citizens' panel would harness the possibility that comes from having multiple points of view and enact a heteroglossia (Bakhtin, 1981) not seen under current policymaking practice.

And where anthropologists had once defined culture as the shared meaning of one ethnic group (Lett, 1987, p. 114), in a diverse democracy that is "by, for and of the people" the term may now be used to validate each family's "meanings shared" with others. And the values urged by FDR? They can be acknowledged for this key function: to bind together a diverse nation. So interdependence on each other, duty, honor, courage, and honesty become the overarching norms that allow distinct family cultural meanings also to be celebrated and shared. Now that would be democracy writ large.

And how might the political economy and layers of motives and secrets of well hidden elites, discussed here, be relevant to the future of educational policymaking and research? It is my strongest hunch that once educated members of a truly democratic public learn the plans of a tiny group to seize U.S. democracy and use it as a vehicle to take control of the world and its resources, they will only be a short step away from fixing the problem; it falls to U.S. education to aid that process and not stand on the sidelines. So if I were to hope for one larger contribution to the subfield from this article, it would be that the peeling back of layers of manipulation and control that I struggled to perform here might lead others to develop even more penetrating and citizen-based methods of applied systemic research—and follow the trail deeper into the rabbit hole:

We are opposed around the world by a monolithic and ruthless conspiracy that relies primarily on covert means for expanding its sphere of influence...It is a system which has conscripted vast human and material resources into the building of a tightly knit, efficient machine...I am asking for your help on the tremendous task of informing and alerting the American people.

President John F. Kennedy Inaugural Speech (January 20, 1961)

ACKNOWLEDGMENTS

Special thanks to Evangelia Ward-Jackson, Katina Conn, Michelle Shaw, Lameka Gratton, Emma Iocono, Cora Sorenson, Lars Henrich, Stephen Gawrylewski, William G. Tierney, and Margaret LeCompte for content and style revisions, and to Rick Worthington for a most uplifting citizens' panel experience.

NOTES

1. This chapter was published in the *Anthropology & Education Quarterly* in December, 2015. It is reprinted here with the permission of its editors Dr. Sally Campbell Galman and Dr. Laura A. Valdiviezo.
2. While care was taken in this chapter to avoid the kind of anti-Semitic bias that has been used in the past to stoke further red-baiting and promote an undemocratic "divide and conquer" outcome among ethnic groups in the United States, there remain several banking related strands in history that do appear to this writer to demand further study. This author urges others to probe more deeply by "following the trail"—and to do so while minimizing ethnocentrism and malice.

BIBLIOGRAPHY

Acemoglu, D., & Robinson, J. A. (2012). *Why nations fail: The origins of power, prosperity, and poverty*. New York, NY: Crown Business/Random House.

Aigrain, P. (2014). *Can bottom-up actions of citizens regenerate democracy in Europe?* Eutopia: Ideas for Europe Magazine, June 27, 2014, in Open Democracy, July 17, 2014.

Alperovitz, G. (2013). *What then must we do? Straight talk about the next American revolution (democratizing wealth and building a community-sustaining economy from the ground up)*. White River Junction, NT: Chelsea Green Publishing.

Alperovitz, G., Imbroscio, D., & Williamson, T. (2002). *Making a place for community: Local democracy in a global era*. New York, NY: Routledge.

Baiocchi, G. (2003). Participation, activism, and politics: The Porto Alegre experiment. In A. Fung & E. O. Wright (Eds.), *Deepening democracy: Institutional innovations in empowered participatory governance*. London: Verso. Pp. 45–76

Bakhtin, M. M. (1981). *Dialogical imagination*. Austin, TX: University of Texas Press.

Bakhtin, M. M. (1929/1984). *Problems of Dostoevsky's Poetics*. Minneapolis, MN: University of Minnesota Press.

Barber, B. R. (1984). *Strong democracy*. Berkeley: University of California Press.

Bartlett, L., & Vavrus, F. (2014). Transversing the vertical case study: A methodological approach to studies of educational policy as practice. *Anthropology & Education Quarterly, 45*(2), 131–147.

Becker, E. (1971/1962). *The birth and death of meaning: An interdisciplinary perspective on the problem of man*. New York, NY: The Free Press.

Bickel, T. (1962). *The least dangerous branch: the supreme court at the bar of politics*. Indianapolis, IN: Bobbs-Merrill Company.

Bishop, M., & Green, M. (2011). *The road from ruin: How to revive capitalism and put America back on top*. New York, NY: Random House.

Black, S. (2015, April 4). Every young person should see the Fed's startling numbers on student debt. Retrieved from SovereignMan.com and reproduced in SilverDoctors.com

Black, W. (2014). How insiders Rob Banks and cause crises. *TED Talks*, March 13, 2014.

Brown, E. (2013). *The Public Bank solution: From austerity to prosperity*. Baton Rouge, LA: Third Millennium Press.

Bucholtz, M., Barnwell, B., Skapoulli, E., & Janie Lee, J. E. (2012). Itineraries of identity in under-graduate science. *Anthropology & Education Quarterly, 43*(2), 157–172.

Carter, P. J. (2013, July 18). *Comments made at Atlantic bridge* (pp. 2–13). Atlanta, GA: Der Spiegel.

Couldry, N. (2004). In the place of a common culture, what? *The Review of Education, Pedagogy & Cultural Studies, 26*(1), 3–22.

Crapanzano, V. (2000). *Serving the word: Literalism in America from the Pulpit to the Bench*. New York, NY: The New Press.

Deninger, K. (2014). *Headed for a 1930's style depression*. Interviewed on USA Watchdog by Greg Hunter. Reproduced in Goldsilver.com (October 1, 2014).

Diamond, J. (2005). *Collapse: How societies choose to fail or succeed*. New York, NY: Viking.

Emihovich, C. (2005). Fire and ice: Activist ethnography in the culture of power. *Anthropology & Education Quarterly, 36*(4), 305–314.

Farrell, P. B. (2014). *4 reasons capitalism is morally bankrupt, dying*. Marketwatch.com (July 31, 2014).

Fenner, D. (2014). Art unbound. Paper presented for panel "How to Construct Citizens for A New Democracy: Moving Away from Neoliberal Policy by Using Participatory Art and Civic Action." American Anthropologial Association Annual Meeting, Washington, D.C. (December, 2014).

Fitts, C. A. (2012, September 4). U.S. Financial Coup D'Etat. Retrieved from Watchdog.com

Flores, A. (2018). Meet the fierce women keeping this radical eastside community space alive: El Sereno's activists and artists find a second home at Eastside Café. *Los Angeles Magazine*, Los Angeles, CA (Saturday, May 12, 2018).

Flores, R. (2008, August). *Chicano artists and zapatistas walk together asking, listening, learning: The role of transnational informal learning networks in the creation of a better world* (Dissertation), University of Southern California.

Freire, P. (1996). *Pedagogy of the oppressed*. New York, NY: Continuum.

Fuentes-Nieva, R. (2014). *Working for the few*. Oxfam, GB.

Fung, A. (2003). Deliberative democracy: Chicago style: Grass-Roots governance in policing and public education. In A. Fung & E. O. Wright (Eds.), *Deepening democracy: Institutional innovations in empowered participatory governance*. London: Verso.

Fung, A., & Wright, E. (Eds.), (2003). *Deepening democracy: Institutional innovations in empowered participatory governance*. London: Verso.

Gailey, C. (1987). *Kinship to kinship: Gender hierarchy and state formation in the Tongan Islands*. Austin, TX: University of Texas Press.

García, M. E. (2005). *Making indigenous citizens: Identity, development, and multicultural activism in Peru*. Stanford, CA: Stanford University Press.

Geertz, C. (1973). *The interpretation of cultures*. New York, NY: Basic Books.

Gilens, M., & Page, B. I. (2014). Testing theories of American politics. *Perspectives on Politics, 12*(3), 564–581.

Gitlin, T. (2006). *The Intellectuals and the Flag*. New York, NY: Columbia University Press.

Gong, J. (2003). *Realizing power: A critical realist's view of participatory policymaking in educational reform* (Dissertation manuscript). UCLA. UMI Dissertation Services.

von Greyerz, E. (2012). $1.5 quadrillion in derivatives. Retrieved July 20, 2012 from KingWorldNews.com

Greyerz, E. von (2014). Global debt a shocking $280 trillion, $200 oil & total collapse. Retrieved July 3, 2014 from KingWorldNews.com

Griffin, G. E. (1998). *The creature from Jekyll Island: A second look at the federal reserve* (3rd ed.). Westlake Village, CA: American Media.

Guajardo, M., Guajardo, F., & Casaperalta, E. C. (2008). Transformative education: chronicling a pedagogy for social change. *Anthropology & Education Quarterly, 39*(1), 3–22.

Guston, D. (1999). Evaluating the first U.S. consensus conference: The impact of the citizens' panel on telecommunications and the future of democracy. *Science Technology & Human Values, 24*(4), 451–482.

Hodges, D. (2014, March 30). The destruction of America. Interviewed by Sheila Zlinsky and Dr. Tim Ball on the Weekend Vigilante Show and carried on SGTReport.com.

Hollenbeck, F. (2014). How central banks cause income inequality. Retrieved February 1, 2014 from ZeroHedge.com

Hudson, M. (2013, March 23). Interview of Michael Hudson by the New York Times, March 9, 2013. Reprinted in Café Americain.com

Hunter, G. (2014, August 8). Weekly News Report. Retrieved from USAWatchdog.com

Janda, D. (2018). We will see movement on the sealed indictments before the November elections. Interviewed by Sarah Westphal on SilverDoctors.com (September 2, 2018).

Joss, S. and Durant, J., eds (1995). Pubic participation in science: The role of consensus conferences in Europe. London: Science Museum.

Kaye, W. (2014, February 16). The Vampire Squid, JP Morgan, Dead Bankers & Criminal Acts. Retrieved from KingWorldNews.com.

Kennedy, P. J. F. (1961). Inaugural address, January, 1961.

Kim, J. S. (2014, April 21). How to rise up from banker slavery and be free. Retrieved from SmartknowledgeU.com

K/RogueMoney.net. (2014, June 13). The Dollar's demise and dead banker update. Retrieved from BeforeItsNews.

Kundera, M. (1984). The unbearable lightness of being. New York, NY: Harper Perennial.

Kwon, S. A. (2008). Moving from complaints to action: Oppositional consciousness and collective action in a political community. *Anthropology & Education Quarterly, 39*(1), 59–76.

LeCompte, M. (2013). *Dialogue at the AAA annual meeting about the history of CAE*. Chicago, IL.

Lenkersdorf, C. (1996/1999). Los Hombres Verdaderos: Voces Y Testimonios Tojolabales. Mexico: Siglo Ventiuno Editores.

Lett, J. (1987). *The human enterprise: A critical introduction to anthropological theory*. Boulder, CO: Westview Press.

Levy, B-H. (2008). *Left in dark times: A stand against the New Barbarism*. New York, NY: Random House.

Light, J. (1974). *Lecture on "the interconnectedness of capital markets," class on capital markets*. Boston, MA: Harvard Business School.

Lipman, P. (2004). *High stakes education: Inequality, globalization and school reform*. New York, NY: Routledge.

Maehrholtz, L. (2014, July 19). *Game changing end the fed rally planned in Europe*. Interviewed on WeAreChange by Luke Rudkowski.

Malaguzzi, L. (1998). History, ideas and basic philosophy. In E. Carolyn, L. Gandini, & G. Forman (Eds.), *One hundred languages of children: The Reggio Emilia approach*. Westport, CT: Ablex Publishers.

Mannarino, G. (2015). Runaway central banks, social decay debt, economic collapse. *SeekingAlpha. com* (April 29, 2015).

McCoy, K. (2013, July 31). Survey questions wall street ethics. Survey by Labaton Sucharow. Cited in Paul B. Farrell. 4 Reasons Capitalism Is Morally Bankrupt. Retrieved from Marketwatch.com

McLaren, P., Flores, R., & Tanaka, G. (2001). Autonomy and participatory democracy: An ongoing discussion on the application of zapatista autonomy in the United States. *International Journal of Educational Reform, 10*(2), 130–144.

Mead, M. (1955). An overview in retrospect: Summary by Margaret Mead. In G. Spindler (Ed.), *Education and anthropology*. Stanford, CA: Stanford University Press.

Mead, M. (1964). *Continuities in cultural evolution*. Piscataway, NJ: Transaction Publishers.

Mirhaydari, A. (2013, December 6). Ghost of 1929 crash reappears. Retrieved from MarketWatch.com

Morgan, D. (2018). What everybody needs to know about silver and the United States dollar. ReluctantPreppers.com (May 1, 2018).

Mouffe, C. (2000). *The democratic paradox*. London: Verso.

Mullins, E. (1991). The secrets of the federal reserve: The London connection. Carson City, NV: Bridger House Publishers. Originally Eustace Mullins (1952). Mullins on the Federal Reserve. New York, NY: Kasper and Horton.

New York Times. (1912, June 19). Tell of Vast Riches in the Grand Canyon: Men engaged in gold dredging operations expect to astonish the world.

Niesz, T., & Krishnamurthy, R. (2014). Movement actors in educational bureaucracy: The figured world of activity based learning in Tamil Nadu. *Anthropology & Education Quarterly, 45*(2), 148–166.

Nussbaum, M. C. (2010). *Not for profit: Why democracy needs the humanities*. Princeton, NJ: Princeton University Press.

Ober, J. (1989). Mass and elite in democratic Athens: Rhetoric, ideology and the power of the people. Princeton, NJ: Princeton University Press.

Orlov, D. (2013). The five stages of collapse: Survivors' toolkit. Gabriola Island, British Columbia: New Society Publishers.

Oxfam. (2014 February 7). Working for the Few. Cited in J. S. Kim, Smartknowledge.com

PB Project. (2013). Vallejo, California residents cast historical vote on how to spend over $3 million to improve their city. www.participatory budgeting.org

Pateman, C. (1970). *Participation and democratic theory*. Cambridge: Cambridge University Press.

Piketty, T. (2014). *Capital in the 21st Century*. Cambridge, MA: Harvard University Press.

Potter, J. (2013). *Keynote address on Chicago teachers union*. Council on Anthropology & Education, American Anthropological Association Annual Meeting, Chicago.

Prins, N. (2014). All the president's bankers. New York, NY: Perseus Books.

Rank O. (1932). *Art and the artist: Creative urge and personality development*. New York, NY: W.W. Norton & Co.

Ricoeur, P. (1992). *Oneself as another*. Chicago: University of Chicago Press.

Roberts, P. C. (2013, April 19). Interviewed on TheKeiserReport.com

Roberts, P. C. (2014a, August 1). *This mega-collapse will terrify people*. KingWorldNews.com

Roberts, P. C. (2014b, May 14) Interviewed by Greg Hunter on Watchdog.com

Robinson, D. (2014). A concrete proposal for revitalizing the education process. Paper presented for panel "How to Construct Citizens for A New Democracy: Moving Away from Neoliberal Policy by Using Participatory Art and Civic Action." American Anthropological Association Annual Meeting, Washington, D.C. (December, 2014).

Rodriguez, M. (1998). *Mito, Identidad y Rito: Mexicanos y Chicanos en California*. Mexico City: Ciesas.

Roosevelt, F. D. (1933, March 4). Inaugural address. In S. Rosenman (Ed.), (1938). The Public Papers of Franklin Delano Roosevelt (Vol. 2: The Years of Crisis) (pp. 11–16). New York, NY: Random House.

Roseberry, W. (1998). Neoliberalism, transnationalism and rural poverty: A case study of Michoacan, Mexico. *American Anthropologist*, 25(1): 53–54.

Rousseau, J.J. (1762). *Of the social contract, or principles of political right*. Amsterdam: Marc Michel Rey.

Russell, R. (2014, July 22). War, $10,000 Gold and Worldwide Change. KingWorldNews.com

Russell, R. (2016). Is one of Richard Russell's last and most shocking predictions now unfolding? *King World News*, November 23, 2016.

Ruti, M. (2006). *Reinventing the Soul: Posthumanist theory and psychic life*. New York, NY: Other Press.

Rymes, B. (2012). Recontextualizing YouTube: From macro-micro to mass-mediated communicative repertoires. *Anthropology & Education Quarterly*, 43(2), 214–227.

Sachs, J. (2013, May 10). Crisis of values. Retrieved from SGTReport.com

Schlanger, H. (2014, July 7). Obama supports ISIS, Saudi Terror & IMF's Magic Number 7. Retrieved from SGTReport.com

Segarra, C. (2013, October 28). So who is Carmen Segarra? A fed whistleblower Q&A. Interviewed by Jake Bernstein, Retrieved from ProPublica.com

Sevastio, R. (2013). Icelanders overthrow government and rewrite constitution after banking fraud—No word from U.S. media. *The Guardian*, December 3, 2013.

Shah, N. (2014). *More Americans go hungry than all but two European countries*. Bloomberg Briefs/Zero Hedge, April 2014.

Shaw, M. (2014). Conversation about how to take ideas from applied research to a wider research public. In course on "Systemic Collapse," Mills College, Oakland, CA.

Smith, A. (1759/2009). *The theory of moral sentiments*. New York, NY: Penguin Books.

Smith, C. H. (2014, September 8). Supreme excellence? Part 5 The World's Plan to Leave the Dollar Behind. Retrieved from SilverDoctors.com

Snyder, M. (2012, February 9). 10 things that every American should know about the federal reserve. Retrieved from TheEconomicCollapse.com

Snyder, M. (2013a, August 5). 40% of U.S. Workers Now Earn Less Than 1968 Minimum Wage. ZeroHedge.com

Snyder, M. (2013b, July 7). 15 signs that the quality of jobs in America is going downhill really fast. TheEconomicCollapseBlog.com

Snyder, M. (2013c, April 4). 21 statistics about the explosive growth of poverty in America that everyone should know about. Retrieved from EconomicCollapseBlog.com

Snyder, M. (2014a, January 23). The global richest 1% have 65 times the wealth of the bottom 50 combined. TheEconomicCollapseBlog.com

Snyder, M. (2014b, April 9). 100 facts about the moral collapse of America that are almost too crazy to believe. TheEconomicCollapseBlog.com.

Snyder, M. (2014c, April 24). Twelve numbers which prove that Americans are sick and tired of politics as usual. TheEconomicCollapseBlog.com

Spivak, G. C. (1988). Can the subaltern speak? In C. Nelson & L. Grossman (Eds.), *Marxism and the interpretation of culture* (pp. 271–313). Urbana, IL: University of Illinois Press.

Stockman, D. (2014, February 12). This financial collapse will be catastrophic. Retrieved from KingWorldNews.com

Street, C. W. (2014, June 2). Inflation now running at 22%. JM Retrieved from Mineset.com

Taibbi, M. (2009, Summer). Griftopia: Bubble mania, vampire squids and the long con that is breaking America. Rolling Stone.

Taibbi, M. (2014). *The divide: American injustice in the age of the welfare gap*. New York, NY: Spiegel & Grau.

Tanaka, G. (2007a). U.S. education in a post-9/11 world: The deeper implications of the current systemic collapse of the neoliberal regime. In K. J. Saltman (Eds.), *Schooling and the politics of disaster*. New York, NY: Routledge.

Tanaka, G. (2007b). Dialogue with chief economist, southern California meeting of investment advisors, Wells Fargo Advisors, Century Plaza Hotel, Century City, CA.

Tanaka, G. (2009). The elephant in the living room that no one wants to talk about: Why anthropologists are unable to acknowledge the end of culture. *Anthropology & Education Quarterly, 40*(1), 82–95.

Tanaka, G. (2010). *Putting the public into public policymaking: On citizens' panels and educational policymaking*. Paper presented at the annual meeting of the American Anthropological Association, New Orleans, November 20, 2010.

Tanaka, G. (2012, December 13). Climate for silver and gold investing. Talk given to Harvard Business School Club of Northern California, U.S. Trust, Palo Alto, CA.

Tanaka, G. (2013). On poverty and systemic collapse: Challenges to education research in an era of infrastructure rebuilding. American Educational Research Association Series. *Education and Poverty: Theory, Research and Practice*. October 2012/January 2013.

de Tocqueville, A. (1835/1945). Democracy in America (Vol. 1). New York, NY: Vintage Books.

de Tocqueville, A. (1840/1945). Democracy in America (Vol. 2). New York, NY: Vintage Books.

Touraine, A. (2000). *Can we live together? Equality and difference*. Stanford, CA: Stanford University Press.

Uhl-Bien, M., Mason, R., & McKelvey, B. (2007). *Complexity leadership theory: Shifting leadership from the industrial age to the knowledge era*. Leadership Institute Faculty Publications. Paper 18.

Wampler, B. (2007). *Participatory budgeting in Brazil: Contestation, cooperation and accountability*. University Park, PA: Pennsylvania State University Press.

Warriner, D. S. (2012). When the macro facilitates the micro: A study of regimentation and emergence in spoken interaction. *Anthropology & Education Quarterly, 43*(2), 173–191.

Weir, B. (2012, September 21). *Friday road trip*.

Weir, B. (2014). DTCC fraud cover-up in progress. *Friday road trip*, RoadtoRoota.com

WilliamBanzai7. (2014, September 16). And the NeXT LeHMaN MoMeNT iS…, Retrieved from ZeroHedge.com

Williams, J. (2014a, September 5). Alternate unemployment charts. ShadowStats.com

Williams, J. (2014b, September 17). Alternate inflation charts. ShadowStats.com

Willie, J. (2014a, July 3). Collapse has occurred: Hyperinflation meets asset destruction. SilverDoctors. com

Willie, J. (2014b, April 16). Fed has lost control, systemic failure flashing warning signals now! SilverDoctors.com

Zero Hedge. (2013a, July 28). 80% of U.S. adults are near poverty, rely on welfare, or are unemployed.

Zero Hedge. (2013b, June 29). Rise in consumer expenses. ZeroHedge.com

From Systemic Collapse
to Social Reconstitution

GREGORY K. TANAKA

> I believe that the only way our nation is saved is by the reinstitution of the rule of law.
> Dave Janda interviewed by Greg Hunter on USAWatchdog.com May 13, 2018

Every once in a long while the largest social systems of a human society—its economy, public education, media, arts, and overall system of governance—can fall into deep crisis and lose their capacity to serve. I suggest it becomes possible then to revisit *de novo* the goals, assumptions, and processes of those very systems and reconstitute the societal infrastructure through means unavailable under normal conditions. The United States is entering such a period now.

When I began writing this book, I used the autobiographical voice, going back several decades in time to describe what I saw as a small, elite group put two social mechanisms into play—race and fiat capital—to undermine the shared meanings of my country and seize its democracy. With the resulting decline in binding cultural meanings, this elite group then had in place the conditions that paved the way for the current, massive US and global economic collapse, and all for their own personal gain.

Worse, by its inattention to these events, U.S. education has arguably been complicit in this dismantling by sacrificing the teaching of critical and strategic thinking skills, values—and in particular civic duty—in favor, exclusively, of rote reading and math that left whole generations of Americans unable to defend, protect, and extend their democracy.

Today, this violation of the idea of America is now *"fait d'compli:"* As shown in Part I, *when the leaders of a representative democracy, intended to be "by, for and of the people," themselves lack the internalized norms and duties to protect and make sacrifices for the people they serve,* there can be no remaining impedance to the destruction of the economy, the rule of law, and now the core elements of the democracy itself. With these events, "systemic collapse" (or the failure of the largest social institutions of a human society) has already been set in motion. In the following pages I shall present eight points that detail some of the sources of this collapse and at the same time, the kind of openings that will appear before us to work together to initiate a "social reconstitution."

SOCIAL DISINTEGRATION AS THE INTENDED OUTCOME OF PUBLIC POLICY

The early chapters of this book were presented to show how a small, elite group could *destroy the unifying norms and duties of a people*, widen the fear and uncertainty that can arise when people from ethnically diverse backgrounds find themselves together (e.g., Allport, 1954/1979)—and then use the resulting social disintegration as a "smokescreen" while seizing control of the democracy. These mechanisms were "race" and "fiat capital" (dollars printed on paper and put into circulation with no gold or silver to back them) and they continue to wreck great mischief today. (Like many others, I suspect, my own wish to acquire status and money as a banker had placed me firmly in that category of Americans vulnerable to these very mechanisms.) Future work to uncover just how a small group of people could use race and fiat capital to convey superficial meaning and value—while (a) diminishing the deeper, shared meanings of a people and (b) creating social fragmentation—to give themselves the opening they needed to hijack a democracy, may one day be conceptualized as the *"anthropology of collapse."*

But in this book, I also contend *the very superficiality of artificial belief in the systems of race and fiat capital creates a fresh opening.* With both racialization and greed becoming increasingly delegitimized as organizing principles for human social behavior in what was intended to be a democratic nation, *a bright opportunity now presents itself to us as Americans to remake our country—by addressing the underlying precondition for this dismantling,* through now *two* sources of meaning:

(a) We can experience the interconnectedness that comes from celebrating an overarching layer of shared and *quintessentially American norms and values*—like "interdependence with each other," "fairness," "honesty," "duty" and "honor" (the *"shared meanings"* urged by President Franklin Delano Roosevelt during the 1930s depression), and

(b) We can share with each other a second layer of culture consisting of *our own individual family's ethnic norms and values*—whether originally from Norway or England or India or countries in Africa, or native America (*"meaning shared"*).

Twenty years of career experience in intercultural education have also taught me that these two ways of assigning value need not be mutually exclusive. In fact, my belief is that the ability to celebrate both "shared meaning" and "meaning shared" is precisely what we will need as we rebuild the democracy for an ethnically diverse United States. *With two sources of meaning, my belief is that we will find ourselves better prepared socially as an ethnically diverse nation—and psychologically as individuals—to renew the democracy while also honoring and celebrating the grounding and re-energizing force that derives from our own families' meanings.* Future work by educators and applied anthropologists to (re)insert these two layers of culture into the U.S. vernacular and way of life—by calling upon citizens to create, celebrate and share their meanings—will constitute a key step in erecting the cultural foundation necessary to rebuild a diverse country's democratic infrastructure. This work might come to be theorized one day as the *"anthropology of renewal."*

In other words, it will not be enough to rebuild the structures of America's social institutions. We will need to do that work *in concert with* (1) the resurrection and celebration of *overarching shared meanings* that will constitute "our national culture," and (2) a re-celebration of the *meanings shared and derived* from of each of our original "families' ethnic cultures." In valuing now two layers of shared meaning, we "re-reap" the "deep culture" and its binding sentiment we will need to reconstruct and sustain the moral foundation for an "intercultural democracy" (after Ortiz, 1947/1940) that better serves the people of an ethnically diverse nation.

MEANING-MAKING

Part I had left us with one very large, open question: *"How will a diverse nation of people, who believe so passionately in democracy, respond in concrete ways to systemic collapse?"* This query was about the loss of meaning in what had been a meaning*ful* democracy. So in Part II of this book, other writers will join me in examining one approach to sharing the meanings for a democracy that is more nearly "by, for and of" a diverse people. In resurrecting the overarching meanings that constitute a *"national culture,"* this act alone can help us make judgments about whether or not our elected officials and members of the High Court have acted properly or improperly. So in place of a dearth of meaning, we resurface it.

The celebration of a national culture will grant us a way to respect ourselves as a nation—and out of this self-regard, we find we will have already taken the first step in returning our country to a place where we are in mutual respect with people from other nations. In other words, we can't respect others until we respect ourselves. Having a national culture will be critical to re-establishing our self-respect as a people and as an honorable nation among nations.

This book thus addresses what I believe to be the underlying cause of the current collapse of the largest U.S. social institutions—the absence of shared meaning—but this time with the specific aim of identifying exactly how the process of self-renewal might begin. I write as an anthropologist who watched in dismay as my country's democratic institutions became ineffectual over the past three decades. As an anthropologist who studies culture in particular, I watched in horror as the binding culture and civility of the country I love was being slowly stripped away in acts large and small:

a. By three tall Marines who "picked on" a smallish senior Hawai'ian standing by himself in an elevator—and then filed charges against him when out of fear he pulled out a knife to defend himself. *Where is the decency in that?*

b. By the white fraternity at UCLA that continued to insist it was just a meaningless ritual when they sang their "Lupe" song to describe what it feels like for young white men to prove their masculinity by stealing the virginity of a 10-year old Mexican girl. *No hay cultura sin verguenza!*

c. And by a heavily funded, white think tank that ran a simulation using top LA city officials as guinea pigs to learn how to better control a city when it is on the brink of race riots—only to see this racially diverse group of high-level and respected city officials *themselves steer the exercise into collapse.*

At the same time, I have been patterned as an educational researcher to look for ways to test and implement positive, concrete change—change that will make an organization or human society better. To do that work now, however, we will *also* all have to rediscover, revalidate and live by the norms and duties, or "meanings shared," *of our own families.* (We will have to bring back ethnic culture.) As the balance of this book will demonstrate, there are some specific ways to do this and schools and colleges can play important roles in making that happen.

So it is this dual training in anthropology and education—along with a romantic combination of optimism and idealism that I acquired from my parents—that lead me today to join others who wish to strengthen, if not "save," the U.S. democracy. I begin my own journey below by "walking" with several other writers and thinkers, and I urge readers to undertake similar journeys of your own, in the company of others.

"SHARED AGENCY" AS A RESPONSE TO SOCIAL FRAGMENTATION

This book thus examines the dual hunch (1) that when a society of people loses its shared meanings, it becomes vulnerable to systemic collapse, from within—but that at the same time (2) that society need not wait for collapse to fully run its course before it initiates a national infrastructure renewal. Indeed, anthropologists had long believed the meanings of a people were passed from one generation to the next through what constituted their "culture" (e.g., Evans-Pritchard, 1940; Geertz, 1973; Levi-Strauss, 1961; Mauss, 1950; Spindler, 1955). From their "culture," the newest members of a society would come to know who they were, enjoy a degree of certainty about how to treat each other, and *learn how to interpret and respond to each new situation by weighing and assigning value—and then make a moral judgment about that event.* The challenge will be to discover and test how to do this today in an ethnically diverse nation.

With the loss of "shared meanings" in the United States that had once constituted each family's "ethnic culture" came the inexorable breakdown in the "webs of significance" that classical anthropologists (e.g., Geertz, 1973) had found necessary to hold a society together. Absent those webs of significance, a society could discover it had compromised its values (Ong, 1987), weakened internally (Sahlins, 1981; Sharp, 1952), fallen prey to deep structural inequality (Gailey, 1987), and ultimately come to experience the collapse of its largest social systems (see, e.g., Diamond, 2005; compare Acemoglu & Robinson, 2012). Even Russian President Vladimir Putin has noted in recent years the great internal threat posed to Western civilization by the absence of moral values:

> People in many European countries are embarrassed or afraid to talk about their religious affiliations. Holidays are abolished or even called something different; their essence is hidden away, *as is their moral foundation*…I am convinced that this opens a direct path to degradation and primitivism, resulting in *a profound demographic and moral crisis.*
>
> Vladimir Putin speaking at the Valdai International Discussion Club, September 19, 2013. Emphasis added.

This book has explored what happens when the most powerful nation in world history, the United States of America, discovers it has lost its sense of shared meaning. In the absence of the binding quality of a common "ethnic" culture, there could be no impedance to the selfish individualism and structural inequalities that Gailey had found to be the direct precursors to systemic collapse in earlier human societies.

And so, in the United States today *it is this absence of shared meaning— the moral center it would provide and our resulting vulnerability to fear and social fragmentation—that gave a small, elite group the opening it needed to further roil the public, manipulate markets impossibly upwards at first and then later into the throes of collapse—and make enormous profits for themselves via extraordinarily high leverage in both directions, at their whim.* They do this because they can and because the norms and duties stating how to treat others and make sacrifices for the good of one's community (what I would today call the ethics of *"deep culture"*) had been replaced over time by "the *thin culture*" of selfish individualism, self-aggrandizement and fear.

BEYOND CRITIQUE TO "SHARED ACTION"

This book also reflects a deep personal wish to extend beyond the abstract critiques of power and asymmetry I encountered in academe in the 1990s, so that we might arrive at a more practical and sanguine mode of infrastructure rebuilding. In my research, I found *it is in fact possible to take concrete steps to reconstitute the social infrastructure and shared norms of a society of people*—and go beyond critique. In that case, the society was a private university in California and we reconstructed the culture of the institution by generating "new shared meanings" that could bind together its diverse members across race and other forms of difference (Tanaka, 2003, 2009; Tanaka & Cruz, 1998).

In that four-year project, we used the methods of "participatory action research" (e.g., Elden & Chisholm, 1993) to give agency and responsibility to interested campus members who wished to improve the culture of their institution and build campus racial harmony. We achieved uplifting results and so much so that the "intercultural model" of campus diversity (Tanaka, Johnson, & Hu, 2001), where there is "learning and sharing across difference and no culture dominates," has since been emulated by other universities and colleges across the United States.

To achieve the same kind of change today—but this time at the level of a national infrastructure reconstruction necessary to launch a more "intercultural democracy" (Ortiz, 1947/1940)—I suggest we begin by undergoing the same sequence of steps that worked so well in constructing a model intercultural university. These were: (1) storytelling in small groups, (2) sharing dreams of how to make a better world, and then (3) group action to begin to put those personal dreams into effect. To strengthen the democracy, we will want to teach this nationwide.

Presented by multiple authors, the models below will demonstrate it is indeed possible to "operationalize" the concept of a "deep democracy" originally envisioned by Fung and Wright (2003, pp. 6–17)—where (1) there is "a practical orientation toward addressing the problems of the people," (2) the public participates in a "bottom-up" process to address those problems, and (3) there is a "deliberative solution generation" that will potentially lead to positive change (see also Couldry, 2004; Pateman, 1970; Touraine, 2000). The sequence of chapters in Part II of this book reflects this very spirit of storytelling, dreaming, and collective action by diverse groups of concerned citizens. As an important offshoot of this approach, seen here, the collaboration and sharing required will also enact the "intercultural" nature of this new democracy.

BEGINNING THE NEXT DEMOCRACY

There is another way to say this. I don't think we can ever have a democracy that is truly "by, for and of the people" until our schools end their "top-down" and robotic fascination with the No Child Left Behind and Common Core regimes of scripted learning and standardized "assessment over-determinism" (Foster, 1997)—*and begin to teach the learned skills of (a) personal agency, (b) social agency and (c) a mutual coming to be.* We can do this by telling each other our stories—and discover how uplifting it is to do that.

In telling our stories (as I attempted to do by way of example in Part I), we as citizens acquire the cultural capacity to share our dreams as a necessary precedent to the collective step of initiating or providing public comment in a new, "bottom-up" approach to policymaking—where members of the public have an opportunity to deliberate in a deep democracy and recommend to elected officials how *they* might make a better world.

So I want to underscore that while I originally set out to tell about systemic collapse and renewal through my own storytelling, I discovered that any move to establish a deep and intercultural democracy would itself have to act out the very multivocality and shared coming to be we would one day hope to see in the democracy itself—by presenting the stories and dreams of multiple thinkers in this book. *Stated in another way, it is by sharing our stories and dreams for positive social change that we create the necessary and constantly evolving narrative foundation to construct and sustain a common public sphere.*

In adopting the mutually reinforcing relation of storyteller and listener, we also pattern a new civility. In effect, we respond to the fragmentation of systemic collapse by enacting the early steps for a new democracy that is interactive, broadly cohering, *and* "bottom-up." As applied researchers, we seek to pattern some of those steps in the chapters below. In fact, we feel a "storytelling" format like this matches up well with a future U.S. social terrain where diverse citizens will want to share their life and family meanings in close acts of civic engagement with each other. In this way, the book attempts to model the direct connection that can inhere between the telling of "life stories"—by multiple storytellers—and the collective enactment of positive social change.

To be sure, there will remain in any period of systemic collapse a threat that the social fragmentation devolves to fascism. Elites may create "false flag" (staged) terrorist events inside the United States, fabricate "out-of-control immigration problems," or even out-and-out "race-baiting." Or a groundswell of populist sentiment may bring sunshine to the existence of extraordinary, secret pyramids and under-the-ice chambers in Antarctica (Quayle, 2017)—and shock our understandings of reality. But the American public has to stand firm and not let those events give rise to further deprivations of Constitutional rights. So the "intersubjective" storytelling approach we use here—where each author is a "subject" and "agent" who makes her/his own meanings and shares those meanings with others—is offered as one way to preempt that default mechanism, give each other strength, and hold the line for democracy.

THE IMPORTANCE OF INTERSUBJECTIVITY IN THE NEXT DEMOCRACY

So in the concluding chapters and epilogue of this book, a large handful of writers and artists will present their dreams about how schools, colleges, public arts programs, local farms and government agencies can begin to generate (and thus "re-reap") the positive meanings needed to push back against the stripping away of value and worth by the forces of race and fiat capital in the late 20th and early 21st centuries. In applied anthropological terms, it is by sharing our stories that we re-foreground and freshly validate the duties, norms, behaviors, and myths that will bind together—and thus ground—the people of a "deep" *and* "*intercultural*" democracy.

This "subject-to-subject" storytelling action is one in which each person becomes an author of her or his own meanings (that is, a "subject" rather than being an "object" on the receiving end of another person's meaning system). In other words, the acts of storytelling and dreaming—by multiple players—will construct a relationship of intersubjectivity where every story counts and no one is turned into an "object" of another person's discourse.

There are also a number of other outcomes produced by the storytelling approach used in this book. *First, my co-authors and I write in a hybrid manner.* Some chapters (1, 3 and 4) were written auto-ethnographically in that they drew a connection between a writer's life experiences and the wider social developments of one's time (e.g., Chang, 2008; Reed-Danahay, 1997). Others are ethnographic portrayals of how a democracy or economy can be hijacked by a small group in power and to the detriment of rest of the people of a country (Chapters 4 and 5). Some chapters (2, 4, 9 and 10) are in the form of visual or intersubjective ethnography where multiple sensibilities help the authors to experience the empowering quality of agency (see also Tanaka & Cruz, 1998). Still other chapters (6, 7 and 8) "dream" acts of future social change through fiction or through the fiction/nonfiction hybrid text (after Bell, 1993). In the Epilogue, a number of authors and artists present their views for how to jumpstart this new democracy—and evoke the kind of human spirit needed to make that happen. My coauthors and I discovered that by being open to nontraditional forms of writing and thinking, we can move fluidly back and forth between stories of collapse and imagined possibilities of renewal.

Second, I found that my own storytelling needed to shift from stories of pain and rage—where I had in a way become "a prisoner to my own critical analysis"—to dreams and acts of personal and social reconstitution where I could then be "free" to make my own meanings, de novo. In this way, I enjoyed a breakthrough in my own felt capacity for agency. Without this capacity to move beyond critique to concrete action—and I feel I have Mari Ruti (2006) to thank for that—I would not have been able to: (a) envision new action that was not merely a response to oppressive regimes and (b) engage in acts of renewal with others who, like me, were also seeking to move beyond oppression *and* beyond resistance to oppression. My suspicion is that the other authors of this text reached the same conclusion as they conducted their own writing.

So while Part I reflects a kind of "victimology" that governed my own soul as a person living under the meaning-sucking forces of race and fiat capital, Part II is presented below to show it is indeed possible *to begin to "remake oneself" as an integral part of a larger process of working with others to reconstitute a country's democratic infrastructure*. In doing this, we enter a new time and space of "liminal possibility"—where we are each a little more free to walk away from the hurtful reach and "totalizing effects" of someone else telling us what to value. No longer shackled to the position of spending all our energies resisting the "dominant discourse," we are free to create and celebrate our own meanings. Indeed, absent this jump shift in personal positioning, we too easily remain locked in a state of "celebrating" the very victimology of which we complain and wish to escape; that is, we too easily remain in that state of "ressentiment" decried by Nietzsche (1989; see also Tanaka, 1999).

Third, I learned that while I had to begin this project by being introspective, I would eventually have to work and write with others if I desired to enter the active, envisioning stage of renewal. So where I had attempted in earlier chapters to be "an agental subject" (Ruti, 2006) who could make my own meanings by telling my stories rather than accepting the meanings of those who held power over me—by the second half of the book, I found myself working "in *inter*subjective relation" with others by listening to and supporting *their* dreams and storytelling—their subjectivity—just as they were supporting mine.

NARRATION AND MUTUAL IMMANENCE AS FOUNDATIONAL STEPS IN DEMOCRATIC RENEWAL

In this spirit of intersubjectivity, Part II therefore contains a number of writings by applied researchers who exchange their "stories" intersubjectively about their dreams of how to make the United States a better country. Collectively and in concert with each other, these expressions enact a rising hope that promises to one day be large enough to trump even the darkest of times. Through storytelling, dreaming and proposals for concrete social change, these expressions thus enact *"a mutual immanence of authors"* where each writer comes into being as a subject and agent *by helping others also to become expressive subjects and agents*. Renewal begins when stories are told—and as we help each other to tell our stories.

Chapter 6, "Letting Go," presents a glimpse into the distant future and from there, a critical look back at the present. In this "prospective archaeology" of the present, I search to know the nature of the idealized self. What will this person be like—this person who is fully aware of the sources of meanness and asymmetry in today's world, who remains him/herself flawed—and yet manages to retain a faith in humanity and develops the skill sets to make that world a better place? Sometimes, *it is by "letting go" of the immediate problems of today that we gain a better vantage point from which to discover a way out of the darkness.*

In Chapter 7, "Looking Past the Target," photographer/MBA Ruth Tate captures the expression of an anonymous street muralist in the heart of Oakland, California: the irrepressible urge of the human condition, always to come together. Aptly entitled "Interdependence," the splash of blue-purple lettering and light green field of this street art is in intersubjective relation with what educational activist David Reed writes in fact-based fiction about a future world where ideas for budget spending are suggested—collaboratively—by staff, students and faculty at a community college rather than reflecting the views of just one or two top college officials. And so, *it is by "letting go" of their own sources of pain and doubt that these two activist researchers—one with Native American roots and the other with African American roots—gain a vantage point from which to "look past the target" to a better place*, a future place beyond immediate predicament or historical limitation.

In Chapter 8, I inter-splice my recollection of a time and place where many strands of history seem to stream unexpectedly into one visual frame. I am emboldened by graduate school classmates to think about my own past and memories of hurtful social branding and social constriction. In this fact-based yet fictive mountain retreat attended by graduate students from UCLA, one encounters the anthropological beauty of "polysemy"—where one presumed "common" U.S. history now admits of very different interpretations by people from different ethnic family backgrounds and meaning systems.

Superimposed on this "new history" (after Schama, 1991), the chapter also presents the vantage point of "Nature" and the fresh opportunity that perspective may give us to re-see our predicaments in wholly new ways, this time where respect for the beauty, grandeur and fecundity of the earth becomes the launching point for a New Human Nature. *In the richness of an ecological and interconnected world, we come to see that by "casting steppingstones" into a pond, this one act can submit of many different paths to take to the other side.* Demonstrating a kind of "polysemy in motion"—effectuated through time and space—this positioning of self and reality may offer fresh modes of action for the social change researcher of tomorrow.

In Chapter 9, applied researchers Derek Fenner and Evangelia Ward-Jackson each present their own take on what life will be like "on the other side of the pond." "Extending the Aura" of their dreams, these public intellectuals imagine themselves already immersed in that new world; in this way, they make it all the more likely they will arrive at that future time and space. Derek Fenner's "narration and art-based project" is offered to teach youth nationwide how to become "subjects and agents" for a democracy that is "performed" in their own communities. In poetic voice, Evangelia Ward-Jackson then enacts/performs her own belief that in making, knowing and sharing our own sources of renewal with others, we construct the necessary *emotive precondition* for one day celebrating a deep, collaborative and intercultural democracy. In this way, the two applied scholar-poets inscribe a path to the future where "the dreamed of social change" and "the inchoate subject or self" begin to merge, each giving rise to the other.

In Chapter 10, Roberto Flores and I reflect on our own personal journeys of self-discovery with the aim of being change agents in our own lives. Outwardly in search of a world better than the one we were born into, we quickly realize we had both been harboring a deep need to find not just social but also personal renewal. In (a) the stories we tell each other, (b) our dreams of a better world—and (c) our subsequent actions to test new models to create that dreamed of world—we gave each other permission to carry out those very dreams. In our dual writing, *it is as if each of us knew exactly how to support—and at the same time benefit from—the agency of the other.* The true joy is that both of our dreams came to fruition in real life—through the creation of an "autonomous community" in the United States in El Sereno at the edge of Los Angeles and in the creation of the first U.S. "intercultural university campus."

But in "going back to the source" of our deepest forms of angst, we also discovered that while we had begun to experience an important time of personal renewal, we were still not at journey's end and perhaps never will be. We are happy to begin each day anew and cherish "the state of the inchoate," which is itself a victory!

But is this possible? *Can* other citizens find a way to renew themselves and engage in infrastructure rebuilding—as part of one integrative process? The Epilogue to this book presents excerpts from 12 papers and artwork offered to impel new approaches to educational leadership during and after systemic collapse. These excerpts show it is indeed possible to proceed from storytelling to dreams of a better world—and thence to the construction of concrete plans to make those dreams come true. Arising out of shared agency and mutuality, these applied researchers and social artists: (1) tell each other (and us) just how they would help to jump-start a national infrastructure renewal in the context of a systemic collapse and (2) enact an "organic approach to leadership development" where new models are hatched in groups, and replication of their models can one day follow.

It is this power of "mutual immanence" that I saw in how these authors treated each other that leads me today to recommend the teaching of mutually reinforcing acts of (a) storytelling, (b) dreaming and (c) collaboratively-developed "social change envisioning projects" across the United States—in schools, universities and arts programs. My deepest hunch is that *teaching "mutuality" will be the key to saving—and re-initializing—the idea of democracy in a diverse nation.*

In other words, the onset of a "deep" (e.g., Barber, 1984; Fung & Wright, 2003; Ober, 1989; Pateman, 1970) and "intercultural" democracy (Couldry, 2004;

McLaren, Flores, & Tanaka, 2001; Ortiz, 1947/1940; Touraine, 2000) would seem to require a human development model that patterns and rewards the broad cultivation and expression of "mutual immanence" (see, e.g., Hand, 1988) nationwide— where every citizen comes into being by helping others *also* to come into being. It may well be that the kind of mutual immanence enacted by the authors in this Epilogue may one day constitute an antidote to selfish individualism, address the nation's vacuum in shared meaning—and prefigure the bottom-up, deep quality of a diverse democracy.

SOME CHALLENGING THOUGHTS ABOUT THE NEXT ECONOMY

Five developments have appeared quite recently and I believe all five will offer fresh insight into how the democracy might best be renewed. These developments also underscore *the crying need for a new model or theory of economics* that can be more local community based and better serve the interests of the people in the context of a bottom-up or deep democracy.

I

Rob Kirby (2016) of Kirby Analytics reports that he has come upon the funding instrumentality for the cabal that had been running the U.S. democracy, sub rosa. By his reckoning, it is the Exchange Stabilization Fund (or "ESF") located within the U.S. Department of the Treasury. Created by Congress in the early 1930s, the ESF was originally funded by gold seized from U.S. citizens by the U.S. government in 1933, and this is believed by some to have been augmented by gold taken during the U.S. invasion of other countries in recent decades.

What is most revealing about the Exchange Stabilization Fund, however, is that it is "off book," meaning there is no public accounting of this hoard. What this means is that the ESF is not in any way accountable to the American public, even though housed within the U.S. Department of the Treasury. Manipulators of this largesse can use its massive funds, now believed to be *over $20 trillion*, to manipulate global markets including the listed prices of all commodities and currencies—and all equities in the U.S. stock markets. With "national security" used as a shield to prevent the average U.S. citizen from seeing what it does or how it operates, Kirby (2016) notes the ESF even employs the New York Federal Reserve branch "trading desk" to complete its trades—another entity that is not accountable to the public or its democracy.

Citing the earlier work of Eric deCarbonnel (2011) of Marketskeptics.com, Kirby argues this fund has long been used to finance regime change, murder for hire, and arms running—again, all without Congressional supervision. "It operates above all laws" and, "it's bigger than London," he concludes. My belief is that *the ideal first step in a U.S. democratic renewal would be for Congress to close down the Exchange Stabilization Fund, seize all its financial, real estate and precious metals holdings, and make those the first assets placed into a U.S. Sovereign Wealth Fund dedicated to serving the human citizens* of the United States (for instance, by guaranteeing free healthcare and free preK-16 education for all such U.S. citizens) and having bylaws similar to those constituting Norway's sovereign wealth fund.

II

A second important development is the finding by former HUD Assistant Secretary Catherine Austin-Fitts (2016a) that over the past two decades there has been a financial coup d'état in the United States during which $40 trillion was stolen from "the Old Economy" by elites—leaving the people of the United States to face old liabilities in the tens of trillions without the benefit of the $40 trillion siphoned off by the New World Order for their "New Economy." This is no small sum. And the average citizen? The average citizen of the United States has not even been made aware of this grand theft and remains stuck trying to address massive personal and private debt accumulated over the past 20 years with little remaining state or personal resources.

As Austin-Fitts (2016a) points out, those who took the $40 trillion still have it and "It belongs to us! We need to get it back." (See also Evans-Pritchard, 2011; Whitehead, 2016.) *An ideal second step in a democratic renewal would be to reclaim the $40 trillion and place it in the same U.S. Sovereign Wealth Fund.* In other words, there is a ready means to fund renewal.

III

So specifically, what has been the cost of losing the democracy for the average American? Public intellectual Gerald Celente (2016) reports that, "Since 2009, *95% of all income gains* have gone to the richest 1% while median household income remains *below* 1999 levels." This is reflected in the fact that "62% of Americans don't have $400 to pay for an emergency bill" (Hodges, 2016). In fact, *from 1960 to 2009, the cost of healthcare in the United States increased by 800% for the average American*, even after taking into account inflation (Heyes, 2016, citing Global Research). This degree of asymmetry would be unfathomable in a true democracy that represents all the people.

Investment advisor David Morgan (2016) adds on USAWatchdog.com (interviewed by Greg Hunter) that in 1985 the top 5% in the United States held $5 trillion in wealth—but that by 2015, the top 5% held $40 trillion. In other words, in the last 30 years the top 5% gained "more in wealth than the human race created before 1980." Meanwhile, it has been reported that over the past 20 years *the Pentagon has misplaced $6.5 trillion in taxpayer funds*. Jay Syrmopoulos (2016) notes that—

> While the Department of Defense can't account for 6.5 trillion dollars of taxpayer funds, in 2014 there were 47 million people, including over 15 million children, living in poverty in the U.S.—15% of the population, which is the largest total number in poverty since records began being kept 52 years ago.

Should there now be a flat tax on all prior contractors that did business with the Pentagon over that time period to make up for that graft?

By the end of fiscal year 2015–2016, the federal government had "lost" another $9.3 trillion from its treasury (Austin-Fitts, 2016b), bringing the total to $50 trillion for bailouts and money simply "lost." It can no longer be denied that *a massive theft has been facilitated by the Federal Reserve, a private bank, as part of a final step "cut-and-run" by elites to move their money offshore before accountability returns*, according to Austin-Fitts (see also Quayle, 2017). But she also argues the people can use the U.S. Constitution, as worded, to get that money back.

So if the average American is wondering why it is so difficult just to get by each month, there is a reason why. The average American is being screwed! In a simple statement, famed financial commentator Jim Sinclair (2016a) concludes the United States has become "a *soul-less* environment, an environment which is without humanity." Is it time to rediscover soul?

Tracing the blame for this sad state of affairs to a specific group, former U.S. Treasury official Paul Craig Roberts (2016) avers, "This is 'the New Economy' that the filthy lying Neoliberal economists promised would be reward for the American work force giving up their manufacturing and professional skill jobs to foreigners. What a monstrous lie....These Neoliberal economists...have not been held accountable for their impoverishment of the American work force deeply buried in debt with no future prospects."

Alastair Macleod (2016) traces the blame for the current invisible, greedy economic policy favoring the wealthy to the "Cantillon Effect." With Richard Cantillon's (1755) work considered by some to be a founding contribution to modern political economy, this concept describes *what happens every time new money is created*, whether that be through the "quantitative easing" of today or given outright by the Fed or Treasury to large banks and hi tech companies in the form of interest-free loans:

> After (all this) new money has progressed through many hands with a tendency to drive up prices every time, the last receivers of the additional money find that prices for nearly all goods have already risen and the purchasing power of their wages and savings has effectively fallen. This is the Cantillon Effect. It amounts to *a wealth transfer from the poorest in society, the unskilled workers, pensioners and small savers to the government and its agents... (the) bankers*. (MacLeod, 2016)

This suggests the Fed as an institution *is intrinsically inimical to the idea of democracy.*

In the *Wall Street Examiner*, commentator Shah Gilani (2016) extends this thread a bit further by drawing a direct connection between the growing wave of economic asymmetry and what he argues has been outright "unconstitutional conduct" by elected government officials:

> (T)he dual mandate (of giving to the Federal Reserve Board responsibility for controlling the money supply and maximizing employment) was Congress punting to the Fed its responsibility for generating growth in the economy and jobs. If there wasn't jobs growth, from then on it would be the Fed's fault, not Congress' fault. *That abdication of Congress' responsibilities, a de facto act of treason which transferred the President's and Congress' Constitutional powers to an oligarchy of banking officers, is worse than frightening*…(Now) there's no fiscal responsibility and no fiscal policies coming out of Congress, because they gave their Constitutional duties the hot-potato treatment and foisted them off on the Fed.

The practical effects of this alleged "unconstitutional conduct" can be seen in the shocking visuality of a chart on "Productivity and Average Real Earnings" published by the U.S. Bureau of Labor Statistics (June, 2015). This chart traces the beginning of the decline in wages of goods-producing workers *to the very time when the Fed-controlled dollar was taken off the gold standard* in the early 1970s and today's unanchored paper "fiat dollar" came to fruition:

Figure I.1: Productivity and Average Real Earnings.

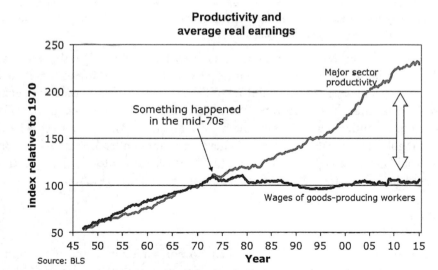

Source: U.S. Bureau of Labor Statistics (June, 2015).

In *The Economist*, Adam LeBor (2014) had this to say about the entity patterned after "the Fed" and Bank of England and now represents central banks worldwide:

Central bankers now "seem more powerful than politicians...holding the destiny of the global economy in their hands." How did this happen? The BIS (Bureau for International Settlements), the world's most secretive global financial institution, can claim much of the credit. From its first day of existence, the BIS has dedicated itself to furthering the interests of central banks and building the new architecture of transnational finance. In doing so, it has spawned a new class of close-knit global technocrats whose members glide between highly-paid positions at the BIS, the IMF, and central and commercial banks...*The bank's opacity, lack of accountability, and ever-increasing influence raises profound questions—not just about monetary policy but transparency, accountability, and how power is exercised in our democracies.*

But it was Danielle DiMartino Booth's (2017) book *Fed Up: An Insider's Take on Why the Federal Reserve Is Bad for America* that perhaps brought to an end the long debate about the value of the ultimate Federal Reserve Bank and its contribution to the decline of America. In this volume, Booth outlines how, among other things, the Fed's decision to keep interest rates low for so long had the result of transforming the U.S. economy into a drug addict dependent upon debt expansion (interviewed by Elijah Johnson and carried in Silverdoctors.com, March 8, 2017).

The upshot? In what he anticipates will be a runaway conflagration resulting from the breakdown of an unregulated "derivatives" market that is part of the transnational finance architecture, gold guru Jim Sinclair (2016b) claims the coming collapse will be epic, even "civilizational," in scale:

There may come a time when there is an entirely new social and political order, one brought about by the dissatisfaction of the disappearing middle class about the difficulty that we're all starting to feel in getting by month to month.

And over the next several years? Egon von Greyerz (December, 2016) suggests "We will see inflation, stagflation, hyper-inflation and deflation. Many of these...will happen simultaneously.... The build-up of debt and derivatives in the last quarter century guarantees that desperate governments will print unlimited amounts of money in a frantic attempt to save the financial system." Von Greyerz concludes that, "If gold reaches $10,000, which I believe is a minimum *without* hyperinflation, that would give a silver price of $665 to $1,000." It is with a note of resignation that "Bond King" Bill Gross (2016) adds: "The system itself is at risk."

IV

Finding it difficult to ignore the above, I am now on a mission to find an economic model that will better serve the democratic interests of a diverse and hard working U.S. population. With the precepts of Milton Friedman's deregulated "free market" capitalism so easily appropriated and misapplied by banker and military industrial elites—and with "Keynesian spending" having failed the people by feeding a bottomless pit of endless wars, bank bailouts, and homeland insecurities—the United

States is in need of alternative and more egalitarian economic frameworks that will not simply play back into the hands of this "power elite" (Mills, 1956).

One model that might work well in concert with a deep and intercultural democracy is "Fusion Economics" (Brahm, 2014), which stands for the proposition that an economy is strongest and most democratic when it is "bottom-up" and "local community-based." What does this mean? Such an economy would feature core characteristics like "compassionate capital," "stakeholder value," "conscientious consumption," "social enterprise," and "green growth"—and even give "power to youth to create economic ventures" (Brahm, 2014, p. 230, xii). So in place of today's sweeping, oligarchistic and top-down model of massive global capital flows and its "greed-based neoliberalism"—where trillions of dollars are manipulated by the hidden hands of a few—international lawyer/economist Laurence Brahm (2014, p. 231) urges a new "financial architecture… that does not see free capital flows as necessarily benefitting economies."

In Brahm's initial fieldwork to test this idea, he is already collaborating with local citizens to jump start hospitals, schools, farms, and ecology projects—in connection with collaboratively owned hotel businesses—so that these functions can operate *as interconnected local social, economic and public enterprises* that benefit synergistically from local cash and human capital flows that support each other. This is the case both with the flagship fieldwork positioned to address melting snow packs in the Himalayas (the "Himalayan Consensus") and famine and under-resourcing in Africa (the "African Consensus")—and in each instance where local community members are made full partners in *boldly linked, cross-enterprise ventures*. Thus, this is an approach to economics that is not Communist but is nonetheless vested in the enacting of economies that are local first, and interconnective, and then from there, bottom-up.

The theme of restoring local economic health to each community—and where local community members are made *partners* in interconnected enterprises and local ecologies are protected from harm—would seem to be an ideal and harmonious pairing with the agency-based, bottom-up and deliberative characteristics of a "deep democracy" (Fung & Wright, 2003).

Given the recent distresses associated with the onset and collapse of today's "global capitalist" economy—as evidenced by (1) the planned destruction of local businesses and public-serving governments around the world (Perkins, 2005), (2) "the automation of factories" on such a scale that now "we must help people to retrain for a new world and support them financially while they do so" (Hawking, 2016), and (3) the silent terror of "malevolent geo-engineering" and its depopulation (Wigington, 2016)—*the call that "fusion economics" makes to merge and facilitate community-controlled cross-enterprise operations of health and schooling services with local business formation and healthy, organic agriculture could not come at a better time.* Perhaps the "loot" we might one day seize back from the ill-gotten, tax-eschewing and anti-democratic gains of the power elite can now be used to fund local cross-enterprise collaborations like these in communities throughout the United States. That would be *"a deep economy!"*

V

This last entry is the hardest for me to set down on paper. It has to do with the moral rise and fall of the public figure I admired most in my life. He was a U.S. Senator of great repute, a man whose accomplishments shall always adorn his reputation for all time, and deservedly so.

But there was one thing he did and I have struggled to reach a decision on whether or not to publish this. This preceded my arrival into a new job in Hawaii as the state cable television regulator. It pains me to write this—and I will always hold my memory of this man in high regard. But it was while he chaired the Senate Subcommittee on Communications that his subcommittee put out new legislation that in effect took away the authority of local city and state regulators to control the monthly rates charged to consumers for cable television service.

The Cable Communications Policy Act of 1984 in essence gave each local cable company *the right to operate as a monopoly while charging rates as high as they wanted.* No competition. No rate regulation. Legalized monopoly. This was from a senator who represented a large population living in deep volcanic valleys rimming the islands of Hawaii—citizens who therefore had no "line of sight" ability to receive direct broadcast television. No cable, no TV.

The result? With many of this senator's own citizens held captive to their cable television company if they wanted to receive *any* television service at all, the operator immediately began raising rates in large leaps. And by the end of the first year after rate regulation authority had been taken away from the local government unit that I now managed—*the profit margin for this fifth largest cable operator in the United States had climbed from 17% to 43%!* In just one year.

What business in America wouldn't want a guaranteed profit margin of 43%?

It used to be that young children were taught that if there was a problem in your community, you could "write your U.S. congressman or senator." It was part of the mythology of growing up in the post-war generation of the 1950s and 1960s. But with this new legislation, that former belief system—and its respect for the will of the people—was brought to an end.

Perhaps more importantly, the ultimate implication of this 1984 legislation needs to be named as it holds great precedential value. While likely written and implemented at the behest of two former legislative assistants to this senator—*one the lawyer representing this very cable television company and the other the chief state regulator*—this legislation was also about how unceremoniously the core principles of "representative democracy" could be pushed aside by the actions of a man whom I had held in such high esteem my whole adult life.

Here I want to note that one of the greatest high points in my personal life was being allowed to play on this very senator's softball team in the U.S. Senate Softball League way back when I was a law student in Washington, D.C. It had brought me great joy and pride to be able to play for this team as it meant that I, as an average American, could be "that close" to an elected official who was a major figure on the national stage: it was like I could "touch" the greatness of representative democracy in a very tangible way. But all those wonderful memories only magnify the level of pain I feel today, as it means I write from such a deeply conflicted position.

And so I find that it hurts to lose one's hero, one's source of personal myth—a belief that there are things in life larger than one's self. But today I decide I will honor this man anyway and in this odd way: by using this personally painful example to demonstrate to readers how the harm from (1) the bottomless pit of "corporate and private donations" that have come to influence the outcomes of U.S. Congressional and Presidential elections and (2) the absence in Congress of "term limits" (indeed, enacted through the machinations of *former* legislative assistants) can mar even in the smallest way the record of the greatest hero I will ever know.

Why is this important? Because *the Cable Communications Policy Act of 1984 is the very first formal act I have encountered in my life of "the selling out of representative democracy"*—in ways that opened the door to the asymmetry and plutocracy of a Neoliberal ideology that went on to destroy the economy and civil society of a once proud and meaning-full nation. This legislation, written on behalf of cable television companies that were already enjoying monopolies in regions where they operated, could therefore arguably be identified as *the beginning point in "the de facto end to representative democracy" in the United States of America.* It became "the test case" that emboldened other counter-democratic initiatives in the decades that followed: the removal of the Glass-Steagall Act that had kept "razzle-dazzle investment banking" separate from more stable and conservative retail banking; the exporting of millions of high paying American jobs under "NAFTA;" threatened surrender of U.S. sovereignty by a "Trans Pacific Partnership" act (abrogated in the first act of President Trump); the approval of unhealthy "genetically-modified food" crops; directed beam forest fires; and the ubiquity of "chemtrails." The list goes on.

It pains me to know all this. And writing about this pains me even more. But I do so on the hope that readers will feel moved to do something about it. *Is it time, once and for all, to bring "campaign finance reform" and "term limits" to Congress?* In this odd way, we would honor the otherwise pristine record—and human vulnerability—of a truly great man.

* * *

In bringing this long interlude to a close, I will refer to a metaphor offered by Chris Martenson (October 8, 2016) that sheds light on how Americans have been traumatized by recent politics—and why this moment may therefore call for compassion. Referring to the psychological concept of "projection" and how it can be used to describe how people who had themselves been abused earlier in life subsequently go on to harm others—Martenson describes how the United States—after having itself invaded and abused so many other nations in since the 1990s—accused Russia of being abusive because it was the first to stand up and point a finger at the United States for its abusive treatment of other nations:

> In psychological terms…*projection*…is what happens when an individual, or a nation, accuses an external party *of the exact same traits that they secretly dislike about themselves.*

Martenson continues,

> *Have you ever noticed this in your own life? When someone who violates my boundaries is met with any sort of resistance at all, they experience it as me attacking them…I remember being yelled at by someone who did that a lot to people in their life and when I'd had enough (and) exactly matched their intensity to simply say 'Stop!' they recoiled and told everyone that I had attacked them.* (Emphasis added)

I too have noticed this in my life. I once knew a professor who had been badly abused as a child. Later as an adult, her practice was to yell at the top of her voice at other faculty members collectively, or individually (including me). When I asked her once to stop yelling at me or I would have to go to Human Resources, she herself went and filed a complaint *against me.* Incomprehensibly, she as my superior had also been trying to get me (a visiting professor with no power) to date her—something I was not interested in doing, and this at times left me feeling like I was being harassed. Would she one day *"project" on to me that same accusation of harassment that she didn't like about her own past?* If so, I would truly insist on believing it is not too late for her to learn how to receive compassion—and forgive the original source of her own pain so that she may one day be free, and stop hurting others.

In the same way, Martenson argues "the neocons and the likuds"—hard-line global leaders who have urged the United States to attack Russia and Syria for being "abusive" countries—can themselves be characterized as "very damaged and traumatized individuals," explaining:

> They carry a set of internal wounds that express on the outside as a very belligerent and hostile set of postures and actions. If I were to guess at their internal wound, it might be something along the lines of "I was really hurt as a child and nobody will ever hurt me again like that…" (So) the best way not to be hurt (again) is to lash out as fiercely and as rapidly as you can… (Their) motto is "Do one to others before they do one to me."

Martenson concludes with conviction: "That is where the U.S. is now. This rush to war is not a matter of anything rational or explicable, it is a function of having too many damaged and wounded people in power operating from deeply unconscious levels."

So if the schemed destruction of shared meaning, the traumatizing effects of one Middle East war after another, and the hurtful economic collapse of today have paralleled and prefigured today's usurpation of democracy, I will ask, *"How will we as a diverse nation of people, who believe so passionately in democracy, rise above the trauma to which we have been subjected and respond constructively to the collapse?"* Kindness, compassion, goodwill toward others, and the courage to dream will make for useful starting points; a larger inquiry into how then to take concrete steps has been the impetus for this writing and reflects my own wish to enter into the era that beckons, an exciting era of "culture, soul and democratic infrastructure rebuilding."

May I suggest there is now at least one alternative to today's empty avatars/ projections of racialization, debt, derivatives and psychological trauma—that we now set in motion the collapse scholarship of Sharp (1952), Sahlins (1981), Gailey (1997) and Diamond (2005) *by showing that at the very moment of collapse, it is possible to rebuild democracy in ways that are co-initiated by the people themselves?*

To achieve that end, we will each have to tell our stories, share our dreams about how to construct a better world, and work together to build that world. Part II outlines one way in which Americans can go about taking this healthy turn—by sharing our meanings, pulling ourselves together as a diverse nation, and beginning the work of constructing the next democracy.

NOTE

1. In selecting and deploying the words "systemic collapse" and "social reconstitution," I honor the wisdom of Christine Gailey who had the foresight to attach those words to the title of a scholarly conference held by the American Ethnological Association in the late 1990s.

REFERENCES

Acemoglu, D., and & J.A. Robinson, J. A. (2012). *Why nations fail: the origins of power, prosperity and poverty*. New York, NY: Crown Business.

Allport, G. (1954/1979). *The nature of prejudice*. Reading, MA: Addison-Wesley Publishing.

Austin-Fitts, C. (2016a, March 6). *Pyramid of lies could implode*. Interviewed by Greg Hunter, USAWatchdog.com

Austin-Fitts, C. (2016b, October 6). Controlled demolition coming—not a crash. Retrieved from USAWatchdog.com

Barber, B. (1984). *Strong democracy: Participatory politics for a new age*. Berkeley, CA: University of California Press.

Bell, D. (1993). *Faces at the bottom of the well: The permanence of racism*. New York, NY: Basic Books.

Booth, D. D. (2017). *Fed up: An insider's take on why the federal reserve is bad for America*. New York, NY: Portfolio Penguin.

Brahm, L (2014). *Fusion economics: How pragmatism is changing the world*. New York: Palgrave Macmillan.

Cantillon, R. (1755/1959). *Essay on the nature of trade in general*. London: Frank Cass & Co., Ltd.

deCarbonnel, E. (2011, June 3). What I have been afraid to blog about: The ESF and it's history. Retrieved from Marketskeptics.com

Celente, G. (2016, June 8). Gerald Celente just issued one of his most prescient trend alerts of 2016. Retrieved from KingWorldNews.com

Chang, H. (2008). *Autoethnography as method*. Walnut Creek, CA: Left Coast Press.

Couldry, N. (2004). In the place of common culture, what? *The Review of Education, Pedagogy & Cultural Studies, 26*(1), 3–22.

Diamond, J. (2005). *Collapse: How societies choose to fail or succeed*. New York, NY: Viking.

Elden, M., & Chisholm, R. F. (1993). Emerging varieties of action research: Introduction to the special issue. *Human Relations, 46*(2), 121–142.

Evans-Pritchard, E. E. (1940/1968). *The Nuer: A description of the modes of livelihood and political institutions of a Nilotic people*. Oxford: Oxford University Press.

Evans-Pritchard, A. (2011, January 9). Deepening crisis traps America's have-nots. *The Telegraph*.

Foster, M. (1997). *Plenary session for conference on reclaiming voice*. Center for Higher Education Policy Analysis, University of Southern California (June 1997).

Fung, A., & Wright, E. O. (Eds.) (2003). *Deepening democracy: Institutional innovations in empowered participatory governance*. London: Verso.

Gailey, C. (1987). *Kinship to kinship: Gender hierarchy and state formation in the Tongan Islands*. Arlington, TX: University of Texas Press.

Geertz, C. (1973). *The interpretation of cultures*. New York, NY: Basic Books.

Gilani, S. (2016, June 7). End the fed…and move the country forward. *Wall Street Examiner*.

von Greyerz, E. (2016, December 11). Global chaos and the road to $1,000 silver. *King World News*.

Gross, B. (2016, May 26). Interviewed on Newsmaxfinance.com

Hand, S. (1988). Translating theory, or the difference between Deleuze and Foucault. In Deleuze, G. (Eds.), *Foucault*. Minneapolis, MN: University of Minnesota Press.

Hawking, S. (2016, December 3). Is this the most dangerous moment in human history? *Zero Hedge*.

Heyes, J. D. (2016, August 23). Cost of U.S. healthcare now 800% higher per person than it was in 1960, even when adjusted for inflation. *Natural News*, citing Global Research and reprinted on SGTReport.com

Hodges, D. (2016, June 1). *TheCommonSenseShow.com*.

Janda, D. (2018). Iran nuke deal—bribes, treason and fraud. Interviewed by Greg Hunter, USAWatchdog.com (May 13, 2018).

Kirby, R. (2016, January 27). America's darkest secret: The covert fund that controls it all. Retrieved from SilverDoctors.com

LeBor, A. (2014). *Tower of Basel: The shadowy history of the secret bank that runs the world*. New York, NY: Public Affairs.

Levi-Strauss, C. (1961). *Tristes tropiques*. New York, NY: Criterion Books.

Martenson, C. (2016). Do we really want war with Russia? PeakProsperity.com. Reproduced in Zero Hedge (October 8, 2016).

Mauss, M. (1950). *The gift: The form and reason for exchange in archaic societies*. New York, NY: W.W. Norton.

McLaren, P., Flores, R., & Tanaka, G. (2001). Autonomy and participatory democracy: An ongoing discussion on the application of Zapatista autonomy in the United States. *International Journal of Educational Reform, 10*(2), 130–144.

Macleod, A. (2016, August 5). Saving the system. Retrieved from Goldseek.com

Mills, C. W. (1956). *The power elite*. Oxford: Oxford University Press.

Morgan, D. (2016, June 7). Interviewed by Greg Hunter on USAWatchdog.com

Nietzsche, F. (1989). *On the genealogy of morals and ecce homo*. New York, NY: Vintage Books.

Ober, J. (1989). *Mass and elite in democratic Athens: Rhetoric, ideology and the power of the people*. Princeton, NJ: Princeton University Press.

Ong, A. (1987). *Spirits of resistance and capitalist discipline: Factory women in Malaysia*. Albany, NY: State University of New York Press.

Ortiz, F. (1947/1940). *Cuban counterpoint*. New York, NY: Alfred A. Knopf.

Pateman, C. (1970). *Participation and democratic theory*. Cambridge, MA: Cambridge University Press.

Perkins, J. (2005). *Confessions of an economic hitman*. New York: Penguin Group.

Putin, V. (2013). Cited in PaulCraigRoberts.com on March 12, 2017: "Putin Speaking About the Collapse of Western Civilization at the Valdai International Discussion Club," September 19, 2013.

Quayle, S. (2017, January 21). Interview of Stephen Quayle on USAWatchdog.com by Greg Hunter and citing Quayle, S. (2015) *Empire beneath the ice: How the Nazis won WWII*. End Time Thunder Publishers.

Reed-Danahay, D. E. (1997). Introduction. *Auto/Ethnography: Rewriting the self and the social*. Oxford: Berg.

Roberts, P. C. (2016, June 9). Where Do Matters Stand? PaulCraigRoberts.com, Institute for Political Economy.

Ruti, M. (2006). *Reinventing the soul: Posthumanist theory in psychic life*. New York, NY: Other Press.

Sahlins, M. (1981). *Historical metaphors and mythical realities: Structure in the early history of the sandwich islands kingdom*. Ann Arbor, MI: University of Michigan Press.

Schama, S. (1991). *Dead certainties: Unwarranted speculations*. New York, NY: Vintage.

Sharp, L. (1952). Steel axes for stone-age Australians. *Human Organization, 11*(2): 17–22.

Sinclair, J. (2016a, June 16). Interviewed by Greg Hunter on USAWatchdog.com

Sinclair, J. (2016b, June 20). Interviewed by Greg Hunter on USAWatchdog.com

Spindler, G. (Ed.) (1955). *Education and anthropology*. Stanford, CA: Stanford University Press.

Syrmopoulos, J. (2016, August 16). Pentagon can't account for $6.5 trillion dollars. Global Research. Reprinted from TheFreeThoughtProject.com.

Tanaka, G. (1999). Ressentiment. *Anthropology and Humanism, 24*(1), 75–77.

Tanaka, G. (2003). *The intercultural campus: Transcending culture and power in American higher education*. New York, NY: Peter Lang Publishing.

Tanaka, G. (2009). The elephant in the living room that no one wants to talk about: Why U.S. anthropologists are unable to acknowledge the end of culture. *Anthropology & Education Quarterly, 40*(1), 82–95.

Tanaka, G., & Cruz, C. (1998). The locker room: Eroticism and exoticism in a polyphonic text. *Qualitative Studies in Education, 11*(1), 137–153.

Tanaka, G., Johnson, P., & Hu, B. (2001). Creating an intercultural campus: A new approach to diversity. *Diversity Digest, 5*(2), 6–7.

Touraine, A. (2000). *Can we live together? Equality and difference*. Stanford, CA: Stanford University Press.

U.S. Bureau of Labor Statistics (2015). Productivity and Average Real Earnings. (Courtesy of Ralph Benko, *ThePulse2016.com* and *Zero Hedge* (June 14, 2016).

Whitehead, J. W. (2016, March 21). Facism, American style. The RutherfordInstitute.com

Wigington, D. (2016). All out assault on life on earth. Interviewed by Greg Hunter on USAWatchdog. com (February 19, 2017). (See also GeoengineeringWatchdog.org).

PART II

Sources of Renewal

It is only…by acknowledging that the fictions we weave can and do make a difference in the world…that we can begin to transform it.

Mari Ruti (2006, p. 55)[1]

---

1 Ruti, M. (2006). *Reinventing the soul: Posthumanist theory and psychic life.* New York: Other Press.

CHAPTER 6

Letting Go

GREGORY K. TANAKA

Frontline journalists, such as Chris Hedges, have concluded that only revolution can correct the imbalance between the interests of a handful of oligarchs and the mass of humanity.

Paul Craig Roberts (January 3, 2017)

I

(February 23, 2117)

The arrival of another Intellect Grade Brown/1 should hardly cause a stir in Santa Fe this time of year. Like hundreds who had appeared in the spring ever since the end of the 16 Years War, the archaeologist had come to study the ruins. But Kainoa Ken Senstrom was unlike the others in one important respect. He was also here to learn the identity of his father.

Senstrom, age 30, IQ 149, 6'1" and slender, had been proud of his mother's Japanese Hawaiian—and his father's European—features. A "hapa" mix always went well, the 20th century Hawaiians used to say.

He was also proud of his "Brown cuff/1st dan" ranking after having so recently finished his apprenticeship at the Harvard/Gorbachev/Tokyo Global University ("HGT")—where he had earned a PhD with honors in Poststructural Archaeology.

"Brown" was the third rank and there were four more to go—a process that would take him the rest of his life, or so they say. Spirit and intellect. Tough to develop both and stay centered at the same time, he always thought. His dissertation had been "A Sensitivity Analysis of Chi Growth in Low and High Psychic-

Communal Posthumanist Societies." To satisfy the mind-body graduation requirements, he had minored in chi kung/internal medicine and tennis, both of which
had come easy.

Kainoa had been sent to Santa Fe by the New Global Government during the
Eco-Human Recovery Period. His assignment: to re-explore the ruins of the All
Sports Hall of Fame (extant 2030–2083 AD). The complex had been built to honor
citizen athletes who exemplified in their careers the highest standards of human interaction and sharing. It was a belief that a mutuality-based approach to sports achievement could serve as a metaphor and symbol for all that humanity strives for under
the new Posthumanist ideal of "mutual immanence." Wax-like figures of women and
men had been in this Hall. Of all ages, races and nation-states, they had stood side-
by-side. Individual achievement was thus enriched by the ritualistic message that one
could help others to achieve and contribute to the team as a component of one's own
achievement. Primitive interactive fiber optic technology had then enabled visitors
to interact with these life-size figures as if in a normal conversation.

But the 16 Years War had greatly damaged the sprawling edifice. Kainoa had
been asked to sift through the physical rubble and public sentiment to find answers
to two questions: (1) Did the militant cells have a spiritual basis for making this
complex their first target in the 16 Years War? And (2) might there be sufficient
psycho-communal sentiment for building a *new* Hall of Fame today, one that departs at last the selfish individualism reproduced by the blinding 1990s–2010s rush
to embrace steroids and bring accolades to "The Isolated Self?"

* * *

The arrival of Zoey Boole Ching, age 28, was another matter. Intellect grade
Brown/4, she had earned a PhD/MPA with highest distinction at the Beijing/
Stanford/ANC Graduate School ("BSA"). Her dissertation had been entitled
"Spiritual Incursion into Post-Structural Equation Modeling." Wiry, 5'10", and
with bright, quick brown eyes, "Z" was known for her IQ of 193 and a silver medal
in three-dimensional chess at the 2114 Olympics. No one in New Mexico knew
that Z had also lived for two years at the Saguaro Institute, meaning she was well
trained in counterintelligence.

Z's assignment was, for public purposes, to study the spiritual-intellectual
profile of the leading intercontinental members of the Super Commerce Class
who lived in Taos during the 16 Years War. But her unofficial assignment was to
confirm the existence of a new deep cover cell believed to be forming, once again,
in the Taos area.

Z opened her eyes after completing a "3-sec" centering exercise—and noticed
an intelligent looking man in his late twenties staring intently at her.

"What do you want?" she asked. Two years at Saguaro left her unwilling to
believe in coincidence.

"I noticed your brown cuff trimming—and your eyes," he answered quickly enough. "You are part Asian?"

"And African. And European."

"There aren't many who would wear their colors to Cliff Dweller's on a Saturday night."

Z looked at him more closely but did not respond. She liked the softness in his voice and the obvious intelligence. But his high sensitivity level could mean trouble.

Her thoughts were interrupted when a thick-necked man stepped out of the crowd and addressed them.

"Heard the latest? Another cell operative was caught trying to administer that synthetic 'fugu' poison to a woman in Dallas this morning. The guy had a huge syringe with him. A roommate walked in just in time to save the woman. Seems like they use good lookin' men and women to prey on members of the opposite sex. You know, to try to catch them unawares? 'Wham,' another convert to the cell."

The guy looked at Kainoa, then at Z. "The poison requires a secret antidote every six months or the person dies a painful death, right? That's how they keep the loyalty of new members to their cell. Do you think it's true they have a preference for direct descendants of old cell leaders?"

Z and Kainoa were now glaring at the thick-set man, who turned abruptly and exited, blending instantly into the crowd.

After this strange encounter, Z and Noa discovered they shared a common interest in tracing the end of the 500-year epoch of Western Civilization (1492–1992) and the launching of the Posthumanist Renewal Period. Z was interested in the decline of Western militarism, the stripping of non-household private property rights out from under capitalism—and resulting onset of Eco-Humanism primed by a sudden switch to non-hydrocarbon based forms of energy in the 2030s and virtually simultaneous adoption of human development models that championed the importance of mutuality. Noa was interested in the merger of rationalism and spiritualism during the same period. The two exchanged tel-net codes and agreed to meet in a few days to talk again about their new jobs.

II

(February 25, 2117)

At his lab in a borrowed room at the Global Government training center, Noa rarely received visitors. He was surprised to hear a knock at his door and rose anxiously to open it. A woman of indeterminate age stood hesitantly at the doorway, holding a crossbow in her right hand. She was positively stunning.

"Excuse me," she said, "Is this the right area for the repair of Parks and Recreation equipment?"

He tried to talk but the words would not come out.

"I'm sorry to bother you," she continued, "but I'm new to the area and I don't know where to go for these things. I'm sure this is all boring you…"

Noa finally found words to respond. "No, no, no. I like crossbows. I mean I always wanted to see one, in the flesh I mean." Feeling his cheeks burn, Noa waited to see if she would talk again or spin and be gone just as quickly as she had appeared.

"Well, I can show you mine. Here," she said handing her crossbow to him. "This is where you grab it with your left hand and this is where you steady it with your right hand."

Somewhere in the back of his mind Noa wondered how this beautiful woman direct from "sci-sensual" movies had known that he was left-handed. But the touch of her hand was already on his arm and the thought was lost. She was close enough for him to feel her warmth and be rendered dizzy.

"What are you doing in this room, off to yourself?" she asked finally, as she moved away from him.

"Oh, I'm doing a study. You know, of the ruins out by Chimayo. I'm an archae-ologist," he said self-consciously.

"Hey, what a coincidence! I'm the new ranger out north of town and some-times I patrol that area. Have you seen the caverns out behind the ruins yet?"

When Noa shook his head, she continued. "It's not a bad walk this time of year. The grass and flowers are just starting to come out. Might be a bit brisk but it's a fun hike. Only about a half mile. Want to see it after work one day?"

Noa was in utter disbelief. This woman's hair was a very light blond and in a way long forgotten, before racial mixing had altered forever the previous norms of beauty. She seemed out of place. Tall and full, she had warm lips and piercing eyes that were set in a perfectly symmetrical face. All these cues were telling him he might indeed enjoy having a walk with her.

Before he could respond, she said, "How's about Friday? That's in two days. 4:00 PM?"

Noa watched as she turned with a smile. She flicked her hair back and was gone.

* * *

Z's third trip into the field was a humdinger. Yesterday, the Old Mansions Clubhouse had turned out to be well maintained but it had held no records that could help her. An earlier search of the Commerce Hall computer records had also failed to show an easy way to cull out the lineage charts for the top commerce brokers—or suspected cell leaders.

But Z knew a Shanghai consortium had recently merged in some twisted way with the surviving leaders of a North American cell. Their plan was to await the right time to come out and strike back at those who had won the non-violent Eco-Humanist Revolution of the 2020s, one that had been foreshadowed a decade earlier by the Egyptian spring and Greek Debt Jubilee and led a decade later to the Constitutional Amendments for Democratic Renewal. Very possibly the cell had established a link to northern Europe as well, but that had not yet been proven.

With uncharacteristic impulse, Z had hopped into her sporty yellow eco-jeep in the early morning and raced over to the old Pueblo de Taos Indian Reservation. The library there had never been purged, by 16-Years War people or hers. Antiquated and not fully computerized, it had been little used by outsiders.

But there, in the second row from the back, along the east wall, she came upon a remarkable account. It was a compendium of stories of sporting events and other rituals hosted by the Reservation for Profit in the years before *and during* the 16-Years War.

Z pulled out her portascanner and ran it along hundreds of pages detailing foreign visitors and performers in the global tournaments. Realizing it was late, she decided to autofax the key pages later to Joelle Valuton. It would take two days for her to review the rest more closely.

It was then that she noticed a movement out of the corner of her eye. As she turned to look, a man scurried around the corner to the rear of the stacks and was lost from sight. She thought he seemed thick-set but wasn't sure.

Immediately Z went into an all-senses prana mode. She gathered her things up and walked firmly out the front door, moving cautiously towards her vehicle. She was so aware she heard the earth beneath her, imagining its sound under her feet in the yards leading to her vehicle. A small stand of trees lay ahead and so she gave them wide birth and angled back towards the eco-jeep.

Z sensed a shadow moving in those trees and stopped to face it, lowering her *ki* and centering herself instantly.

"Hi! Remember me?" A thick-necked man emerged from the trees and began walking slowly in her direction. He was smiling and carrying a briefcase. He was also dressed in a lightweight Morningstar suit. He was the same course man who had rudely interrupted her first meeting with Noa. Noa...

"I'm sorry," Z said as nonchalantly as she could. She moved quickly to her right, skirting the next row of vehicles and jumped into her eco-jeep. As she started the Prosper fuel cell engine and whirred out of the parking lot, she looked in the rear view mirror and saw the thick-necked man get into a large Electro-glide car that had been parked at the far curb.

III

(February 26, 2117)

Noa glanced at a serene looking Zoey Ching and felt proud of himself for his good fortune. Z was guiding her little yellow eco-Jeep through the tight curves of

Route 64 with all the uncelebrated confidence of a person who had always combined natural gifts with hard work.

In the short time it had taken them to drive to Taos from Kit Carson Peak, Noa and Z had tested each other's intellectual and emotional mettle.

"What do you mean?" Noa asked when Z opined that America had turned totalitarian during the 1990's. This was far earlier than the 2020 date that was accepted lore.

"You know how everybody talks about 'The Great Depression II,'" Z continued.

"Starting with the Cascading Crashes of 2000–2016? The Dot.Com bubble of 2000, the subprime crash of 2008, the derivatives market breakdown of 2019, the sovereign debt collapse of (2019–2020), and what else? In fact, by the 1990's where pieces had already been put in place for a desperate turn to a fascist form of U.S. government, where the interests of big capital and government merged? You know, jobs for the middle class had been exported and the 'full-time employment rate' was down to a record low 62%."

"Okay, okay," Noa interjected. "Let's say there was a scheme by some group that planned all this—even the stock market crashes—for their own gain. How could they have duped the public? I still can't believe it!"

"By the early-1990's," Z responded, "The Elites had taken their own children out other local public schools and placed them into private schools. And public schools were turned into 'factories' that were forced to compete with each other to graduate obedient workers who performed well on standardized tests, rather than becoming critical, independent thinkers, problem solvers and democratic citizens. The great American universities were by then fully marketized, and this had produced deep, subtle messages about economic power and race hierarchy. And by then the ruling financial elite had already gained full content-control of the media. It was all part of their plan. We know that this was how the ruling elite had sneaked up on the public, right? Total control of the media, and no more independent reporting?"

"Yes, we do know all that now," Noa added. "The democratic function died the moment that independent media reporting came to an end. But worse, the public had continued to believe it had a working Constitution anyway. With many lulled into believing they could afford to buy an expensive house or car on easy, low interest loans made available by U.S. banks, those very banks were repackaging and selling those mortgages as "derivatives" for a fat commission. What was initially a kind of "systemic euphoria" ultimately gave way to "systemic despair" where the effects of an economic depression could no longer be ignored.

Noa paused before continuing. "Come to think of it, the 1990's and 2000's were when those government dollars were used to fund a massive build-up of local police forces in the U.S.—and all under the guise of controlling drugs and youth gangs. But the real goal all along was to put in place a foundation for martial law in anticipation of widespread social protests."

"Ah…" Z said, "and you know how the public was manipulated into *accepting* the need for infrastructure for a police state in the first place, right?"

"Yes, I see what you mean," Noa said, reading her thoughts. "The same way—yes, the media. The media frightened the public with news about one terrorist event after another. This was all part of *The Narrative* the Elites had continued to trot out and use over and over again to hoodwink the public, and over a long period of time. The public never got it—until it was too late. And this was all because the media was controlled by those same Elites."

"I think we're on to something here," Z added. "The ensuing 9/11 catastrophe—shown later to have been a manufactured fiction funded and directed *by members of the U.S. government no less!* From there it was easy to steer the American public into buying into terrorism—to believe that all acts of terror were being caused by dark-skinned people from the Middle East. And then on top of that, we had the food riots of 2019. By the late 2019, the public was fairly begging for more police protection.

"But it all sounds too neat, too schemed out. In other words, somebody funded this narrative, somebody planned it, somebody benefitted from this. Who was pulling the strings behind those Elites?" Z asked. "That is the real question."

"I, uh…" Noa paused. "I think you are right. There was a small group benefitting from all those so-called acts of terror, all those mini wars in the Middle East that drove the U.S. economy into the tank—just like the Afghanistan War had crippled the Soviet Union economy in the 1980s."

"Yes, and it had to have been the same group that benefitted from all those stock market crashes—of 2001, 2008 and 2019," Z responded. "Think about it. It was those global bankers, the ones that many have since argued were really ambassadors of the global control arm called the New World Order that was really just operating for the Rothschilds, the Rockefellers and the successors to the Morgan bank."

"And then so where does the 16 Years War figure in?" Noa asked pensively. "Might that whole thing be connected in some way with the same New World Order bankers who initiated those currency, commodity and stock market manipulations of the early 21st Century? What economists then called 'central bankers?'"

"Wait," Z said with growing excitement. "That might have been the same secret organization that fanned public fear about the Chinese.

"My mom used to tell me jokingly that this fear was aided by naming all those viruses and flu bugs after places in China, 'Z added.' You know, the 'Hong Kong Flu', the 'Beijing Flu,' the 'Shanghai Flu.' That was part of the plan. It was all pretty insidious. And then it was almost too late—"

"Yes," said Noa. "But suddenly there were military tribunals with top politicians placed on trial for treason, including the trial of a former President, top CIA and FBI officials, and two former Secretaries of State! Altogether, there were over 50,000 sealed indictments written."

"So of course the American public was shocked," Z added. "People could not figure out if President Trump was the *savior of democracy* or instead, a Hitler-like fascist riding a wave of anti-globalist public sentiment for his own ego-gratification."

Noah thought for a moment and then said, "It was a stroke of genius, really, how the President set everything up with his December 20, 2017 executive order. That gave him the authority to not only arrest and try U.S. citizens in the interest of national security but *also* to seize their assets. This means the evil cabal members who had plotted to take over the democracy—whom some then called the *Deep State*—had their trillions of dollars seized."

Feeling the excitement, Z chimed in. "Seizure of their illegal off-shore bank accounts alone amounted to almost $100 trillion! And *that* signified the return after many years to the *rule of law*, a moral basis for democracy, and a Constitutional republic."

"And ultimately," Noa said, "*all* that made possible the end of the Federal Reserve Bank and a reset of the currency away from a cheap, flimsy paper dollar to a new currency backed by gold and silver. But the biggest surprise of all was the deeply personal decision President Trump had to make, as commentator Dr. Dave Janda predicted in September 2018, whether to extend his term as President—or terminate his work then, abjure fascism, and become the greatest President in U.S. history. We all know which route he chose."

"But what I like best," Z said., "is how this all paved the way for the Constitutional Amendments of 2029, where the people demanded by a 5-to-1 margin that the new amendments add five "core elements" to the U.S. Constitution: (1) a permanent provision barring the establishment of a private central bank, (2) an annual public accounting of all gold and silver and other monies held by the U.S. (which then included the Exchange Stabilization Fund, the $21 trillion stolen from HUD and the Department of Defense, and the gold and silver in the Grand Canyon and Chocolate Mountain), (3) creation of a *"U.S. Sovereign Wealth Fund,"* much like Norway's, that would be funded by the gold and silver and other monies held by the U.S. and used to fund health costs, free preK-12 public education, welfare, and the arts for all Americans, (4) a *"News Media Non-Profit Status Clause"* that turned news distribution vehicles—like newspapers, online news entities, cable programming, and television channels—into regulated utilities that were required to operate as non-profit organizations and offer both balanced reporting and investigative journalism, and (5) a *reaffirmation of the original version of the U.S. Constitution of 1789—*

Moved by Z's words, Noa could not contain himself. "Yes, like the use of barium bars superheated by focused sunlight and then plunged into plain old H_2O— and then combined with the unhealthy nitrogen effluent from coal plants to form ethanol. Those technologies were available by the early 2000s but were blocked by the oil and automobile industries. But when they did arrive, the onset of those forms of cheap, non-polluting energy marked the beginning of the 'Age of Democratic

Renewal,' the onset of a strengthened U.S. democracy that would finally be 'by, for and of the people'—and really, just a human way of being that was no longer in the tradition of selfish individualism of Emersonian or Ayn Randian philosophy and instead rooted in a mutuality of souls."

"Yes," Z added. "The promise made by the founding fathers had finally been kept…Hey, you know what I think? I think the seeds for the 'Democracy II' had already been sewn the moment global capitalism and its greedy cabal stopped serving the needs of wider humanity, in favor of just padding their off-shore bank accounts."

Noa looked at Z again. She could not be more alluring than she was now, with her minimal make-up, minimal flash-attire, understated femaleness. She had a beauty that surely humanity was meant to have—a shimmering world aesthetic of racial mixing. There was a permanence about her, too, a steadiness that seemed to move gently like the rising and falling of tides. It made him recall the term from the Russian literature that he had studied and loved in college—*pochva*, a sentiment that reflects one's all-abiding connection to mother earth, a feeling of being anchored in time and space. And best of all, he was quite sure she was unaware of this.

Right at that moment, at 5,000 feet, racing downhill to a place where every night sparkling lights sought to re-define the meaning of human existence, Noa felt a little giddy. At the same time, he had never been more centered.

IV

(The next day, mid-afternoon, warm but cooling.)

"These ruins say lots," Noa said to himself as he stood perched on the cliff edge looking out across the wide red-stained canyon below.

"Still, there has to be something this all represents, taken together as a whole," he continued silently to himself. I must figure out what it is. If it were just an idea, it would be easy. But it's not an idea. Hey, I went to the academy to learn how to do this, to comprehend emotion. But now I'm out here alone and it all seems so elusive. I'll ask Z when I next see her. She will know."

At that very moment, he looked up and saw an eagle sweeping from right to left across the sky. Off in the distance he saw that a tiny eco-jeep was bouncing with great speed as it jitterbugged up the same rutted road that he had taken a moment earlier. "That one looks yellow," he thought, "but a lot of them are yellow. Must be the fourth yellow one I've seen today."

A crunch from the sound of dry rock broke him from his reverie and the warmth of a soft laugh just as quickly washed over him. In that very instant, the serenity of his being in a place and time without measure was ripped away and replaced by another sensation.

As Noa swung back to look behind him, his eyes focused on an inspiring sight. It was the new park ranger. There she stood on two straight, powerful legs. The sinking sun now splashed over her yellow-white hair and it seemed as if all the sunlight from the canyon below had just as been captured and directed instead into her eyes. He had no choice but to be pulled in, too.

Her light field jacket was zipped half way down. She held a worn leather rucksack over her shoulder. She wore a shiny gold belt buckle, unseasonably short shorts, and Vibram-soled boots. All this detail registered upon his senses like an unexpected gust of warm sirocco wind.

Knowing she had his full attention, the Park Ranger extended her right hand toward him palm up, pointed her index finger at him, then slowly curled it once, twice.

"Come," she said playfully. "Shall we take that hike?"

V

(Earlier that day)

It was noon at the Taos Ski Lodge. Hundreds of tourists were milling about, moving in the blurred Dostoyevsky-like chiaroscuro of a Raskolnikovian world. But deeply immersed as she was in humanity, Zoey could still not be a part of it—so preoccupied was she with her dilemma.

"This morning I suddenly accomplish all that I had come here to accomplish," she told herself. "And after only one week on the job, not even the vaunted Joelle Valuton would have believed the old reservation library might hold the key to all the answers we needed. It's all right here in my electronic eco-copies."

"So why am I so unfulfilled?" she asked herself tentatively. "I'm so angry at being pressed into a corner. What I feel is—is rage."

"The video newspaper accounts show exactly what I don't want to see: that on 17 September 2086, 31 years ago, an obscure Swedish doubles team defeated the #1 seed U.S. team at the Taos World Tennis Doubles Tournament. That one of the two victorious Swedes met and fell in love with a young Hawaiian women's singles semi-finalist whose beauty was overwhelming."

"Name? Senstrom. K. T. Senstrom. Always known as 'K.T.' to the admiring public in Taos. But the story then added briefly that they fell in love and later produced a child whose first name was the same as his father's, 'Kainoa.'"

Zoey knew there was no going back now. She had to decide, right or left.

"So what if the video had reported that this tennis god went on to become a cell lieutenant in the 16 Years War. Noa may not know any of this. The thing is, if the local cell finds out this guy was Noa's father, Noa's a sitting duck. He will be their next target for conversion."

"I must tell him! What's his tel-net number? I'll call and leave a message to meet tonight, never mind our silly disagreement."

But the impulse was blocked by another just as strong. "What if he's already tagged? Oh my God, what if they tagged him years ago? That would mean he's been fooling the Global Government all along. Maybe he's even spying *on me!*"

"So, what are you, Kainoa Ken Senstrom, one great actor—or one dear, dear vulnerable man?"

And then it struck Zoey. "It doesn't matter one rational iota which way I go on this. If I try to warn him and it's too late, he will have to tell his cell and they will kill me. They win."

"But if I don't warn him and then they tag him, the cells win again. Whatever I decide, I won't know in advance the mischief I will cause."

As Z ran to get into her eco-jeep, tears of confusion and anger welled in her eyes. She knew there was a third possibility, however remote, and she held on to that feeling with all her soul. "I *must* hurry."

NOTE

This chapter was inspired by the work of Derrick Bell (1992) and Simon Schama (1991).

REFERENCES

Bell, D. A. (1992). *Faces at the bottom of the well: The permanence of racism.* New York, NY: Basic Books.

Janda, D. (2018). *Criminals in top positions in the U.S. government will be indicted* (Greg Hunter, USA Watchdog.com), Silverdoctors.com (September 21, 2018).

Roberts, P. C. (2017). Can Trump fix the economy in 2017? *Institute for Political Economy*, January 3, 2017.

Schama, S. (1991). *Dead certainties: Unwarranted speculations.* New York, NY: Alfred P. Knopf.

CHAPTER 7

Looking Past the Target

RUTH COTTON AND DAVID REED

Figure 7.1: Interdependence. Anonymous street art painted on the side of the old Parkway Theater at the corner of Park Blvd and East 19th Street Oakland, CA.

Photo taken by Ruth Cotton, November 2011.

Never doubt that a small group of thoughtful, committed people can change the world. Indeed, it is the only thing that ever has.

Margaret Mead (1964)

THE RE-DEMOCRATIZATION OF THE UNITED STATES (2020–2120) BY DAVID REED

Institutionalizing Phase: 2072–2120

November 13, 2120

As I write this historical sketch of the evolution of the Participatory Budgeting and Governance ("PBG") movement that has within the last ten years become firmly established across all fifty states and within the federal government of the United States, it is apparent to me how long the road has been to arrive at this point. Was it really one hundred years ago that a few pioneering city council and non-profit organization leaders in cities like New York, Chicago, and Vallejo, California began their experiment with what was then known as Participatory Budgeting (PB)? In spite of the fact that over 1,000 cities around the world were using some form of PB in 2020, did it really take 100 years for what we now know as PBG to be implemented in our state and federal budgeting processes? Yes, it did. What follows is a brief journey through that past.

In general terms Participatory Budgeting was originally described as created via "reforms that devolve decision-making to local units"—where community members decide how to spend part of the public budget (Baiocchi, 2003, p. 46). This was accomplished through the interface of deliberative citizen planning councils with existing local government agencies, in a bottom-up decision making format. Fung and Wright (2003) articulated a three-point framework in their description of processes, which they described as Empowered Participatory Governance (EPG).

Although now over one hundred years later, this model is still the foundation for processes such as PBG. The main features are as follows: (1) *Practical Orientation*, meaning a focus on community-level efforts such as infrastructure repair, public safety, or other community needs; (2) *Bottom-Up Participation*, in that ordinary citizens form the constituency and have access to participate, as opposed to only elected officials or experts; and (3) *Deliberative Solution Generation*, which is distinguished from other means of group decision making in that it requires people to articulate reasons for supporting a particular action and to work collaboratively to construct what eventually becomes a final plan, as opposed to advocating exclusively for a predetermined outcome. Basic criteria were and continue to be commonly applied in both the historical PB and modern-day PBG processes, where competing proposals are ranked in importance by number of people affected, contribution to health and safety, and urgency of need demonstrated by popular support.

The Emerging Constitution: Toward a More Participatory Democracy

Shortly after the Supreme Court ruling of 2097 upholding the PBG constitutional amendment, an unexpected alignment between the far-right Homeland Party and the center-left New Democracy Party paved the way for nearly universal support in the United States, which is holding strong now for fifteen years. Even though a two-thirds majority of both houses of the legislature and a majority of the states approved the amendment, there was still an entrenched far-right segment of the population led by the Homeland Party that seemed ready to obstruct implementation on a local level in many areas of the nation. What led to their acceptance of the model was the realization that through participation in PBG in local areas, each could actually be more successful in driving their own agendas than they would through obstruction.

So what, you might ask, has changed in these past twenty-five years? It would appear that democracy itself, as practiced in the United States, has undergone a significant and lasting change. Simple measures such as voter turnout in state and national elections are up 22% (from 51% in 2068 to 72% of eligible voters in the 2092 national elections). What is more striking is the demographic change: percentages of young voters, low-income voters and other traditionally low-turnout groups have all seen double-digit increases.

Major national policy decisions have also changed considerably. The nation has seen a massive increase in infrastructure spending from previous years. The decrease in number of aboveground electrical and utility lines are a useful measure of this, as their presence indicates the progress made toward the federally mandated goal of moving all utility lines to underground fiber optic systems. From 2062 to 2082, there was a 15% reduction in aboveground lines, commensurate with the installation of below ground fiber optic systems. In only five years beyond the passage of the constitutional amendment to adopt a federal PBG process, there has been a 67% reduction in aboveground lines as a result of the tripling of the federal budget to implement this goal, but equally as important is the role of the state and county PBG Councils who largely direct the prioritization—and hiring—for this massive public infrastructure project.

Other notable measures include an ongoing year-to-year decrease in military spending, now 22% lower in adjusted dollars from ten years ago. Changes in local tax policy, requiring that corporations pay some taxes directly to municipalities, have resulted in an influx of new funding to state and local governments. This in turn fed the expansion of PGB in many areas, as more funds are on the table to be allocated and therefore more at stake for those who participate.

Promoting/Spreading Phase (2042–2072)

April 4, 2035
Mobile, Alabama
News of the adoption of PBG in the city government took many Americans by surprise. After all, the Deep South has always been a region of the United States where tradition and conservatism as opposed to progressive policies are known to take precedence. Upon further examination though, we can see what might have led to its early adoption here. In Birmingham, Alabama, PBG was intentionally introduced as a means to advocate for local priorities, and as a counterpoint to the state and federal government and their perceived control over local decision-making. Local PGB supporters did extensive preliminary work with local churches, members of the Homeland Party and other local power brokers to determine which priorities would gain wide support in terms of being opened up to a participatory process. Looking back, it is thought that Mobile was a major turning point in the nationwide acceptance of PGB because it represented a very conservative area of the country taking on a form of participatory governance that had been commonly referred to as socialist and un-American prior to that time. It was also shown that small government advocates had something tangible to gain through PGB, namely a sense of being in control of their own affairs.

The experience of Mobile also provides a counterpoint to theories of democracy that assume widespread direct participation in democracy by citizens with low levels of political sophistication will beget at best mediocre civic governance, and at worst can lead to tyranny (Tocqueville, 1838). Many of the PBG participants in Mobile are newcomers to civic involvement, have low levels of education, and are from low income communities. In spite of these factors all indications are that these bodies are able to deliberate in a collaborative manner over complex decision-making processes, and the individuals involved report gaining considerable levels of understanding of the functions of civic governance far beyond the level at which they began.

Proof phase (2030–2042)

Case Study: Pacific Community College District, 2030–2032
The following is an excerpt recovered from a blog documenting the work of staff and faculty from several colleges within this district. Due to effects of the Polarity Shift of 2031 it is not possible to verify the names of the authors, I am thus very thankful to the work of the Forensic Digital Recovery Project (FDRP) for their efforts in finding this document.
April 2032
The Participatory Planning and Governance policies have now been in place in the Pacific Community College District ("PCCD") for one full year, and some of the changes to decision-making and inclusion in governance have been wonderfully transformative. The recently passed bond measure, Measure B1, has already

set a new precedent for participatory governance in several regards by expressly providing for:

- Direct student and community member voting in the expenditure of municipal bond funds
- The use of a prioritization plan that is collectively decided upon (students, faculty, staff, community members and administration)
- A representative oversight committee empowered to enforce recommendations and verify expenditures and fiscal oversight

From its shaky early beginnings, the PBG process has grown to become an active and involved collection of individuals and groups. The initial process involved convening the main constituent groups: Student Council, Faculty Council, Staff Council, Administrative Council and an Ad Hoc Community Council. From a starting point of 5% or fewer of the total student body, current overall participation has stabilized at around 10% annually. A byproduct of the student involvement has been an increase in numbers of students participating in other forms of civic engagement, such as running for local political offices and voting in local and state-wide elections. The transition to a participatory budgeting and governance model at the PCCD is in stark contrast to the former processes which were largely top down and had routinely excluded the participation of key constituent groups such as students, staff and the local community.

Although PBG has taken root in this school district, it was not long ago that things were done quite differently. It is striking to examine the difference in decision-making structures that existed a mere seven years ago, in that they were highly exclusionary and often resulted in questionable decisions. Although several prominent area civil rights and political leaders are alumni, and one of its colleges was an incubator for several key leaders of the Black Panther Party in the 1960's, the district had historically been besieged by poor leadership at all levels. Students had mostly been only peripherally involved in the governance process of key issues such as infrastructure development, budget allocations, or curriculum development. In 2005 the voters in that county passed a $400 million bond measure to improve infrastructure and equipment throughout the 20,000-student district.

A key contrast from the current PBG form of governance prior to Measure B1 being passed can be seen in the choices made then versus those made in the past twenty-one years. Under the old system of governance, over $200 million was poured into the two most sparsely attended colleges in the district, Veranga College and Grove College. Even at Pacific College, the largest in the district, over $25 million was spent on the construction of a baseball field and a well-appointed field house for the Athletics Department. Given the decrepit condition of many classroom buildings on the Pacific campus and what was at the time a 40 year-old library, these seemed a particularly inappropriate misuses of funds. Yet the board of trustees and chancellor at the time were able to push through by fiat nearly any funding decision they saw fit.

Under the current PBG system such one-sided decision-making is no longer possible. The Pacific Student Council, which represents all four colleges and the entire student body, is required to conduct through survey or referendum, a measure of student consensus on spending priorities on a biennial basis. These results are forwarded to the district Planning and Budgeting Committee, which in turn reviews the results from the respective representative Councils for faculty, administration and the ad hoc Community Council, made up of residents who are required to live within the boundaries of the district service area. As a result of this input, no large capital spending projects can be undertaken that are not aligned with priorities as specified by the PBG Councils.

Besides shifting power to students and the community in an unprecedented way, the PBG process has radically altered the manner of prioritizing expenditures and other key decisions in this district, and has had other democratizing effects as well:

1. The student governments have become much more active and engaged. The increased number of students participating as officer's in their respective student governments evidences this, as well as the number of students attending shared governance meetings at the colleges and the district. Students also report feeling an increased sense of agency in the functioning of the district as demonstrated in the annual surveys;
2. Community-based organizations play a more active role as a result of being included in the oversight committees and community advising councils;
3. Perhaps most importantly, traditional measures of student success such as persistence and degree completion are also higher than at any previous point. Although these measures can't be definitively tied to the PBG process, the correlations are very compelling.

Emergent phase: 2020–2030

Changing the Behavior of Elected and Appointed Officials: The Road to Good Governance

The blog post below was found in a series of historic entries from the Participatory Budgeting Vallejo organization, a group of citizens involved in the first citywide use of PB in the United States:

The early part of the twenty-first century saw egregious examples of elected and appointed government officials betraying the public trust through fiscal mismanagement. In 2010 in the city of Bell, California, the City Manager and entire city council used low voter turnout and an undemocratically implemented charter to award themselves salaries hundreds of times higher than officials in comparative locations. Cities and school districts have seen similar mismanagement of public funds, often through bond measures that were given minimal oversight toward the expenditure of tens of millions of dollars in public funds. The common theme in all of this is low to non-existent citizen oversight, and deliberately undermined governance regulations that allow corrupt officials to ignore or cherry pick appointments to citizen oversight committees.

In contrast, applying a PB model to civic governance processes makes corruption far more difficult to engage in because of the multiple levels of consultative bodies (unelected citizens) working in tandem with the traditional elected city council representatives. This is a fundamental change because it places the responsibility onto these public bodies to include the electorate, whereas in the early 21st century we saw a willful exclusion of the electorate on the part of many elected bodies, presumably because they preferred to operate without interference and accountability. Many school district governing boards even operated in closed-door sessions circumventing state public notice laws such as the Ralph A. Brown Act.

Changing our Schools

Education Through Action Research and Participant Agency

Taken further, the PBG model can also be extended to local school systems in the form of preparing young citizens to be future participants in an engaged democracy. Research long ago pointed to the correlation between youth participating in some form of civic engagement at an early age, with ongoing engagement such as voting and taking part in other forms of political advocacy (Kahn & Cohen, 2011).

1. Starting in elementary schools, children will be introduced to their role in participatory governance through exposure to a required curriculum that describes in basic terms the form and function of the PB process. This can be thought of as similar to a traditional Civics or Government class, however in this case there will be a distinct element of modeling participation, in contrast to memorizing information.

2. Starting in middle and high school, students will be encouraged to become part of the neighborhood and popular councils in the areas in which they live, and it will be understood that this is a duty for them as citizens. Participation will be optional, however, as the age of the student increases from middle school on, there will be a combination of incentives to participate and penalties for those who opt out of participating, such as not receiving certain public benefits (free use of community facilities, receiving free bus passes, etc.). The message will be clear: everyone must take part in order for a participative democracy to work, and "opting out" will require some tangible sacrifices for the individual.

Schools will see a dramatic reinvention of their curriculum as well as in the manner in which the content is delivered. Certain models of Action Research and particularly Engagement Theory give us a way to envision how this new learning will take place, that is, where: (1) students are meaningfully engaged in learning activities through interaction with others and (2) tasks must have an external meaning and benefit beyond the walls of the classroom.

Engagement theory also stresses an emphasis on collaborative efforts, project-based assignments, and an outside "authentic" focus (Kearsley & Shneiderman, 1998). So one major departure from traditional classroom instruction is that students must define the project or problem domain and apply their own ideas to a specific context. They may not always choose the topic, but because they are required to define the nature of it and this accords them agency in their own learning experience. Placing an emphasis on authenticity will provide students an opportunity to learn how to identify real world problems an outline a scope of work—skills they will be able to use later in life. To prepare students for involvement in participatory democracy, as early as middle school there will also be Student PBG Councils included as part of the school week. Under the guidance of school staff, these students will have the opportunity to have input into the allocation of resources toward their school districts and individual schools.

Conclusion

When we look back over these past one hundred years we can answer at least part of the question of what happens when a revolutionary movement "wins." In this case it can be argued the PBG process did in fact win and along with winning, it has changed major aspects of governance and democracy in the United States. Throughout the time period described above, people openly wondered if the basic concepts that drove the struggle to implement PBG could remain intact, and if the very structures they hoped to influence would themselves remain the same or be radically altered after being exposed to such extreme change.

Table 7.1. Historic Timeline Depicting the Onset of Participatory Budgeting in the U.S. Century of Emergence: U.S. Participatory Budgeting and Governance Timeline: 2012–2120. Source: Authors.

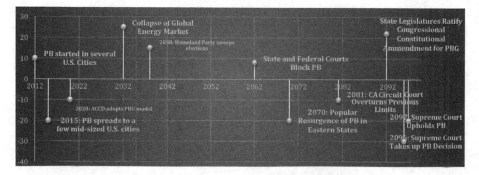

As the timeline above shows, there have been many bumps in the road and many doubts along the way, but clearly a paradigm shift has prevailed and it helped to contribute to nothing less than a *re-democratization of the United States.*

Implications and Considerations for Future Research

To be sure, the "participatory public budgeting" (PPB) practice of Porto Alegre, Brazil, served as an early model for successful citizen entry into civic engagement and functional governance in neighborhood, city and state governments:

Figure 7.2: Diagram of PB Model in Porto Alegre, Brazil.

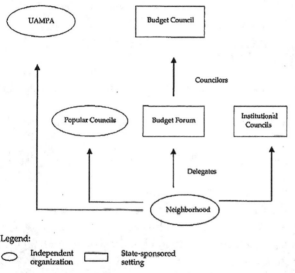

UAMPA
Budget Council
Councilors
Popular Councils
Budget Forum
Institutional Councils
Delegates
Neighborhood
At the citywide Budget Council, councilors chosen from among delegates make final decisions on the budget. At the municipal level, UAMPA is an independent organization that represents the interests of neighborhood associations.
In the districts, at weekly meetings of the Budget Forum of the Orçamento Participativo, delegates from the neighborhoods decide on local projects and priorities. Institutional councils with delegates from neighborhoods advise the municipality on service provision in areas such as health. Popular councils are independent organizations that represent neighborhood associations and local movements.
In many of the city's working-class and poor neighborhoods there are neighborhood associations and cooperatives. These are independent and voluntary entities, and most participate in the Budget Forum.
Legend:
Independent organization
State-sponsored setting

FIG. 1. Civil society organizations and participatory settings in Porto Alegre

Source: Baiocchi (2005).

That the PB model in this part of Brazil has been sustained is certainly a measure of its success, but there remain questions of scalability and application in other areas even within Brazil. For example, in areas of Brazil with much lower revenues from taxes and other sources, PB has not been established nearly as successfully, which is partly explained by the simple logic of there not being much revenue to allocate and therefore not as much to "participate in."

At the same time, a symbiotic relationship between participatory budgeting and overall civic participation has now been confirmed over time. Assessments of the PPB process in Porto Alegre, for example, reported that the process had come to act as a tool for learning about and spreading democracy as well as an entryway into civic life (Baiocchi, 2005). This was a key point in the re-democratization of the United States in particular, as measures of civic participation such as voting and involvement in local governance had prior to its institutionalization been historically low for young people, marginalized ethnic groups such as African Americans and Latinos, and low-income people in general.

The quote below from one of the historically important PB initiative in Porto Alegre neatly sums up the early challenges, as well the work that lies ahead to maintain democracy.

> The transition to democracy in Brazil has juxtaposed a largely unresponsive, corrupt political system, dominated by patronage, particularly at the local and state levels, and an emergent civil society, based on citizenship and public policy. Resolving this dichotomy is the fundamental challenge faced by Brazil today.
>
> Gianpaolo Baiocchi (2005)

FUTURE RESEARCH QUESTIONS

1. How will these new models establish themselves while maintaining their essential attributes?
2. What kind of engaged citizen do we need to move democracy forward in the United States?
3. How can the role of unions be adapted to support this model? Should they be?
4. How do we measure success, how do we define success?
5. What is the role of existing community college governance systems in this new model? Do they still exist or are they obsolete?
6. What is the process by which social movements can come to change the state, or become the state?
7. What happens when a social movement "wins"? Is the integrity of the change maintained?
8. How does the nature of leadership change when participation and engagement are paramount?

REFERENCES

Baiocchi, G. (2003). Participation, activism, and politics: The Porto Alegre Experiment. In Fung, A. & E. O. Wright, eds (2003). *Deepening democracy: Institutional innovations in empowered participatory governance*. London: Verso Press. Pp. 45–69.

Baiocchi, G. (2005). *Militants and citizens: The politics of participatory democracy in Porto Alegre*. Stanford: Stanford University Press.

Fung, A., & Wright, E. O. (2003). *Thinking about empowered participatory governance*. London and New York, NY: Verso.

Kahn, J., & Cohen, C. (Eds.). (2011). *Participatory politics: New media and youth political action*. Oakland, CA: Mills College.

Kearsley, G., & Shneiderman, B. (1998, September–October). Engagement theory: A framework for technology-based teaching and learning. *Educational Technology, 38*(5), 20–23.

Mead, M. (1964). *Continuities in cultural evolution*. Piscataway: Transaction Publishers.

Tocqueville, A. (1838). *Democracy in America*. New York, NY: Saunders and Otley.

CHAPTER 8

Casting Steppingstones

GREGORY K. TANAKA

---

*(M)yths enable us to access an imaginative world that empowers us to construct alternatives to the
social fictions that are handed down to us at birth.*

Mari Ruti (2006) *Reinventing the Soul*, p. 54

Roj flipped the red and gold Thomas Buoyant into the lake and retrieved it me-
thodically. Earlier he had seen an impossibly large fish break the surface, twist in
mid air and land not far from where he was now playing his lure. In the flash of a
millisecond, the trout had turned, caught the angle of the sun, and reflected back
a speckling of well-spaced, large red spots on a gold background, signifying it was
female and a German brown.

The sun still warmed his back as it had all afternoon, but it was now descending.
Turning to look at his rucksack, he saw a soda and a half-eaten sandwich peeking
out. They reminded him of the conversation he had at lunch with his friends, all
doctoral students at UCLA.

* * *

The large bay window of Fisherman's Lodge had looked right out on to Twin
Lakes, Mammoth. In the distance two massive mountains rose up sharply trailing
a cascade of silver talus on to the far shore, a silent waterfall of glistening stones.

The five had seated themselves at a table covered with a red and white-
checkered tablecloth. Mounted fish decorated the varnished knotty pine walls of
an otherwise simple dining room.

"You think there's democracy in America? Well, there isn't." Billy looked directly into Constance Cruz' eyes and watched her stiffen slightly. He was tall and meaty with light brown skin and dark brown hair.

"See, the U.S. Constitution came from Iroquois law—" Billy continued.

"Wait, wait, wait, wait!" Constance interrupted. She wore her long black hair straight and tied in back. Chuckling, she added, "Where did you get this…*bold* idea?"

"Let him finish," Liz Stevens interrupted. Like Constance, she had not missed the twinkle in Billy's eye.

Billy told his four friends how the Iroquois had been practicing the structural features of the U.S. Constitution long before the white man arrived—three branches of government, consent of the governed, one person/one vote, the right of public debate, peaceful succession of power, impeachment procedures, women's suffrage, and a federation of independent states with a central government for common defense. All this was new to the Europeans whose cultural histories had long been governed by monarchy.

Billy explained how these concepts had been introduced to the Constitutional Convention in Philadelphia via "The Albany Plan," a thick manual that Benjamin Franklin wrote immediately following his meeting with Iroquois leaders in New York in 1754. Historians Grinde and Johansen have argued that Constitutional Convention delegates had this plan on their laps thirty years later.

"Is that how you got your middle name, from your Indian nation?" Constance asked, this time with a note of seriousness.

Billy softened as he told his story. His middle name "Peacemaker" had been given to him by a great uncle who said he had traits similar to another Onandaga long ago called "Deganawidah." Deganawidah was the mythic hero who united the six nations—Onandaga, Seneca, Oneida, Mohawk, Tucarora, and Cayuga—into one federation. It was Deganawidah who told these nations about the Great White Pine tree—a symbol of harmony and unity. Later, when rising up against King George of England, the colonialists used this symbol as their "Tree of Liberty."

"Are you upset about this—this borrowing?" Constance asked.

"Oh, I'm upset. Many of the Revolutionary War leaders were plantation owners and big city bankers. They took our Iroquois principles and translated them into a document that protected their own interests first. Today's democracy is only a shadow of what it could be. It leaves out the Iroquois spirit."

* * *

Roj bent down and released another slippery 10-inch rainbow trout into the stream that entered the upper end of the lake. Fishing alone, Roj had caught and released four other rainbows, the largest a fat 13-incher. At 8,500 feet, with tall pine trees rimming the lake, blue sky overhead, and a stream gurgling at his feet, this was where he wanted to be. What gave him pause was the feeling that he belonged here, in this time *and* place.

He turned back and squinted into a sun that was dipping fast behind Mammoth Mountain. He knew he had only a few more hours to fish. It would soon be twilight, when large trout stirred from deep water to forage closer to shore.

* * *

"To understand my middle name you have to know where I come from. I may look black to you, but I'm not."

Noting the confused looks on her friends' faces, Liz continued with a smile, "I'm Indian…*and* Portuguese…*and* African." She had high cheekbones and wore her thick, black hair in long braids.

"My mother's side was from Brazil. The family story is that my African fore-fathers came to the Americas before Columbus. They came not as slaves but as ad-venturers on strong ocean currents directly from West Africa to the northern part of South America and Central America." Her friends were now leaning forward intently.

"Even now, people are discovering huge ceremonial stone heads and clay figu-rines in Central and South America with unmistakably African features—the hair, lips, noses, the decorative details."

"But what makes these discoveries so completely powerful is the radioactive carbon dating. The figurines and Olmec heads in Mexico were carved in the 1300's!"

"The 1300's?" Benjamin asked. "That's way before Columbus!" Benjamin was tall and thin with a baby face and neatly trimmed, light reddish-blond hair.

"Liz, this is amazing," Roj added with enthusiasm. "But why isn't this in our newspapers or on TV?"

"Yeah, well, maybe it strikes too close to home," Liz continued in a lowered voice. "I mean, what would happen if white Americans lost their Columbus myth?"

Hearing no response, Liz continued. "Anyway, one of the African leaders who did this was a guy named 'Abu Bakiri II,' a Mali ruler from West Africa." African oral history says he set off in a large flotilla toward what is now South America in the early 1300s and never returned.

"So that's my middle name, 'Bakiri.' My mom wanted me to know that before Africans came to the Americas as slaves, we came as adventurers, using our own technology and navigation—"

Liz stopped and looked at each of her friends. Her eyes were glistening. "You know, I never really told this to anyone else before."

* * *

Roj felt the sharp tug on his rod. It had to be a large fish. The thin monofilament paid out of his reel for several long seconds before the pressure on the rod began to lessen. The fish was resting for a second run. Roj quickly wound his reel several times—but then the fish took off again.

Suddenly, there was a splash on the surface of the lake about thirty yards out. In the fading sunlight, Roj could just make out the trout's features. Small black dots on a dark green back: a rainbow.

After several more minutes, Roj pulled the trout closer to shore and picked it up by the gills. It was 17 inches long and at least a pound and a half. After admiring his catch, Roj slipped the fish back into the water and gently guided it back and forth, forcing water slowly into its mouth and through the gills to return precious oxygen to its system.

* * *

"What about you, Constance?" Billy asked. "Do you have a middle name?"

"Yes," Constance said with a broad smile, "but promise not to laugh. My middle name is 'Primavera.' It means 'spring' in Spanish—like in 'winter and spring.'"

"'*Constance Primavera Cruz*,'" Liz said. "That's pretty."

"Thanks. Well, I don't have a fancy story behind my name. We were mostly from Mexico and we lived in Texas and Chicago. My father's side is originally from Guadalajara and Monterrey. My mother's side has some Mexican Indian and Peruvian Indian in her. I guess you could say we were from all over—and we kept changing. My mom says my name describes this constant rebirth."

"That's great," Roj said, and Constance gave him a smile. Roj was Asian and had straight black hair to his collar. "If you think about it, Constance, you are All People. You are European by way of Spanish conquerors. You are Native American—and since Native Americans supposedly came to North America from China, you are Asian, too. In fact, with what Liz said about Africans coming before Columbus, you could have black American blood, too."

"You know," Constance continued, "It feels good to talk like this—about where I really came from. I'm so tired of people just thinking I'm a gang member when they hear I'm Mexican."

When everyone nodded in agreement, she spoke again. "What about you, Benjamin? You've been silent."

* * *

The sun was down and Roj was surprised to see trout beginning to queue up in the shallow water where the stream entered the lake. This was surreal. Here he was trying to catch fish, and now over a dozen slender shadows were waving slowly in the current directly facing him as they nudged their noses into the entering stream.

Roj caught his breath. Not 20 feet away two large shadows had swung into the current. They were gigantic, each weighing as much as seven or eight pounds. In the shallow water these thick rainbows seemed like tuna.

Separated from the trout by the thin film that divides water and air, Roj knew he was of a different world. But standing on small, flat rocks and straddling this stream, he felt the sky and pure water and knew that man and trout shared a common existence.

* * *

"I don't really have a story," Benjamin said finally.

"Oh, come on, Benjamin," Roj said quickly.

"No, Roj, I mean it. I'm not going to try to compete with the ethnic histories at this lunch table."

"We can't let you off so easily," Billy interjected.

"Well, I'm such a mish-mash of cultures that came from Europe so long ago I don't really have a story to tell," Benjamin said.

"Wait," Constance said, "what about Western technology and capitalism? Isn't there a positive Western identity from that?"

"Yeah, well other countries around the world have the same things now. So I guess I'm just an American," Benjamin said.

"No, wait, you can't say you're 'just an American' because I am, too," Liz said as she tucked her chin down into her chest and leaned back in her chair. "And I'm also black!"

"Okay, then I'm just happy to be a modern white person," Benjamin responded a bit more flippantly than he intended.

"No, I won't let you hide behind white identity. There has to be something behind it. You have to have to tell us a story," Liz continued.

"—Well, I don't think I'm ready to—"Benjamin said.

"Wait, this is not Benjamin's fault," Constance interjected. "I mean, what is identity for Whites going to be based on if not race? Christopher Columbus? That was white colonialism. Thanksgiving? Stealing land from the Indians. None of this was Benjamin's fault."

"Look," Benjamin said trying to calm his friends. "I've always wanted to talk about where we get our history from. For a long time now I've wanted history books and Hollywood to 'come clean.' Take the way they portray the 'winning of the West.' Did you know almost *one third* of all cowboys were black? Another one third were Mexican. There's stuff on this at the Black Cowboy Museum in Denver. So, if published history is all that wrong, don't we have to restart history?"

But the mood at the table remained tense as Liz spoke. "The problem is, today's rituals are hurtful and they affect me viscerally. That history is hard to change. Remember when Pasadena Rose Parade officials said they would rather move the parade to Arizona than add even one person of color to their 36-member board of directors? All of America knows this story—"

* * *

Roj felt a sharp tug on the line. The line played out quickly and, this time, he struggled to hold up the tip of the rod. He had just changed lures to a three inch long Rapala, and the large fish was now taking it instinctively out to the middle of the lake. The reel screamed as yard after yard of line paid out.

* * *

"What about you, Roj? What's *your* middle name?" Billy asked.

Roj considered ducking the question as he had all his life. The fear inside came from an ancient time when children were mean and memories became etched forever.

"Actually, you already know my middle name. It's 'Roj.' I'm Winston Roji Ishibashi. 'Roj' comes from 'Roji,' pronounced with a long 'o.' A 'roji' is the garden path one takes from the outside world to the entrance of a Japanese teahouse."

"Teahouse?" Billy smiled, barely suppressing a chuckle.

"Well, one group of our family in Japan apparently designed, built, and cared for teahouses. They say that while walking down the path to a teahouse you re-connect with your ancestors and honor nature and life itself."

"It is on this path to the teahouse that your preparation for the spiritual world begins. When you go down this simple, winding path, you leave the outer world behind, let go of worldly cares, and start to go into yourself."

"When you get to the teahouse you have to duck down real low. Once inside, the whole ritual of sitting for tea is also purifying. The pathway is the first step. I did this once at a real teahouse in Japan."

"Roj, that's a great story," Constance said.

"But your family has been in the U.S. for several generations, right?" Liz asked. When Roj nodded, she asked softly, "Was your family taken to U.S. concentration camps during World War II?"

"Yes," Roj said as he looked down, "my father's family and my uncle and his parents were rounded up in L.A. and put into camps in different parts of the country."

"Even though they didn't do anything wrong?" Benjamin asked.

"Well, there was a lot of hysteria back then." His eyes glistening, Roj continued. "But our family has this story about how Grandpa saw a tiny little flower sticking up through the snow—up in cold Missoula, Montana—and kept that one tiny flower in his mind as motivation to keep living."

"What about your mom's side?" Constance asked.

"They were in New York. In New Rochelle just north of the city. My grandfather was taken to Ellis Island and held there for a long time."

"Why?" Billy asked. "That's nowhere near the war with Japan."

"My mother says he was a gifted dental technician who made the best false teeth in New York. I guess the dentists must have kept calling him for his services even after Japan attacked Pearl Harbor. He didn't want to let them down, and so one day he was arrested for making deliveries after curfew. And get this, they froze my grandmother's bank account so she was forced to raise four kids without an income."

"How did she survive?" Benjamin asked.

"Neighbors helped. Caucasian neighbors. It was hard for her to talk about this."
"Is there a Japanese word for that, you know, where you just take it?" Billy asked.
"'*Shi-gata-ga-nai*,' Roj said with a note of finality." "It means 'it can't be helped.'"

* * *

Now the big fish was running to Roj's right. The line continued to pay out, but not as quickly. Roj sensed the trout's energy beginning to wane. After three long runs, the fourth run was about to end. Carefully Roj pulled up on the rod and then let the tip drop down slightly while winding the reel, just as his father had taught him to do many years before.

Suddenly the line moved rapidly to Roj's left. In the growing darkness, Roj could see the small wake left by the line as it sliced rapidly across the surface of the lake. The fish was now erasing all the gains he had achieved by pumping the rod.

Then, just when he thought the big fish was about to tire, Roj felt a quick jerk and a rat-a-tat-tat. The fish was leaping high into the air. Large dots on a creamy side. It was the German brown he had seen earlier. It was close to 10 pounds!

But just as suddenly, the line went slack. Roj quickly wound the reel six or seven more times expecting, hoping, waiting to again feel the weight of the fish. But with each wind he began to accept that the fish had shaken itself free by jumping high into the air. That leap from one world to another and back again had been defiant. This action, sudden and symbolic, had signified the end of one life and beginning of another.

* * *

"Okay, you know that stuff about gang-bangers on t.v.?" Benjamin asked. "And the 'Tailhook' scandal where 100 Navy officers and admirals were reprimanded for covering up the fondling of women officers? You know what? It's all the same thing."

"What do you mean?" Roj asked unable to hide his distrust.

"Well, you might think this is crazy, but aren't they all 'rites of passage?' You know, where boys become men? The *real* problem is, once we sweep aside these 'bad' rituals, we have no new ones to replace them with."

"And?"

"And, so what if something like this conversation today was used as a kind of ritual to create new history for the U.S.?"

"What do you mean?" Roj asked with new interest.

"Okay. Let's say all high school seniors—or college freshmen—are required to do storytelling like you have done today. Each student would have to delve into his or her own past and come back with a narrative, a work of art, a video. It could start by capturing the joys, fears, mistakes, victories based on a personal experience in relation to race or ethnicity. Then maybe from there it could move on to the person's family history in the U.S."

"Benjamin, give us an example," Constance said. "From your own life."

Benjamin sat back hard against his chair and thought for several long seconds. "Well, okay, there was one thing I remember. It was right after the L.A. riots in 1992. I was talking with a young black woman I worked with on campus. When I told her how the riots made me feel angry, she ripped into me for not crying—for only being angry.

"Well, it hurt me a lot to hear that. See, she didn't know that where I come from you aren't allowed to show emotion."

"My father's side is from Boston. Stiff upper lip and all that. And my mother's side is from New Jersey. They're mostly Irish and love to tell stories, especially stories that make people laugh. So Mom always had a ready quip for anything. The problem is, in New England people thought because she laughed so much she should never be taken seriously. She always felt hurt by this."

"So sometimes I feel out of place, too. I get caught between two conflicting commands. And sometimes the wrong side comes out."

"Like when you said the riots only made you feel 'angry?'" Constance asked.

"Yes."

"Benjamin, that's a story!" Constance announced mischievously—

* * *

At precisely 7:45 PM—when it was too dark to see his wristwatch but too compelling to turn away forever—Roj retrieved the Rapala for the last time, flipped it up, and fixed it to the lowest guide on his rod. Turning to look out at the lake, he saw a large fish rise out of the water not 50 yards from where he stood.

A full two feet above the water's surface, the trout appeared in the darkened sky to be silver with large black spots along the side. As the trout completed its roll and landed on its side with a flat smash, Roj knew in sunlight the spots would have been red and the sides yellow-gold.

Blinking his eyes and looking one last time into the spot where pure memory and endless time disappeared into wet darkness, Roj could have sworn he heard the trout whispering one last message to him, "Catch me if you can, you must do better next time."

Light from a campfire winked between the trees far off to his left. He'd better get moving. He didn't want to keep his friends waiting.

NOTE

1. This is a fictional account that drew its founding idea and strength from a mountain retreat that I attended with several UCLA graduate students at this very lodge in the early 1990s. It is inspired by work detailing the influence of the early democratic structures of the Iroquois Nation on the writing of the United States Constitution described by Grinde and Johansen (1991) in their book *Exemplar of Liberty*. It draws in addition from and seeks to extend the narrative courage of

Simon Schama (1992) portrayed in his book *Dead Certainties* and Derrick Bell (1993) in *Faces at the Bottom of the Well*.

REFERENCES

Bell, D. (1993). *Faces at the bottom of the well: The permanence of racism*. New York: Basic Books.

Grinde, D. A., & Johansen, B. E. (1991). *Exemplar of liberty: Native America and the evolution of democracy*. Los Angeles, CA: UCLA American Indian Studies Center.

Ruti, M. (2006). *Reinventing the soul: Posthumanist theory and psychic life*. New York: Other Press.

Schama, S. (1992). *Dead certainties (unwarranted speculations)*. New York: Vintage Books.

CHAPTER 9

Extending the Aura

DEREK FENNER AND EVANGELIA WARD-JACKSON

Some day, though the work may be long and painful, a new world will be born.
Jacques Derrida (November, 2004)

ART UNBOUND: THE ARTS AND JUVENILE JUSTICE EDUCATION BY DEREK FENNER

Introduction

I stumbled into the field of education. I graduated in the lower tenth percentile at my high school and was told repeatedly by teachers that I'd amount to nothing. I got accepted into college on academic probation and struggled for the first year and a half. Then I took a photography class. I got an A, my first, and I was hooked. It was only then, as an art major, that learning became relevant to my life, because I could see myself in the curriculum. After 12+ years of struggling in learning environments I went on to earn both my Bachelor of Fine Arts degree in painting and photography, as well as my Master of Fine Arts degree in writing and poetics.

After finishing graduate school I ended up pursuing work as an art teacher, where I honed my skills in the most unlikely of settings, inside the walls of juvenile justice residential facilities. While I have continued to exhibit and publish my work, as well as to give public readings and lectures, it is from my position as an educator and an arts administrator in those settings that have allowed me to see that the real power of the arts is in allowing the invisible to become visible. After spending over 10 years in the juvenile justice system, I have seen first hand that many youth are being tossed aside and given little for education that is relevant to their lives, or rigorous in its expectations that every one of them can succeed. When I moved to Massachusetts in the summer of 2002 and began my career with the state's juvenile justice system, the Department of Youth Services (DYS), I entered a world of policies, bureaucracies, and had my introduction to the school-to-prison-pipeline.

Frustrated with the lack of arts in juvenile justice settings, and knowing first hand the power that the arts have in creating engaged lifelong learners, I began to form conversations around building support for the arts in these settings. Within these multifaceted constraints, while working for the Collaborative for Educational Services, I applied my first-hand experience as a teacher in the DYS education system and designed an arts-integration model that was awarded a $1,000,000 U.S. Department of Education grant for a program I named, Unlocking the Light (UTL). This statewide program provided a vehicle for court-involved youth to engage in school-based learning through the arts, using job-embedded professional development for DYS teachers. Art Unbound is deeply indebted to UTL, where the design concepts for this type of program were formed and tested.

The Setting and Pedagogy

The school-to-prison-pipeline. In direct correlation with the cutting of arts programming in school and community settings, schools have continued to have a rising number of youth that they are failing (Bahena, Cooc, Currie-Rubin, Kuttner, & Ng, 2012; Eisner, 2002). These students when pushed out end up in communities with very little opportunity, or worse yet they are caught up in the free-market driven privatization of those communities through industrial complex feeder systems like the school-to-prison-pipeline (Giroux, 2012; Nocella, Parmar & Stovall, 2014). What hope there is left to uncover often goes hidden for generations. These are the young people that Giroux (2012) labels America's "disposable youth." They are on the edge of disappearing into the government-supported and society-accepted school-to prison/deportation/hospitalization/military/low-wage-earner pipeline(s).

The American Civil Liberties Union defines the school-school-to-prison-pipeline as, "…the policies and practices that push our nation's schoolchildren, especially our most at-risk children, out of classrooms and into the juvenile and criminal justice systems" ("School-to-Prison Pipeline," n.d.). For many youth, once their lives become submerged in the juvenile justice system, a lifetime of institutionalization follows resulting in high levels of recidivism as minors, and in turn acts as a "feeder" modality for the Prison Industrial Complex. Marian Wright Edelman has expanded the field of research on the school-to-prison-pipeline calling it the "cradle-to-prison-pipeline" ("Cradle to Prison Pipeline Campaign," n.d.).

The very fact that we can isolate and name how children are funneled into these strata of institutional settings emphasizes a need for systemic change. Numerous studies have pointed out that school disciplinary policies such as "Zero Tolerance" have contributed to the astonishing rate at which young people are moved from classrooms into incarceration (Bahena *et al.*, 2012). For young people who are pushed out of school through suspension and expulsion there is a crisis of limited opportunities for them to enter the workforce (Wald & Losen, 2003). Increased policing in our communities also leads to youth finding their way to the juvenile justice system. Society on the whole has failed these youth, and while there may be conversations about these travesties across multiple fields of study, held in closed-door institutions, not much is being done in raising a more systemic awareness that youth of color have become profitable through being criminalized. "Prisons in this view have now become a primary constituent of the neoliberal state (p. 36)" writes Giroux (2011), who explains how deregulation and privatization of prisons is parallel to the stripping of civil liberties and the "increasing criminalization of social problems" (p. 35). The aims of the institutions studying these problems have run into a media-sphere that doesn't allow their findings to be reported broadly to society.

It's important to know who these youth are and to understand how they have entered the juvenile system, often directly from the educational system. 81,000 children are held everyday in juvenile justice residential treatment. Nationally, 1 in 3 Black and 1 in 6 Latino boys born in 2001 are at risk of imprisonment during their lifetime ("Juvenile Justice," n.d.). This trajectory, specifically for youth of color, toward a life in the margins of society is our national pipeline to prison. Over time youth begin to normalize their experiences within the oppressive structures of capitalism, eventually believing the dominant narrative that says they deserve the oppression. Ruti (2006) terms this a "psychic colonization" of the human in order to impede their potential from ever surfacing.

This is a form of what Foucault would call "biopower," and was made possible when security was added as an instrument of disciplinary power, in order to aid economic growth by delineating new boundaries for what the public accepts. Foucault's (2000) four apparatuses of security—the spaces of security, the treatment of the uncertain, the normalization of security, and the correlation between security and the population—have all paved the path for the unjust adjudication for many youth into confinement within the juvenile justice system.

Every day, there are youth in the United States serving "dead time." Simply defined, dead time, often linked to pretrial detention, is any time you spend locked up that does not count toward a sentence you must serve. For young people involved with the juvenile justice system, the matter is further complicated by the fact that many of them have not committed the crimes to end up institutionalized. There are a variety of factors that can land children within the walls of the juvenile justice system, stemming from heavily policed communities to schools that utilize prison related disciplinary measures (Bahena *et al.*, 2012; Giroux, 2011). Believing that only "bad" kids go to "juvie" is the very convention that has allowed this injustice to continue since the system was implemented in the early 19th-century United States. For every young person serving dead time in the juvenile justice system there are countless others being continually targeted for entry into the system.

The juvenile justice system and school-to-prison-pipeline have become feeder systems for the adult prison industry, which currently houses just over 2 million people costing taxpayers nearly $60 billion dollars a year (Alexander & West, 2012). We have allowed a neoliberal agenda to create a trajectory for many of our nation's youth—disproportionally youth of color from underserved communities—to become commodities to be traded in a system that amounts to institutional slavery (Alexander & West, 2012; Nocella *et al.*, 2014). That it happens in the open, its effects have been quantified and measured, and that we do nothing, is a statement on the blinding state of capital in the 21st Century. We are living in a time where the top 1% of the population controls the techniques of power in the name of free market expansion (Giroux, 2013). What are we saying to our young people when we prioritize institutionalization, which cost four times more than school (Bahena *et al.*, 2012)?

The obvious outrage of the system outlined above is that there are many individuals and organizations that have been working against the oppressive structures for a great number of years in effort to positively impact the youth most affected by the pipeline. Art Unbound allows those practitioners the opportunity to move beyond the statistics of the pipeline and imagine a utopia. "To imagine the justice to-come is not to think of an infinitely deferred future but to imagine the present otherwise than it is, to see the world as it is and, at the same time, to be able to think of what it might be" (Larson, 2010, p. 110). In writing about the importance of utopian discourse in a dystopian world, Larson (2010) makes it clear that to dismiss it is to allow authoritarian power to remain in control.

There is a paralyzing fear to go against the status quo for many Americans; privilege becomes blinders we wear, shielding us from our responsibility for the success of ALL youth. We need to reframe personal responsibility as human responsibility; as educators it is one thing not to know about the conditions by which this oppression occurs, and another to know and do nothing.

Culturally Relevant Pedagogy and Contemporary and Community-Based Art as Social Justice in Education

Culturally responsive teaching (Gay, 2010), culturally relevant pedagogy (hooks, 2009; Ladson-Billings, 1995) and social justice youth development (Quinn, Ploof, & Hochtritt, 2011) have been shown to be successful in work with youth in juvenile justice settings, increasing the achievement of those youth. So in building on what we already know as educators, I am calling upon the work of prominent multicultural educator, Geneva Gay (2010), known for her scholarship in education around the intersections of culture, race, ethnicity, teaching, and learning. Gay articulates that "culturally responsive practice" serves to empower students to the point where they will be able to examine critically educational content and processes and ask what its role is in creating a truly democratic and multicultural society (Gay, 2010). It uses the students' culture to help them create meaning and understand the world, emphasizing not only academic success but also social and cultural success (Gay, 2010). An educational program steeped in culturally responsive practice affirms the perspective of the young person taking into account knowledge and understanding of how the personal and cultural experiences of a young person can be assets in supporting her or him toward future success. To be a culturally responsive educator requires that we put our relationship with the students at the center of our practice. The educational culture must then reflect a relationship that is mutually enriching for both students and teachers.

A number of studies conducted over the past decade have demonstrated that all students, but particularly those with a history of academic failure, perform at a higher academic level when the arts are part of the curricula (Cahnmann-Taylor & Siegesmund, 2007; Clewell, Campbell, & Perlman, 2007; DeMoss, 2005; Eisner, 2002). DeMoss and Morris (2005) explored the learning processes and outcomes associated with arts integration units versus those in comparable non-arts units. They found that the differences were most notable in lower performing students, who scored higher on analytical understanding of the material than students participating in non-arts units who were middle range performers. Other studies confirm this study's results: "that while the arts have a positive impact on academic achievement for all students, these effects are most powerful for struggling students" (DeMoss, 2005, p. 91).

One of the reasons the arts are uniquely positioned to close the achievement gap is that teachers integrating arts into the classroom find that their expectations of students increase as they see students demonstrate new strengths and talents. Increasing expectations has long been shown to positively impact student achievement (Clewell et al., 2007; Eisner, 2002; Weinstein, 2004). I am particularly interested in the interstitial relationships existing among contemporary art and literature, art education, and theory and how they illuminate the possibility of engagements when imagination and innovation provide the light in an otherwise dark place. "Contemporary art provides one such location; a dynamic site of learning that opens other ways of seeing, being, thinking, and feeling" (Desai, 2010, p. 440). When the arts are activated as a mechanism of social justice, they can serve teachers and students by offering counternarratives by actively uncovering in students their own sociopolitical context in order to resist the dominant narratives that serve to oppress. "Curriculum should be rooted in the life experiences of students, and explore how personal perspectives are intertwined with broader study" (Tavin & Hausman, 2004, p. 48).

This is especially important in juvenile justice and urban educational settings where the cultural and linguistic diversity of the students does not exactly mirror that of the educators. The juvenile justice student population is demographically diverse and differences in cultural, racial and gender-influenced experiences impact the ways in which youth engage or do not engage in learning. In order to meet the needs of this very diverse student body, contemporary arts learning can provide opportunities for educational staff to deepen their learning, understanding, and hone their practice of asset-based, culturally responsive approaches to learning both in and out of the classroom (Gay, 2010; Hanley, Sheppard, Noblit, & Barone, 2013).

When teachers see arts learning as a modality of positive youth development it helps them to identify the strengths and needs of each student. In order for teachers to make the learning relevant, they need to develop a concrete but flexible knowledge of who their students are, in order to better meet their needs and connect their content with what is truly relevant in their lives. In this way, teachers act as "creative intellectuals," rather than as mere "technicians," by developing a critical analysis of their students' cultures to reach all their students more effectively (Nieto & Bode, 2011).

Contemporary visual art is the perfect partner in an effort to provide counter-narrative and is useful when exploring issues of race/racism, diasporas, immigration, and other racialized inquiries in the classroom. Jackson (2012) highlights the cultivation of a "transformative perspective" in students by examining the need for "teachers and students to critically examine themselves through the lens of their sociocultural experiences" (p. x). Sociocultural awareness is a primary characteristic of all culturally relevant pedagogy and when accented with the sociopolitical context of contemporary artists, students and teachers are able to engage in meaningful discussions around race in a triangulated way, learning about each other's experiences in relation to the artists studied (Gay, 2010; Nieto & Bode, 2011). Jackson (2012) paints a vibrant picture of how classrooms can function as epicenters of affirming attitudes toward students from diverse backgrounds. She says, "Likewise, a culturally responsive teacher cultivates in students a better understanding of how their personal experiences and social practices are, in part, one of many in our global community" (Jackson, 2012, p. x).

Desai (2010) adds to the call to consider contemporary art as pedagogy for helping students understand in complex ways topics, such as immigration, which can be as charged a topic as any for the classroom. Desai's (2010) notion is that these highly politicized experiences can be confronted directly when dialogue is stimulated through the study of public art works on immigration. This is but one way to continue "confronting and then responding to the racialized spaces and discourses of immigration in our country and its relationship to neoliberal economic policies" (Desai, 2010, p. 440).

As schools tighten budgets and discount contemporary art education, there is still a solid escape available through the very nature of creative problem solving. Empowering artistic pedagogies in this way will help schools stay relevant to new "ways of knowing," which in turn will better serve students at all ages in learning to navigate the very complex world they inhabit. The National Endowment for the Arts (NEA, n.d.) builds a case that arts learning has long been associated with improved cognitive, social and behavioral outcomes, citing studies that demonstrate positive academic and social outcomes for students who receive arts education.

As an example of these new "ways of knowing," Gude's (2000, 2004, 2007, 2010) collaborative art project, the Spiral Workshop, has for years been at the epicenter of quality cutting-edge arts learning that aims to help youth participants learn to "become more fully human" (Freire, 2000).

> Much significant contemporary art is not the result of an investigation by an individual artist who reaches an endpoint or conclusion, but rather is the practice of creating frames for participatory investigation, enabling experiences that are deeply engaged and deeply reflective. (Quinn et al., 2011, p. 78)

The Spiral Workshop coincidentally offers this co-construction of knowledge and meaning in an effort to liberate its participants' imagination, creativity, and dialogues. Gude (in Quinn et al., 2011) writes,

> Spiral curriculum is not so much to definitively categorize and figure things out as to observe how the recognitions, representations, and figures of our imagination create meaning, and to then expand the discursive spaces within which these figures can move and interact, creating shifting and unforeseeable patters of being. (p. 81)

There are a maddening number of values that arts learning can claim and many of the articles presented reach similar conclusions—arts learning is critical in forming future generations of caring, conscientious adults. The process of making and responding to art allows young people to see their own thinking present in the curriculum, by activities that connect their art processes with their own personal values (Tavin & Hausman, 2004).

Contemporary art can also serve teachers well as a way to engage students in multiple content areas. As my own research has shown, in 2010, at a Massachusetts juvenile justice residential treatment facility, I led a team of teaching artists in integrating a contemporary art curriculum in all subject area classrooms (Bode, Fenner, & Halwagy, 2013). After many days of researching imagery through painting and collage, students ended the study by comparing the work of Shepard Fairey to the work of Bernard Williams. They spontaneously spoke in terms of the artists' "sociopolitical context," or the artists' "intended discourse" when pointing out the references to US history and the layering of meaning. The students achieved academic knowledge and artistic production that far exceeded their own expectations and reached beyond classroom teachers' imaginations. Some of the teachers who had demonstrated initial resistance to the value of art in their classroom asked us to leave art supplies, inviting us to return to co-teach with them again. The teachers, who were already engaged in meaningful curriculum, felt supported and rejuvenated in their work.

It's not to say that there is any one way to use contemporary art in the classroom. There are a multitude of uses in all of our complex settings. The literature is conclusive, though, that when properly done, contemporary art offers relevant issues to surface between the learner and what is being learned. Rolling (2011) reminds us that sometimes teaching can be an act of resistance and requires a flexible inquiry-based approach, saying that this kind of teaching, "…generates a continuum of possibilities in the address of the kinds of educational research and curriculum approaches worth valuing" (p. 103).

The Art Unbound Model

In preparing a model for systemic change I considered the following guiding questions:

- How does one battle the outrage we feel about the civic, political, and educational neglect that push so many of our youth into the juvenile justice system?
- How does one create a model of hope with measurable results for both teacher accomplishment and student achievement in a system that has chronically failed our youth?
- Since we've tried a lot of other things, isn't it time we really give the Arts a chance at helping in the liberation of all youth?

Detained youth, too often resistant to learning and disengaged from and marginalized by their peers and communities, pose some of the greatest challenges to educators. At the same time, these youth have tremendous potential. As survivors of complex trauma, many of these youth have developed both the resiliency and creativity to deal with the challenges they face. Art Unbound is designed to provide teaching artists and educators with powerful, creative tools that will help reach and engage these students. Based on this need to reach students who are underperforming, multilingual, multicultural, or disengaged and who are often from high crime and high poverty backgrounds, I have imagined a multi-year comprehensive professional development program—Art Unbound—focused on using the arts as a vehicle for engaging students involved in the juvenile justice system in learning.

Through intensive, job-embedded training and coaching to teachers serving students detained within the juvenile justice system, the program aims to: 1) increase the capacity of juvenile justice teachers to provide high quality, standards-based arts education linked to the core curriculum; 2) increase the academic achievement of students in juvenile justice facilities in core subjects through active involvement in the arts and 3) increase the capacity of the juvenile justice system to provide standards-based arts instruction to youth in residential and community settings. The design for this project mirrors these goals and is based upon my federally funded Unlocking the Light project, which introduced art integration into Massachusetts's juvenile justice classrooms through job-embedded professional development with measurable success.

The juvenile justice student population is demographically diverse and differences in cultural, racial and gender-influenced experiences impact the ways in which youth engage or do not engage in learning (Nocella *et al.*, 2014). In order to meet the needs of this very diverse student body, Art Unbound will provide opportunities for juvenile justice educational staff to deepen their learning, understanding, and hone their practice of asset-based, culturally responsive approaches to learning both in and out of the classroom. Art Unbound will also help teachers see the arts as a modality of positive youth development and help to identify the strengths and needs of each student.

Through classroom-based residencies, teaching artists and teachers collaborate in developing, teaching, and refining curriculum units that deliver arts instruction and standards-based academic content to students. Utilizing a gradual release of responsibility approach to professional development (Reigeluth, 2012), teachers observe new techniques as the artist demonstrates them, then collaborate and work with artists in implementing those techniques, and finally practice the techniques on their own toward the end of a residency.

Art Unbound is a program that integrates the arts into juvenile justice classrooms giving students a chance to find successes that build upon each other, developing confidence, self-expression, and a willingness to accept and meet higher expectations. As students develop in awareness and confidence, teachers grow as well, gaining new skills, new awareness of student strengths, and new ways to encourage students to reach their potential.

The design for the Art Unbound program builds upon the lessons learned from Unlocking the Light to focus intensive, sustained and job-embedded professional development for teachers serving students in juvenile justice facilities. Art Unbound utilizes a lab site model in order to encourage the collaborative and collegial planning and implementation process that was found to be so successful in sustaining the Unlocking the Light project. Confirming experiences around the efficacy of teacher collaboration, research by Gleckel and Koretz (2007) shows that teachers who worked collaboratively were more likely to follow new and recommended practices than those who worked independently. While teachers who worked independently were in favor of these practices, they did not incorporate them into their classroom practice (Friend & Cook, 2012; Gleckel & Koretz, 2007). This project builds on collaborative planning and teaching for the participating juvenile justice teachers and also gives teaching artists who provide the job-embedded professional development the opportunity to form their own learning community to strengthen their work and learn from each other.

In Art Unbound, I envision a model of dissemination, which involves ever widening spheres of influence. In the research around Kaupapa Māori theory and practice, Mahuika (2008), has defined a similar "inside-out" model of education that seeks "to both challenge mainstream attitudes and understandings towards issues of relevance for Māori and make space for the articulation of Māori ways of knowing and being" (p. 11). In a similar way, Art Unbound, wants to achieve for youth in the juvenile justice system, the same sense of understanding both of who they are as well as what is necessary for their success and to prepare partners from a wide array of communities in aiding them in overcoming their struggles.

The first sphere of influence is the lab site. One overarching goal of the program is to build capacity of educators in each lab site facility to continue to practice and enhance arts-rich strategies. The second sphere of influence includes the juvenile justice educational system, as well as a general community of teaching artists. Perspective shifts from program participants and Arts curricula developed at the lab sites will be presented to all juvenile justice teachers in workshops. Materials and resources will be available on a dedicated webpage that juvenile justice educators will be able to access. An online, Professional Learning Community (PLC) will be developed so that educators within the lab-sites and throughout the juvenile justice system can share their experiences with arts-based strategies. Also in the second sphere of influence, this project will continue to recruit and develop teaching artists through webinars and workshops. These trainings will provide artists interested in working in juvenile justice settings the background knowledge needed to be successful.

The third sphere of influence includes public school districts that serve a high number of underserved youth. These tend to be larger cities with high populations of families below the poverty level, high dropout rates, and large achievement gaps. Outreach by project staff will target these districts to inform them about the project and invite their educators to participate in the online PLC, as well as have access to all materials and resources on the web site. Professional development in the Art Unbound model will also be made available to these districts, at cost.

The final sphere of influence in this systems change model is the broader community of educators, including those in other juvenile justice programs across the country. The resources and materials on the website will be available to all educators. In addition, Art Unbound staff will publish about and present the Art Unbound arts-based model at a variety of educational and juvenile justice conferences.

Goals and objectives. Goal #1—Increase the capacity of juvenile justice teachers to provide high quality, standards-based arts education linked to the core curriculum.

Objectives:

- Increase teachers' skills integrating project-based arts experiences in course content.
- Build on-going collaboration among juvenile justice teachers (and with teaching artists) and sharing of strategies/projects for using the arts to effectively engage students.
- Deepen juvenile justice teachers' understanding of Positive Youth Development and Culturally Responsive Practices and enhance teacher skills in using these approaches.
- Increase teacher awareness of students' strengths and capacity to master academic content and communicate their understandings.
- Increase teachers' experience with assessment of visual and performing arts products.

Goal #2—Increase the academic achievement of students in juvenile justice facilities in core subjects through their active involvement in the arts.

Objectives:

- Provide weekly exposure to all students in juvenile justice facilities to multiple art forms through standards-based arts projects taught by juvenile justice teachers and teaching artists.
- Use Universal Design for Learning approaches to ensure that all students—including English Language Learners and those with special needs—are engaged in standards-based art projects.
- Build student knowledge and skills of standards-based art content.
- Support students in using the arts to understand academic content and problems.
- Support students in using the arts to express their interpretations and understanding.
- Use the arts to enhance student attention and engagement in the classroom.
- Use the arts to increase understanding and mastery of academic content.

Goal #3—Increase capacity of the juvenile justice system to provide standards-based arts instruction to youth in residential and community settings.

Objectives:

- Demonstrate to juvenile justice administrators and policy-makers the value of the arts in engaging high-risk students in school and promoting academic achievement.

- Develop and disseminate evidence on the effectiveness of the arts as an intervention strategy for juvenile justice youth, increasing engagement and achievement.
- Collect and disseminate promising project-based arts curriculum units on a website for use by all juvenile justice teachers and as a resource for future professional development trainings.
- Work with juvenile justice officials to support and expand arts education for juvenile justice youth.
- Develop a cadre of teaching artists able to work with the juvenile justice student population.

The primary intervention of Art Unbound resides in the job-embedded professional development led by teaching artists. During multiple-day residencies, typically distributed over several weeks, teaching artists collaborate with their juvenile justice teacher hosts to explore creative new approaches to curriculum, instruction, and assessment. The residencies focus on engaging students in learning about academic subject matter while actively exploring the arts. Residencies are integrally tied to standards-based and Common Core teaching concepts, such as literacy, numeracy, critical and reflective thinking, and meta-cognitive skills. The teaching artists support teacher experimentation with "at-the-elbow" assistance and constructive feedback as they coplan and coteach integrated curriculum units which focus both on studying existing works of art and creating and performing works. Residencies will culminate with a final student product, such as an art exhibit, a published collection of student poetry, a mural, or a performance. The residency's goal is to develop the hosting teachers' capacity to use and to meet arts and core academic area standards when the teaching artist is no longer present. It is vital that the juvenile justice system hire community-based teaching artists who are already offering opportunities in the youths' home communities, so that there will be a continuity and the youth can follow up on their interests upon release.

Conclusion

Unfortunately, community-based providers of arts-rich programming tend to be disconnected from the traditional juvenile justice system. These providers tend to be smaller, underfunded struggling organizations without the resources necessary to cultivate relationships within the multiple agencies and organizations within the juvenile justice system. In other words, the people most ideally situated to provide liberating and engaging arts-rich educational experiences for our nation's most vulnerable young people have the least access to the juvenile justice system, a system created to support those same young people. Art Unbound seeks to address this.

As an artist, researcher, and educator it's aggravating to write about utopia, especially in a society that has no real commitment to the cultivation of imagination. In his book, *The Emancipated Spectator*, Jacques Rancière (2011) confirms what I learned through the arts, that being a spectator is the opposite of knowing: "Being a spectator is to be separated from both the capacity to know and the power to act" (p. 2). In the processes of art one finds pure contemplation, which brings to light the value of meaning. One need not become an artist, writer, or performer to gain insight into the power the metacognitive possesses. So I'm forced to navigate a range of emotions as an administrator who has for years been trying systemically to agitate from the top down, while at the same time serving youth and teachers from the bottom-up. But this mid-slope Promethean act has many of us begging the power structures to allow us to re-humanize the discourse, when in actuality, it's there for the making.

Every decision we make says something about what we believe. Through a liberatory and critical pedagogy, Freire (2000) showed us that no child comes to us as a blank slate, looking to "bank" enough knowledge for a lifetime. In the 1970s Illich (1983) asked us to value hope above expectations, to liberate through "de-schooling" by blurring the distinctions between economics, education, and politics. One could go on in this way, forming the perfect literature review to rebuild our educational system, from Byzantine manuscripts to the most recent hip, pedagogy of hope and change. Knowing all along, however, that a crisis looms in the waiting, we have to start somewhere. Why not within the waiting rooms of the Prison Industrial Complex?

One could provide an adequate metaphor between the school-to-prison-pipeline and "the long emergency" of peak oil (Kunstler, 2006)—yet I would argue we are already out of time and must focus to save our most precious natural resource—our nation's youth. It is only through their liberation and success that we could ever dream of being a global utopian benchmark. While we may have a distance to travel, there is light in the shadows.

Many of our nation's adjudicated youth show extraordinary talent in and appetite for creative and imaginative pursuits. Unfortunately, these strengths are not commonly encouraged or rewarded in their educational settings. Integrating the arts into the overall intervention plan offers these young people a crucial opportunity to express themselves in a constructive way. New approaches must be integrated into the current system—new alternatives to offer young people on their return to their home communities, new modalities integrated within our curricula, and new opportunities for building agency/mission within youth. Young people are most likely to succeed when they can be connected to options within their community, and the community-based teaching artists of Art Unbound will provide young people with those opportunities and help them develop a strong sense of self-efficacy. They will also come to "feel connected"—to their teachers, peers and communities—and develop the social competencies and sense of purpose that are necessary for their liberation.

Walking the walk and knowing the walk are different. The form of the prisoner is the form of our unfinished lives. All of us hold the innate possibility of being the prisoner—and in this regard we also already have the capacity for utopia. It's not valued, though. Capital makes imprisonment more profitable than freedom, charging four times more per year for a youth in residential treatment than for that same pupil in the public school system. In this sense, the funding is already in place. It's time to re-sort our priorities and utilize the arts as an intervention mechanism for our most marginalized youth. It is only with infinite possibility placed in their hands that we could ever dream to realize any sort of utopia.

"GIVE ME BEAUTIFUL" BY EVANGELIA WARD-JACKSON

Give me beautiful
Here are the ashes
The shadows of my imperfections
The remnants of my past
The bitter memories and recollections

Give me beautiful
Take these ashes
The inadequacies that quest to dominate
The questions that like to linger
The doubt that wants to hover over my fate

Give me beautiful
Remove these ashes
The traces of an esteem unborn
The leftovers of a mortified self
The cry of a heart brutally torn

Give me beautiful
Give me bright
Give me breath
Give me transparent sight
Flame these issues to ashes
Bury them no longer again to rise
Let them dissipate into the earth
And become one with the passing of time
New joy, new hope
New air, new life

All for me
Take these ashes
And give me beautiful
So all will see
The fresh new break of morning
And know that you have given me

Beautiful

REFERENCES

Alexander, M., & West, C. (2012). *The New Jim Crow: Mass incarceration in the age of colorblindness.* New York, NY: Jackson, TN: The New Press.

Bahena, S., Cooc, N., Currie-Rubin, R., Kuttner, P., & Ng, M. (2012). *Disrupting the school-to-prison pipeline.* Cambridge, MA: Harvard Educational Review.

Bode, P., Fenner, D., & Halwagy, B. E. (2013). Incarcerated youth and arts education: Unlocking the light through youth arts and teacher development. In M. S. Hanley (Ed.), *Culturally relevant arts education for social justice: A way out of no way.* New York: Routledge.

Cahnmann-Taylor, M., & Siegesmund, R. (Eds.). (2007). *Arts-based research in education: Foundations for practice* (1st ed.). New York: Routledge.

Clewell, B. C., Campbell, P. B., & Perlman, L. (2007). *Good schools in poor neighborhoods: Defying demographics, achieving success.* The Urban Institute.

Cradle to Prison Pipeline Campaign. (n.d.). Retrieved October 2, 2013 from http://www.childrensdefense.org/programs-campaigns/cradle-to-prison-pipeline/

DeMoss, K. (2005). How arts integration supports student learning: Evidence from students in Chicago's cape. *Arts and Learning Research, 21*(1), 91.

Derrida, J. (2004). Enlightenment past and to come. *Le Monde Diplomatique* (November, 2004).

Desai, D. (2010). Unframing immigration: Looking through the educational space of contemporary art. *Peabody Journal of Education, 85*(4), 425–442.

Eisner, E. W. (2002). *Arts and the creation of mind.* Yale University Press.

Foucault, M. (2000). *Power: Essential works of Foucault, 1954–1984.* New Press.

Freire, P. (2000). *Pedagogy of the oppressed: 30th anniversary edition.* Continuum International Publishing Group.

Friend, M., & Cook, L. (2012). *Interactions: Collaboration skills for school professionals.* Pearson Higher Education.

Gay, G. (2010). *Culturally responsive teaching: Theory, research, and practice.* Teachers College Press.

Giroux, H. A. (2011). *Zombie politics and culture in the age of casino capitalism.* Peter Lang.

Giroux, H. A. (2012). *Disposable youth, racialized memories, and the culture of cruelty.* New York, NY: Routledge.

Giroux, H. A. (2013). *America's education deficit and the war on youth: Reform beyond electoral politics.* Monthly Review Press.

Gleckel, E. K., & Koretz, E. S. (2007). *Collaborative individualized education process: RSVP to IDEA.* Pearson/Merrill/Prentice Hall.

Gude, O. (2000). Drawing color lines. *Art Education, 53*(1), 44–50.

Gude, O. (2004). Postmodern principles: In search of a 21st century art education. *Art Education, 57*(1), 6–14.

Gude, O. (2007). Principles of possibility: Considerations for a 21st-century art & culture curriculum. *Art Education, 60*(1), 6–17.

Gude, O. (2010). Playing, creativity, possibility. *Art Education, 63*(2), 31–37.

Hanley, M. S., Sheppard, G. L., Noblit, G. W., & Barone, T. (2013). *Culturally relevant arts education for social justice: A way out of no way*. Routledge.

hooks, b. (2009). *Teaching critical thinking: Practical wisdom*. Routledge.

Illich, I. (1983). *Deschooling society*. HarperCollins.

Jackson, T. (2012). Introducing Charly Palmer: Tar Baby and culturally responsive teaching. *Art Education, 65*(6), 6–11.

Juvenile Justice. (n.d.). Retrieved May 7, 2014 from http://www.childrensdefense.org/policy-priorities/juvenile-justice/

Kunstler, J. H. (2006). *The long emergency: Surviving the end of oil, climate change, and other converging catastrophes of the twenty-first century* (1st ed.). New York, NY: Grove Press.

Ladson-Billings, G. (1995). *Culturally relevant teaching*. Ohio State University's College of Education.

Larson, M. (2010). *Immature dreams, inauthentic desires: Utopia in a precarious world*. Retrieved May 1, 2013 from http://www.academia.edu/429915/Immature_Dreams_Inauthentic_Desires_Utopia_in_a_Precarious_World

Mahuika, R. (2008). Kaupapa Māori theory is critical and anti-colonial. *MAI Review, 3*, 1–16.

Nieto, S., & Bode, P. (2011). *Affirming diversity: The sociopolitical context of multicultural education*. Allyn & Bacon, Incorporated.

Nocella, A. J. N. II, Parmar, P., & Stovall, D. (2014). *From education to incarceration: Dismantling the school-to-prison pipeline* (2nd ed.). New York, NY: Peter Lang International Academic Publishers.

Quinn, T. M., Ploof, J., & Hochtritt, L. J. (2011). *Art and social justice education: Culture as commons*. Florence, KY: Routledge, Taylor & Francis Group.

Rancière, J. (2011). *The emancipated spectator* (Reprint ed.). London: Verso.

Reigeluth, C. M. (2012). *Instructional-design theories and models: A new paradigm of instructional theory*. Psychology Press.

Rolling, J. H. (2011). *Circumventing the imposed ceiling: Art education as resistance narrative. Qualitative Inquiry, 17*(1), 99–104. doi:10.1177/1077800410389759

Ruti, M. (2006). *Reinventing the soul: Posthumanist theory and psychic life*. Other Press.

School-to-Prison Pipeline. (n.d.). *American civil liberties union*. Retrieved May 1, 2013 from http://www.aclu.org/racial-justice/school-prison-pipeline

Tavin, K., & Hausman, J. (2004). Art education and visual culture in the age of globalization. *Art Education, 57*(5), 47–52.

The Arts and Human Development: Framing a National Research Agenda for the Arts, Lifelong Learning, and Individual Well-Being | NEA. (n.d.). Retrieved May 7, 2014 from http://arts.gov/publications/arts-and-human-development-framing-national-research-agenda-forthe-arts-lifelong

Wald, J., & Losen, D. J. (2003). Defining and redirecting a school-to-prison pipeline. *New Directions for Youth Development, 2003*(99), 9–15. doi:10.1002/yd.51

Weinstein, R. S. (2004). *Reaching higher: The power of expectations in schooling*. Harvard University Press.

CHAPTER 10

Going Back to the Source ("Caminando Juntos")

GREGORY K. TANAKA AND ROBERTO FLORES

The "development" of self—reconfiguration, reconstruction or transformation of self—comes through arduous self-examination.

Heewon Chang in *Autoethnography as Method* (2008)

In an era of anxiety and fear about a traumatized global/U.S. economy, few have presented concrete alternatives to a neoliberal governmental and education regime that leaves future citizens without the skills to rebuild the infrastructure of their nation. Written in auto-ethnographic style, this article summarizes findings from two parallel applied research projects with the aim of outlining a "mutuality-based pedagogy" that might one day be deployed more broadly in schools, help an ethnically diverse nation to renew its democracy, and heal the soul of that nation.

Through the highly personalized pedagogy of (1) storytelling, (2) dreaming, and (3) social action, the authors demonstrate how the change projects they experienced in their own lives can serve as models for systemic reform while also promoting growth at the level of the individual or self. In posing a place where individual learners come into being (as subjects and agents) by helping others *also* to become subjects and agents, this pedagogy enacts "a mutual immanence of subjects" and offers one foundation upon which to construct a more participatory and egalitarian democracy.

In this time of "liminality"—where global economic systems and democracies are in various stages of collapse—a pedagogy that combines fiction/dreaming with concrete model building would match up well against the moods and social needs of a people who find themselves in need of ways to overcome the harsh effects of systemic collapse, bind themselves together, and remake their public sphere.

* * *

Peabody Wilson made a fortune from the Crash of 2019–2020. Asking in her will that her entire estate support the creation of a new college, she directed that it dedicate its work to "constructing and sustaining a deep and more participatory democracy." She wanted to trigger the launching of new frameworks, new artwork, new science and technology, and new writing that would provide a depth of human interconnectedness and soul she had not enjoyed in her own life.

The Zapitista encampment was in a clearing. A mile across, it was close to the mountainside where the road snaked in big turns beneath a canopy of colors of green I had never before seen. In las milpas, I did not know my life would be forever changed—or that the fear and joy elicited by this place would pierce so deeply into my soul.

ON STORYTELLING AND SUBJECT FORMATION

In this chapter we call on education researchers to formally take up the question of how to initiate a redesign of the national education system during an era defined by systemic collapse and in a way that directly involves the American public. While we do not go into the causes of failure of free market capitalism and its neoliberal ideology as the guiding determinates of human social behavior in the United States today (see, e.g., Bartlett & Vavrus, 2014; Bremmer, 2009; Diamond, 2005; Flores, 2008; Gailey, 1987; Giroux, 2004; Lipman, 2003), we want to underscore the importance of putting in place an education based approach to civic engagement that is opposite the "top down" tendency of the current corporate free market ideology to make policy (e.g., NCLB and Race to the Top) that impacts children, families and schools without their input.

In this regard, we urge the practice of a more bottom-up, horizontal and participatory democracy (e.g., Couldry, 2004; Pateman, 1970; Touraine, 2000) where members of a public become directly involved in their own governance and policy-making along with an approach to formal education that prepares future citizens to do just that. It is precisely during moments of systemic breakdown and collapse, we contend, that the researcher acquires a special duty to move out of a mode of critique and deconstruction to one of "system creating"—redesign and rebuilding—and we present one way of enacting that here.

Set in a microcosm, this chapter is about what happens when two people have an extended conversation over a period of years in which they tell each other stories about their family's immigrant histories, the difficulties their families faced along the way, and their dreams of a future world where the harmful hierarchies and oppressions their families encountered are removed or side-stepped. It is through this form of auto-ethnography (e.g., Chang, 2008; Reed-Danahey, 1997)—between two very different people and set in motion through concrete, formative projects—that we seek to demonstrate the operation of a particular vehicle for systemic creation and reform in a highly diverse United States. In telling each other our dreams of a better world, we find ourselves wishing for a horizontal and egalitarian imaginary that might invoke a new yet old democracy, one that is not controlled by authoritarian economic or bureaucratic elites. We tell these stories below.

So in abstract terms, we propose the narrative construction of the individual as *a subject* (Ruti, 2006) who—through collaborative storytelling, dreaming and steps taken to test those dreams via concrete change projects—can make her/his own personal and social meanings and then act to put those meanings into effect. It is for this reason that we intentionally make a significant part of this chapter story-based.

Part auto-ethnographic and part dreamed, we demonstrate in the narratives that follow the notion that a person who arises out of mutuality—and where one is equal because one is different (Subcomandante Marcos, 2007)—acquires a special capacity not just to confront one's own fears or oppressions but also to help shape a rebuilding or formalization of the social systems in which one lives (extending the work of Solnit, 2010, and Wood, 2010), at times, even co-existing with and parallel to "the official system." In this work, we reaffirm the curious and striking power that listening and support of one storyteller, by another, delivers to the process of subject formation and to the creation of an interconnectedness, or shared and collective soul, based on the embrace of difference so necessary to reconstituting a diverse public sphere.

* * *

Committed to equality in every way, Malibu College sits high above the Pacific Ocean overlooking the multi-million dollar homes of Hollywood actors and producers. Nestled half way up Chumash Canyon, its quaint Southwest Indian style buildings are caressed daily by westerly trade winds that bring with them a hint of salt air.

A highly successful land developer in the 1980's and 1990's, Peabody Wilson invested early in high tech stocks. By the late 1990's, when her holdings had tripled, she began to unload her high technology stocks and invest the proceeds in long-term Treasury bonds. Later, following the high tech rout of 2001, she switched to precious metals bullion and mining companies. With the subprime crisis of 2007–2008 and debt driven collapse of the free market economy in 2019, her 1980s holdings had appreciated significantly. Anticipating a sudden period of hyperinflation and massive "disintermediation"—or wholesale departure by foreign investors, central banks and governments from U.S. Treasury bonds and other dollar denominated instruments—Dr. Wilson then positioned herself to turn her vast wealth into an enormous largesse for public good.

With her success, Peabody Wilson retired and vowed to fund public ventures that would solve stubborn problems facing human society. One project that immediately caught her eye was the idea of an experimental college devoted to building and sustaining a new and uplifting human condition.

Dr. Wilson asked that this college be built on a belief that all people and cultures can be equally valued and where future citizens would learn to pattern a kind of *mutual reliance where each would grow by helping others also to grow. She urged the creation of programs that would teach students the cross-cultural skills they would need to be successful citizens in an increasingly interdependent, global human society—and go on to make decisions and recommendations in their own democracy. Funded by the yield from her $3.2 billion endowment, she further decreed that there be no tuition or student activities fees charged to admitted students.*

An African American female, Dr. Wilson had known the importance of constant reminders about equality and maintaining her own voice in events that affect her, and so she asked that all employees participate in summer workshops on race, gender, sexual orientation, class difference and other historical sources of asymmetry. To this day, her request is honored to a person as a condition of employment for all faculty and staff.

The amazing thing is that Peabody Wilson's vision has been a success. Now eight years into its existence, the new college attracts the best high school graduates in the United States and from around the world. The faculty is first rate and diverse. The curriculum is ground-breaking. And with tuition fully subsidized, many students come from underprivileged or middle class backgrounds. Over 30% of the students are of color with another 20% from foreign countries. The sustaining belief is that its graduates will go on to become leading citizens in participatory democracies around the world.

But now there is an unexpected problem. A group of white students is expressing how difficult it is to participate in this "intersubjective" campus where everyone is supposed to have a voice. With the inequities of Western Eurocentrism deconstructed and eliminated by its progressive faculty, the students are saying they now have no basis for identity or meaning. Hurt, marginalized and feeling deprived of culture, they have started what they call a "White Student Union."

* * *

To reach the rebel Zapatista encampment, Quetzal, Gabriel and I left the highlands at dusk, traveled by car to a "safe house" in Las Margaritas where we rested for a couple of hours, then boarded a dented, gray, two-ton truck that took us on rumbling wheels past the government immigration post at 5 AM—the only time the station was left unmanned. We knew this road would be blocked at other times by soldiers with machine guns and military tanks. On board the truck were 25 people who had come to Las Margaritas to buy provisions for the next two weeks. Nearly half the truck was filled with sacks of beans, corn and other sundries—some, we speculated, headed for the Zapatista Army hiding high up in the mountains.

While waiting to board the truck, I noticed several chickens and one pig tightly held by its owner who was looking very concerned. A discussion soon ensued about how the pig should travel and five minutes later, a resolution was announced by the squealing pig itself which fought with all its might as the owner and truck driver tied it up by its feet and hung it outside the truck.

The sunrise was beautiful, sending rays of light through the thick canopy that reached us with filtered warmth and softness. Thirty minutes into the bumpy trip, however, several people in the truck got motion sickness and this started a chain reaction of people quickly making their way to the side of the truck. I remembered having read that many of these indigenous people had intestinal and liver problems because of the lack of potable water. About six months earlier, I had been diagnosed with Hepatitis. Mine was "Hep C" and soon I too awkwardly made my way over to the back rail. As I finished I embarrassingly looked back to find my way over sacks and people and saw many faces giving me a welcome-to-the-group smile.

With such thoughts, my mind raced back to my own childhood. I was the fourth in a family of 14 children in a rural farming community 70 miles north of Los Angeles. While Oxnard had Caucasian, Asian and black families, Colonia, my barrio, was predominantly Chicana/o. Behind our house at the edge of town ran a large dirt ditch that often became filled with larvae and pesticide-contaminated water running off the ranchers' land bordering our community. When mosquitoes from the ditch started biting the children, I decided something had to be done about it. At 18, I went to City Council meeting to request that something be done, waited about a month—and nothing. Then I went door-to-door and talked with mothers because they were the ones at home. We went to the City Council with tested water sample results and demanded immediate help. Within three days, big rigs came and dug out the ditch, filling it with concrete. This was a period of "symptom treating" and reform oriented activities when I was timid, self-critical and apologetic. Part of me saw my community as if it were in a "deficit" and I harbored to some extent a sense of self-hatred. It was also a time when I thought that if we wanted change, all we had to do was organize. I felt that the system could be reformed.

As time passed, I was hurt, alienated and angry at the rejection and intimidating air of superiority I felt from others in the elite white society. It pained me to see the humiliation that minorities and the poor were subjected to as they attempted to obtain services to meet their rightful basic needs. Eventually, my anger turned inward and for a three-year period I self-medicated my pain and open wounds with alcohol and drugs. Heroin and other drugs were common in Oxnard, known to many as "the heroin capitol of the world" because of its seaport. Among us In Colonia, it was common knowledge that a significant chunk of this trade was financed by the big ranchers themselves. It was then that through careless use of syringes I picked up Hepatitis C—now a constant reminder of that self-defacing process.

* * *

SUBJECTIVITY AND AGENCY

In the storytelling above, Roberto describes how it feels to be a Fulbright scholar who goes to live and learn with Zapatista rebels in the secluded mountainous region of Southern Mexico. Seeking to understand how senior women, many of them *abuelas* or grandmothers, sustained the foundation for a horizontal and participatory democracy and facilitate intersubjective schools—where children develop a natural inclination to help each other grow rather than a sense of individual achievement (Flores, 2007)—he experiences a kind of culture shock. As a Mexican American/Chicano entering a civil society that enjoys a sense of autonomy and intersubjectivity in which each citizen is a "subject" who has voice and helps others also to have voice in a way he did not experience in his own upbringing in the United States, Roberto finds himself straddling two worlds. In the United States, difference had always meant inferiority, exclusion, marginalization but in the Zapatista liberated zone it meant equality. Assailed by the new sights and sounds of *la selva*, he is simultaneously reminded of his own childhood in a small, rural, Latino community in California and draws the courage to speak out about a childhood where he himself was sprayed with pesticide while picking strawberries, where polluted water ran through a ditch in the backyard and he felt compelled as a teenager to challenge those harsh conditions.

In this way, Roberto probes the meaning-making that others have offered in the powerful work of *testimonio* (Beverly, 2004; Cruz, 2006; Menchu, 1983), wherein a storyteller acquires an enhanced capacity to envision actual social justice as a result of her/his storytelling (also Cruz, 2001). At the same time, Roberto cannot help but think that some of the lessons he learned in Chiapas might prove useful one day in redesigning the U.S. education system—perhaps even in an applied ethnographic sense—and it is about this that he is led to ruminate.

In contrast, Greg begins above by telling Roberto his dream about a future place. Finding Roberto a supportive listener, he describes a future campus that he calls Malibu College, where the kind of racial patterns he had encountered in his own life are eliminated. Not yet ready to delve into the distant spaces of his own family history, he instead insists on looking forward, into a future where a better and brighter place might be imagined that is free of the hurtful forces that had harmed him in his youth. It is the unrestricted quality of this form of dreaming that Roberto would also find useful when dreaming of an alternative place where the harsh conditions of his own childhood in Colonia would be relocated to a distant past.

In one case through dreaming and in another case by describing a recent stay in a foreign country, we submit we experienced a mutuality-based form of "subject formation" in which each person comes into being by creating his/her own meanings and sharing those meanings with another. We also came upon something *other than* the Western, ego-based individual who is conceived as moving through life in sequential stages replicating a linear pattern of traditional human development theory.

At the same time we felt that if this were an act of subject formation, it was already quite different from the cynical view of a "dissolved subject" theorized by early poststructural thinkers that individual is solitary and destined to be subservient to a dominant discourse (e.g., Foucault, 1976/1990, p. 101; Guano, 2002; Ortner, 1995; but see Ruti, 2006; Johnson, 2008; Tanaka, 2009; Viego, 2007). In making our own meanings as storytellers—and sharing with each other our dreams of a better world—we lessened our own internal fears and oppressions, let our dreams give rise to practical creation and change projects, and helped each other to move out of victimhood to a new kind of personal and social agency (Booze, R, 2006). Where would this lead—and what kind of agency? We wanted to follow this strand. And if no longer a dissolved subject (after Foucault), we also wanted to know what kind of subject this would be.

* * *

I, too, am a southern Californian. One of my earliest memories is of an event that occurred in the early 1950's. My father had taken the family on a fishing trip to Big Bear in the mountains high above San Bernadino near Los Angeles. Born in Los Angeles to Japanese-American parents, this was to be the first time in my life that I can recall where race made a difference.

Arriving at Big Bear Lake—a large body of water that sat between the crests of two 5,000 feet evergreen covered mountains—we went to Gray's Landing to rent a boat. My father had been excited for weeks about going trout fishing. But when we got to the boat dock, the dock operator, a white man, said, "No, there aren't any boats left." As we looked out at the docks, we could see several dozen boats, bobbing in the water, ready to go out.

Soon enough other customers came, white customers, and we watched as the dock operator ran to get them seat cushions that would double up as floating life preservers. What made this especially difficult for my father to accept was that he had served in the U.S. Army during World War II. Born and raised in East Los Angeles, he had attended UCLA and been working to help his father run a small photography studio when Japan attacked Pearl Harbor. Having lived the life of an all-American boy, my father continued to encounter anti-Japanese sentiment long after World War II was over.

It was partly as a result of this inhumanity that my father seemed impelled to instill in all his children a desire to achieve and make our lives more secure and better than the one he had. But at the same time, there was a kind of amnesia in my family's understanding of its history because of my father's unwillingness to talk about or confront those difficult times in his past. Worse, my siblings and I were acquiring from this amnesia an inability to ever feel satisfied with ourselves or our accomplishments. Ironically, we could never feel secure. It is this sense of denial that I struggle to push through today.

* * *

Arriving mid-morning in San Jose near the Guatemalan border and deep inside **la selva***, we alighted from our clumsy truck to find the earth spongy and covered with light green moss. It was just starting to rain. Throwing my rucksack over my shoulder, I took a few tentative steps on the soft earth and smiled. Tiny, warm drops grazed my face. In the steamy jungle, the light rain seemed to evaporate as soon as it touched the hot ground.*

I was lucky to meet Ramona on a previous visit and then on a later visit to Mexico City. A Tzotzil Indian, her aura of power defied her diminutive physical presence. With a red kerchief over her mouth and nose, this slight-of-frame woman was one of the visionaries of the Zapatista movement fast spreading throughout Mexico. The words "Chiapas" and "Zapatista" had become the exotic cachet of the international press. On their part, leaders of the national government were harboring growing fears that they were losing legitimacy in the eyes of a public that saw how these calm people could govern themselves and thrive independently of federal rule. "Todos somos Ramona" was what people were starting to say all over Mexico: "We are all Ramona!"

Yet it was here in Chiapas that I also found a new way to view my own rage as dignified—in the practices of my ancestors. Here in **la selva** people had long practiced a form of government that would have to be called a "horizontal and participatory democracy." Carried through the ages by women, in particular the grandmothers who directed informal education, the idea of intersubjectivity "evolved" early by being intersubjective and by developing in the children a deep sense of responsibility for helping each other and putting the group ahead of oneself. The philosophy was one of complementarity and mutual interdependence where to be different is a necessary asset, a gift to the collective community that needs to be developed.

So while the outside world often reduced the Zapatista movement to media images of the black ski masks—called pasa montanas—of the Zapatista army, the far larger event was the emergence all over Mexico of "autonomous communities" based in intersubjectivity. These communities were self-governing and wholly independent of the national government. In a time of dying representative democracy—where elected officials are bought off by transnational economic interests—the time was ripe for a new democracy closer to the hearts, experience and needs of the people. The words "Todos para todos, nada para nosotros" and "Mandar obedeciendo" encapsulated a new political ethic that began to echo in the corridors and backrooms of the Mexican national government: "Everything for everyone, nothing for us!" and "We lead by obeying."

By U.S. standards, every autonomous community I saw seemed poor. The one or two room huts were made of mortar and wood or brick, had dirt floors and no running water. There were no beds, only metates. There were no modern appliances—no televisions, gas stoves or refrigerators. The one exception was that occasionally there was a computer. In such economically depressed conditions, the irony was that the Zapatista uprising had already gone global and become known as the first technological "netwar."

Finding this autonomy here in Mexico, I realized some of the weaknesses in my own thinking about myself. I remembered that by the late Sixties I was in college and had become necessarily very critical of the system. But there was a lack of seeing our own failures, and I began to attribute all problems in the community to the unfairness of the existing vertical social structure. While the existing social structure generated in us an extremely negative mindset, I began to see that the ideal strategy wasn't to be in permanent resistance and deconstruction. While critique and resistance are absolutely necessary, I began to see that I had to put the majority of my energy into changing the conditions around me. In 1967 I helped co-found UMAS then MEChA at UCLA. When I went home, I co-founded the Brown Berets of Oxnard. While non-violent, we *were highly distrusting of social institutions and became somewhat militant. During the 1960's and 1970's many groups like ours pushed for systemic change and in some ways we succeeded—through the creation of civil rights laws, the Equal Rights Amendment, bilingual education, ethnic studies programs and affirmative action.*

By the 1980's, however, "The System" had appropriated, redefined and absorbed every gain we had made. Those in power had adapted by redirecting our hard won programs in ways that kept them in power. Under the guise of democracy, this had translated into keeping indigenous people down. Realizing that "representative democracy" was not working, I turned to Marxist organizations that advocated violent overthrow. But I quickly found that while Marxist economic analysis was quite valid, the Marxist top-down social-organizational paradigms did not lead to positive solutions either. With the fall of the Soviet Union in 1989, there came a vacuum and a call for something new. I soon turned away from the top-down Marxist-Leninist approach. I was again without tether but oddly felt a liberating hope in finally admitting that I didn't know how to get there but knew that in caminando juntos *(walking together), we could one day make the road.*

What I was now seeing with my own eyes in Chiapas, Mexico, represented the direct opposite of what I had experienced in my own life as a youth.

* * *

ON DREAMING—AND MUTUAL IMMANENCE

Hearing Roberto's earlier story of polluted water in ditches behind the home where he grew up, Greg finds this continuing dialogue a safe place to dig into his own past and tells a story he had never told to anyone before about a childhood fishing expedition that went awry. In this extended narration, he both dreams about a future time and place, Malibu College, *and* revisits a memory that had in some ways fueled this dream but remained repressed for decades. In contrast, Roberto finds it more expedient to tell the stories from his own past first and then describe an ideal democracy operating in the southern one-third of Mexico. In a storytelling that comes much later in this text, both his family stories and the Chiapas ideal would figure heavily into the Roberto's own dream of social change.

Looking back, we believe it was the simple give-and-take nature of our telling and listening that was the key foundation for a personal transformation that was to follow. Telling and listening gave us a "sense of permission" to be bold, take risks and explore what might have been too painful otherwise to unearth. In a dual telling, neither storyteller is ridiculed, doubted, judged or chastised. Instead, we each felt supported and encouraged by the other narrator who would "double" as a willing listener. And it was out of this process of storytelling and dreaming that we would one day discover a mutual release from pain.

In her book *Reinventing the Soul,* Mari Ruti (2006) develops in some depth the idea that a downtrodden individual can escape her/his feeling of "Lack," or emptiness of soul by having one's own stories witnessed and by witnessing the stories of others, and I find a close kinship between her abstract work and our field experience. Combining self-reflection and witnessing for others, or what Ruti (2006, pp. 83–84) calls "sociality," she argues an oppressed person can escape a tendency to resist or overcome social inequity in isolation, shift from lack of soul to soul reinvention, and become what she calls "an agental subject" (p. 59).

Drawing from Lacan, Ruti goes on to define soul as "the subject's attempt to find its place and purpose in the world" and "infuse the necessities of daily life with *forms of meaningfulness* and value that translate to inner satisfaction" (id at p. 20, emphasis added). It is this work that "connects the individual to the world in loving intersubjectivity with others" (id at p. 20). It is also Ruti's definition of soul—combining one's own meaning construction *and* one's ability to connect with others in one analysis—that helps us better understand the importance of the form of dual storytelling presented here. This analysis parallels the work of Native American therapist Eduardo Duran (2006, p. 27, 44, 46), who conceptualizes soul as the feeling that inheres when people connect with their "Native ways of being… in both the personal and collective spheres" (id at p. 46), and of narrative therapists who explain how the renewing power of alternative storytelling will have a willing listener (e.g., White & Epston, 1990; also Popkewitz, 1998, pp. 49–50).

In our own storytelling experience, we see to a certain extent the "interconnectedness" addressed by both Ruti and Duran. This does not come easy as we had been trained all our lives to think in terms of the individualistic, ego-based soul of Western psychoanalytic thought. We now believe, however, that a *mutuality-based approach* to human development is better suited to the collapsing world of a transnational, global human society and diverse United States—where more than at any other time in recent history it is now crucial for a fragmented and battered human society to begin to pull together and aid each other's renewal and fresh coming to be.

So when storytellers begin to dream of social change—and support each other's dreaming process—we suggest a special kind of "mutual immanence" unfolds that heightens the agency of each participant. As Ruti theorizes, that mutual support empowers storytellers to help each other move out of Lack. Operationalized in this way through storytelling and dreaming, we hypothesize that a fresh capacity for interconnectedness—like the intersubjectivity taught to children in Chiapas—is a skill set that can and must be taught and assessed in U.S. schools now. It will help the next generation to move out of the Lack generated by a crashing global economy and troubled democracy and steer them to a place from which to renew.

So in our view, this capacity to move from victimization to renewal can have special traction in times of systemic stress, like today when the economic superstructures of a society are collapsing, traditional norms and duties of a shared ethnic culture have given way to superficial, money based meanings, and there is little left but nostalgia to bind a large and diverse nation together. Stated in more direct terms, the widening de-legitimation of class and race based hierarchies concretized in recent decades by the free market ideology and its corresponding education law No Child Left Behind (e.g., Giroux, 2004) provides applied researchers with an opening in which to launch a new, more egalitarian, pluri-ethnic, meaning-based social system.

Specifically, we hypothesize that intersubjective storytelling and dreaming— where each participant becomes a subject who is urged to create his/her own meanings—will pattern for future citizens the habits and attitudes they will need to participate in performing civic engagement and social change later in life. Some have already begun to test an "intersubjective storytelling and dreaming pedagogy" in pre-K to 12 settings (Arroyo, in press; Chagolla, in press; D'Urso-Cunningham, in press; Thompson, in press; Toscano, in press) and find that it can enhance both sense of community and an expansion of individual agency. We suspect this mutuality-based form of applied human development human will have special significance during systemic distress, and we address that possibility in the storytelling that follows.

* * *

My father's side came to East Los Angeles from Japan by way of Hawaii and central California. His father was a photographer and ran a retail photography store on the second floor of a two-story building on 1st Street in Little Tokyo in Los Angeles. Later, he moved the store around the corner and across the street from the downtown Los Angeles Police Department headquarters on what is now called Judge John Aiso Street.

My mother was born in New York and raised in New Rochelle, where they lived in a fine two-story stone house on Oakdale Avenue. Her father came to the United States from Japan just after the turn of the century. I remember the day I discovered that when he told his stories, my grandpa in New York—who spoke English well after having lived in the United States for 60 years—would always refer to white people in America as "Americans," as if he himself didn't belong in that category. I had not noticed this until one fall when a college roommate from Missouri came down with me to stay at my grandparents' house during Thanksgiving break. Steve asked me why my grand-father did that, calling only white people Americans. "I guess he doesn't see himself as an American yet," I said maybe as much to convince myself that this was the case.

That was in 1968. I still recall the flat, silver gray stones that made up the facade of that house in New Rochelle, New York. These stones had tiny flecks of silver-gold, very unlike the white granite with black striations I had become accustomed to seeing in the Sierra Nevada mountains of my youth. I always liked the sparkle in the stones on that house at 16 Oakdale Avenue and sometimes, I used to think those silver-gold flecks could give me energy and hope in my own life. I also remember the tall, thick trees on Oakdale with their dark gray-brown bark. In the winter they stood especially tall when the sky was overcast and wet and the air was very cold for a southern Californian.

On some days I am convinced those gray stones and tall trees are the stuff of which my mother was made. One of the first parents to push for special education in California schools during the 1950's, she was a true pioneer. In the city of South Pasadena, then 98% white, my mother became the first person of color to be elected PTA president. Tall trees, indeed, and stones that sparkle with wit.

My mother's father had also been a natural leader. At the age of 14, he climbed aboard a tramp steamer in Hiroshima, Japan, and emigrated by himself to San Francisco. One day, after being kicked out of the local San Francisco public school because he was Japanese, he was sitting on the steps of a church and looking dejected when a Catholic priest happened by. The priest felt sorry for him and took him into the church's parochial school. Later, he decided to take a train to New York and on that train met an older couple from Long Island who befriended him. They took him in and he ended up graduating from a high school on Long Island. Due to his bubbly personality and high intelligence, my grandfather was elected class president.

These traces of memory, the silver-gold flecks and tall trees, a grandfather who always smiled and had stories to tell, and my mother who went to PTA meetings as a leading citizen—these all instilled in me a strong sense of duty to be a team player, to make things better for others, always to build harmony. But it was only decades later, when asked to share my stories, that I can begin to accept myself.

So if my life has been about a search for harmony, I can tell myself that I found "partial harmony" on a bright summer day in 1960. That year the Rafu Angling Club, a Los Angeles based Japanese American fishing organization, was having its annual trout fishing tournament at Big Bear Lake. My father, twin brother and I (the two oldest of five children) were there along with our church friend Ronnie. At age 12, I caught the one and only trophy fish of my life, a two-pound rainbow trout that pulled and tugged mightily on my line for almost twenty minutes.

I still have the trophy to prove it—a 16-inch tall, heavy metal, gold-colored trophy stand with a leaping fish—celebrating the fish I caught, on a boat from Gray's Landing.

* * *

It was while sitting with my back propped against a large gray boulder at the edge of a thick patch of tall plants—leafy, ten-foot high elephant ear plants not uncommon to **la selva**—*that I dreamed of a mystical place back home that I called Aguas Calientes. Located just north of Los Angeles, this town is 70% Latino with the rest Caucasian, African American, and Asian American. The high drop-out rates in schools pale in comparison to the mounting importation of drugs, growth in gang activity, contamination of the city water supply, and high incidence of cancer. The leukemia rates for children of Aguas Calientes is 20 times the national standard.*

Two years ago, a group of concerned citizens got together in the back room of Padilla's Bar and Grill. The 45 gathered souls voted to create a parallel system of governance and exchange for Aguas Calientes. Canvassing local businesses, they asked for money to create a "Directory of Skills, Occupations and Professions"—an inventory of skills of each member of the community including children and seniors. The people also printed paper that looked like a dollar bill but had a family pictured in the middle instead of Abraham Lincoln or Benjamin Franklin. These bills became the new currency that all members of the community could use to buy each other's services. 2,000 bills were given to each person including children.

In the ensuing weeks, small events began to occur. Dona Sipriana, who was 80 and too old to walk to the drugstore to get her medicine, looked in the directory and saw that little Ruben who was 12 years old had a bike. She paid him to go buy her medicine for her. For this, she paid him six community dollars, more than the four that was normal for that kind of service. Over time they became good friends. Over an 11-month period, there were thousands of ties created between community members who otherwise would not have known each other. It was the beginning of people starting to rely on each other—a mutual interdependence of individuals and a healthy reliance on one's own community.

Soon this community set up a coordinating council, an education committee, an economic projects committee, a youth council, an elders council, and a pluri-ethnic committee. Between members of the council and the assembly, there was a "mandar obedeciendo" relationship meaning that all members of the community had a duty to place the community ahead of their own aggrandizement. At assembly meetings, people were welcome to bring their children.

After 12 months, the people of Aguas Calientes closed the main street downtown and held a big fiesta called "La Quema del Dolar," or the burning of the dollars. People brought all kinds of food and put them on tables for everyone to eat. People also brought all their community dollars and threw them into a roaring bonfire. Why would they burn all their community dollars? The message people wanted to celebrate was that it's not the dollar that counts anymore, it's you that matters most and what you do for others. What was developed was a relationship between people of helping each other, and with this the people of Aguas Calientes realized they had all the solutions within themselves.

* * *

RETHINKING DEMOCRACY, RETHINKING THE SOUL

Something happened in the years following our storytelling that we did not anticipate: both the dreams we had described to each other in the 1990s had come true. From his vision of a mystical place called "Aguas Calientes," Roberto went on to work with youth in East Los Angeles to launch the kind of self-governing community vehicle he had seen while living in Chiapas, Mexico (Flores, 2008). By 2003, the Eastside Café had become a place where Mexican-American youth and young adults could share their stories through dance and music—and build a capacity to govern and manage their own job training and health programs, economic development projects, and youth activities.

Performed without relying on the city government of Los Angeles, this experimental "autonomous community" served as a concrete alternative to the deficit based, "progressive model" of social services that had stripped Roberto of worth and hope when he was young. Reflecting back on the hurtful U.S. representative democracy of his youth, Roberto had found a way to test an alternative democracy—one that made horizontal civic engagement its lynchpin and taught teenagers and young adults the skills and habits of direct participation and intersubjective communication they would need to govern themselves in a truly "civil society" (Flores, 2008). Importantly, he also put his own dream into action by testing a specific civic practice inside the United States and redefined himself as a "citizen subject" no longer separated from or at the mercy of a state apparatus but instead intimately connected with its civic reconstitution. For Roberto, development of the self and the concrete steps he took to help evoke democratic change had become interconnected operations.

In a similar way, by 2000 Greg's utopian vision of an "intercultural" Malibu College—where individuals from diverse ethnic and racial backgrounds can learn from each other across difference—had also become a reality. In a four-year action research project he directed from 1996 to 2000, he helped a small private university turn itself into "the first intercultural university" in the United States (Tanaka, 2003/2007, 2009). Through workshops, courses, staff training sessions and other interventions, the campus sought to promote "learning and sharing across difference where no culture dominates." The students, staff and faculty at this highly diverse campus began to move out of prior tendencies to stay in racial or ethnic enclaves and instead supported the growth of each other *across difference*—just as he had once dreamed might happen. Pre/post quantitative and qualitative analysis demonstrated that after three years of intercultural programming there were already significant increases in sense of community, cross-cultural skills, and sense of personal control over race issues on campus—and most importantly, significant declines in racial stress (Tanaka 2003/2007, 2009; Tanaka, Johnson, & Hu, 2001).

Recapitulating the dual storytelling we had ourselves performed, it was intercultural storytelling that worked best in this university change project. Like the personal growth Roberto had experienced when his dream came to fruition, the practical work of helping a campus become a model intercultural university *made smaller* the pain Greg had kept buried inside him all those years from an earlier, race-defined childhood—and helped him move to a new place that was soul regenerating.

Applying Ruti's analysis, there was a greater "connection to the world" for us both. And in addition, we found that when we engaged in storytelling, dreaming and a concrete social change project to put our respective dreams into effect—there came what we now see as a tangible, felt *departure from Lack*. In Ruti's words, we had in some small way begun to "reinvent soul." And we had done this by both generating projects to enhance a community to bind its people together. It is this same kind of shared, storytelling-based success that we now hope to see youth perform across the country as a foundational step toward mutuality-based subject formation and enhanced civic engagement.

So what next? As the years passed we began to wonder if our change projects could not in some way be joined. Could there be a new U.S. democracy that is *both* participatory *and* intersubjective? This question has been raised persuasively by public intellectuals Alain Touraine (2000) of Paris and Nicolas Couldry (2004) of London. In *Can We Live Together? Equality and Difference,* Touraine (2000) explains why the U.S. market-driven or "neoliberal" democracy of today—where moneyed capitalists control an "elected" government through interest group lobbies and fragment the population along race and ethnic lines—should be replaced by *a new "democracy for the subject"* that directly engages a diverse public in its own policymaking.

Indeed, with the current "representative" U.S. government controlled since the early 1980s by free market interests—"free" only because businesses are deregulated and can leverage up their gains well beyond safe proportions and without government oversight—the result has been not only a dissolution of "real societies into globalized markets and networks while destroying culture and causing divisiveness between groups" (id at 158; also Bremmer, 2009) but also a collapse of the very free market system itself (see Ferguson, 2008; Flores, 2008; Roubini & Mihm, 2011; Taleb, 2007).

To initiate this democracy, Touraine urges the creation of schools that specifically teach the next generation of U.S. citizens the "*intercultural* communication skills" they would need to interact closely with each other in a more participatory democracy. In language and outcome sounding remarkably similar to the "intersubjective society" Roberto described seeing in Chiapas and subsequently tested by launching the Eastside Café in Los Angeles, the democracy for the subject envisioned by Touraine would be managed *in intersubjective fashion* by the people themselves. It also mimics the intersubjectivity achieved in Greg's project to build an intercultural campus.

To support his argument, Touraine calls for the creation of "schools for the subject" (p. 269) that teach youth the cross-cultural skills for a diverse and participatory democracy (see also Arratia, 1997; Fabian, 2002; Garcia, 2005; Hornberger, 2000; Lenkersdorft, 1996; Tanaka, 2002, concerning other venues worldwide where intercultural education has already been tested). What is different here is that both of our visions are more local community based and not tied to the rigid structure of a state apparatus.

In a similar vein, British writer Nicolas Couldry (2004, p. 5) translates Touraine's abstract thinking into more concrete steps by urging Western democracies to (1) end their practice of destroying culture on behalf of free market forces and instead (2) develop public schools that teach *the skills and attitudes of listening, mutual reliance and storytelling* while nurturing a "self" who focuses on the well being of others.

Mirroring Ruti's "loving intersubjectivity," Touraine's schools for the subject—and our own experience of mutual immanence in building an autonomous community and an intercultural university campus—Couldry urges the teaching of mutuality and storytelling in public schools to provide the tools that citizens in a diverse society will one day need if they are to work closely together in a more participatory democracy. In the work of Couldry, Ruti and Touraine, we found kindred souls while performing our own work.

This is not new. In addition to the *autonomous communities* of Chiapas, Mexico, there are other participatory democracies and supportive education systems not examined by Touraine or Couldry. Collectively, these successes add significant momentum to the possibility that there can one day be an improved and more participatory democracy in the United States. These include the Freirean effort toward a *participatory public budgeting,* or PPB, in Porto Alegre, Brazil (Baiocchi, 2003; Deantoni, 2004); the community based process of "extending participation outwards" of the *Kaopapa Maori* in New Zealand (Smith, 1999); a Swedish effort hypothesizing *children as agents of social change* (Lancy, 2006; Poluha, 2004); and the Helsinki practice of having education policy embedded within a larger state process of nurturing *holistic support of the whole family* (Grubb, 2005).

Further, there is the Bolivian *intercultural education project* in which the national education system accords value to all cultures in a diverse society (Hornberger, 2000); the *direct democracy* of Kerala, India (Isaac & Heller, 2003); the *citizens panel* used with success to form public policy in London and Denmark (Guston, 1999); and the *local school councils,* or LSCs, of Chicago where local citizens voted on the budget and had hiring and firing power over local public schools (Fung, 2003; Lipman, 2003; also Tanaka, 2007).

What all of the above systems have in common is a grounding in community-based approaches to learning and decision-making in which the skills and habits of mutuality and direct participation are held dear and, accordingly, taught in schools. Here we should point out that the pedagogical needs of a public education system that sustains a participatory democracy are fundamentally at odds with the assessment-driven, privatized and top down administration of schools codified in the policies of "No Child Left Behind," "Race to the Top" and "Common Core" that place emphasis on individual success to the exclusion of sense of community, artistic creativity, strategic thinking, and learning how to achieve mutuality between learners (e.g., Cochran-Smith, 2005; Kim & Sunderman, 2005; Tanaka, 2015).

We note therefore the timeliness of an inquiry into fresh examples of direct democracy offered at the end of an era where a "representative" democracy has so failed its people by allowing a small group of wealthy elites to deploy reckless amounts of debt and left their public and nation holding the empty bag of a hollowed out economy and broken "social fabric" (Krieger, 2016; also Austin-Fitts, 2016; Celente, 2016; Farrell, 2010; Manarino, 2016; Roberts, 2016; Tanaka, 2007; von Greyerz, 2016).

To support his argument, Couldry harkens back to Paul Ricoeur (1992, p. 161) who reasoned in *Oneself As Another* that in an increasingly diverse world "the life history of each of us is caught up in the history of others." We reaffirm the significance of that thinking here. While we did not know it then, we now believe the reciprocal and mutual immanence we experienced in our own dual storytelling—where we had reinforced and supported each other's coming to be—constitutes one way of patterning the mutuality across difference called for by Touraine, Couldry and Ricoeur. In human development terms, we suggest that *learning in a diverse and participatory U.S. democracy might now be theorized and assessed as a process of expanding mutuality in which one's own growth and dreaming become interwoven with the act of helping others also to dream and grow.* This is an area that begs for more field research.

What was most encouraging to us, however, was that our dreaming and implementation enabled us to envision new meaning construction at the higher level of large social institutions—that is, *systemically*—by becoming subjects who could help design and test new approaches to civic engagement (as in the imagined Aguas Calientes) and diversity education (as in the dreamed of Malibu College), successful models that might one day be combined in a concerted effort to reconstitute and reinvigorate the democracy itself. It is our belief that the wider practice of field-based testing will be closely interconnected with the onset of new stories, new dreams.

* * *

In May of 1970, when still in college, I stood with great anticipation on the edge of a walkway between The Ellipse and the back lawn of the White House. With a massive crowd starting to gather, I was to become one of 20 college students who had been asked to escort speakers opposing the war in Vietnam to the dais—speaker John Dellinger, famous singer Judy Collins, Senator Mark Hatfield, and others.

Forming a tight ring around the speakers, we walked the speakers down from All Soul's Church a mile away. It is not an exaggeration to say it made my heart sing to be walking right beside Judy Collins. At the point of our procession, a man in his forties led the makeshift parade, wearing an old Davy Crockett style, yellow-tan buckskin coat with hair down to his shoulder blades and strumming a beat for us on a dilapidated six-string guitar. Had it not been for the solemnity of the moment, he might have seemed comical.

I did not have a camera since we had been told to leave them behind in the event of a riot when one would need to run quickly without catching oneself on a branch or other object. We had large clear plastic bags to pull over our heads in the event of tear gas—to buy precious seconds to run from the smoke. We each also wore a thin, light green cotton strip around our left biceps, armbands to signal that we were "strike marshals" and were there to keep peace. In my eyes, the thin green armbands probably also symbolized my own heightened sense of importance as a college senior not-yet-ready-for-the-world.

What I remember most clearly was what happened when John Dellinger was speaking. Leading up to the event, he had been the most vociferous and controversial of speakers now sitting on the dais. Those who had escorted the speakers to the platform were asked to join thirty other strike marshals and form a shoulder-to-shoulder semi-circle in front of the stage, to keep the crowd from getting too close. While the crowd of a hundred thousand stretched for half a mile away from this platform in back of the White House, here we were standing not ten yards from the stage.

Just when Dellinger was getting into his most aggressive attack on President Nixon and his Vietnam War, I felt someone brush hard against me from behind. Before I could react, a figure had rushed the stage, jumped up on the six-foot high railing, and grabbed the microphone stand away from Dellinger. The on-rusher, a thin, shirtless young white man with a shaved head and in his early twenties, had sprinted past me when I wasn't looking. I had two thoughts as the police came in to take the young man away. First, I felt sorry for this foolish young person who had wanted so badly to disrupt a peaceful protest. But second, I realized I had failed to do my duty. This was the Japanese American in me—the pull to constantly fulfill one's duty—and the rush to blame myself said much about both the kind of citizen I would go on to be and a sense of self-blame that would be hard to tamp down for the rest of my life.

My father's relocation during World War II did not go away when the war was over. As his future children, we would one day be on the receiving end of unintended yet palpable emotional abuse. To assuage that pain, I learned at an early age that it was easier to just aid my younger siblings. Since those early days, this way of being in the world became set in stone and I went on to seek one context after another where I could render succor to others. I still remember how in the 8th graded, I first told myself I would go on to do my best "to make one big contribution to the world." But from this entrenched habit of always having to save the world, I blew myself out on more than one occasion in my life where my health suffered as a result.

And so it was through my extended conversations with Roberto, that I began to see that it's okay to receive gifts from another. And as I let go of the self-imposed role of always having to be the savior of others, I found more vistas opening up. I found a deeper, shared connection with others. I discovered I did not have to extend the life of the pain and abuse by staying entrenched in a rigid "savior" mode. Where before I had been the initiator, the facilitator, I became in this practice of dreaming and storytelling with Roberto the recipient of another person's humanity, cosmology and succor.

Is this what it feels like to begin to experience soul? If so, it is a process of mutual support, departure from Lack—and re-energizing that is continuing today.

And with this thought one thing becomes instantly clear: that many things are starting to come together in the same visual frame in my life—a thin green arm band, silver-gold flecks and tall trees, the dream of an intercultural campus, and a two-pound rainbow trout from Gray's Landing.

* * *

Xamay sits on the eastern banks of Lake Chapala, a body of water so rich and immense the Huichol Indians still make yearly pilgrimages to pay homage to it as a holy shrine and source of life. I am told my ancestors, the Gonzalez family, came to Xamay in northern Mexico in 1810 to escape the encomienda, where they worked as campesinos. After 300 years of genocide and domination by Spain, the indigenous rebels who had wrested control of the country felt obligated, in an ecomienda in Guanajuato, to kill all light-skinned people and slaughter every white person including children because they believed the white children would grow up to become white oppressors.

My mother, Elvira Gonzales Flores, vividly recalls an incident that occurred when she was 12 and growing up in Xamay. One night her friend Lupe Partida came running to tell her that there was a fire in the old firecracker warehouse on the edge of town and her little brother, Alfredo, was badly burned. Throwing a rebozo over her shoulders, Elvira ran to the warehouse to find a crowd gathered around a small body on the ground. It was Alfredo, covered with a sheet. The priest, El Senor Cura, was administering last rites. When Elvira's father gently removed the sheet, they could see that Alfredo had been burned all over—but was still breathing.

As the adults made ready to take Alfredo to the hospital, Elvira fainted. For the next three days, she ran a high fever and went into periodic convulsions. When a week passed and the doctors could do nothing to help Elvira, her father became very concerned. While Alfredo was making a quick recovery, Elvira's condition continued to worsen for over a year. Elvira had no control of her limbs and could not speak. Her father decided there was only one thing left to do—take Elvira to La Basilica de Tepeyac in Mexico City, where La Virgen de Guadalupe had appeared in 1531 to an Aztec Indian named Juan Diego. At La Basilica there existed a natural spring of water that was visited daily by thousands who made their promises—mandas—and asked for favors and miracles in return—favores y milagros.

In 1936, Elvira's father took Elvira to La Basilica. Since roads had not been built, he carried her two miles from the train station to the church. Arriving at La Basilica, they saw to their dismay that the fountain had almost gone dry. In desperation, Elvira's father gathered mud from the fountain and rubbed it all over her arms, legs and neck. He even made her eat some of it. Finished, he sat down in exhaustion and went into deep prayer. He promised La Virgencita that he would be a good man from here on, name one of his children after her, and come once a year—and asked if she could please give Elvira control of her body and voice.

Eyes swelling with tears of hope and profound faith, he went to Elvira and told her to stand up. Holding his arm, she rose up spasmodically but determined, and stood. Crying and silently joyful, the two held each other. In a barely audible voice, Elvira said, Gracias Virgencita por todo lo que has consedido—thank you Virgin for all that you have conceded.

Ten years later, in 1944, Elvira married Alejandro Flores. Under a stellar night, as the cool, fresh, sweet-water scented winds came to them off Lake Chapala, they decided *to leave Xamay and travel to the United States for new opportunity. With the war still raging in Europe, there was a need for workers in San Diego. Leaving her beloved Xamay, Elvira whispered once again, Gracias Virgencita por todo lo que has concedido.*

Ten years later, Elvira and Alejandro took their seven children and moved to Simi Valley outside Los Angeles and six months later, they moved to Oxnard where they both worked in the fields and then the packing house, the normal progression of seniority for migrant workers. After a number of years, a young pocho—a U.S.-born Mexican—who lived on Hayes Avenue came by and helped workers in their desire to organize in order to gain health benefits, sick pay, and grievance rights. Two months later, with the help of a young Cesar Chavez, a campaign of union recognition ensued. From that date, however, Elvira and Alejandro were marked people and one day on returning from a trip to see Alejandro's mother in Mexico, Alejandro and Elvira both received termination notices from company officials.

"Okay," Elvira told her children, "Everyone from Carlos on up, join your father to pick fruit up north. You too, Roberto." Early the next morning, Elvira made una altera de tacos and asked everyone to kneel down to give a blessing. I was nine on the day she said, "Que la divina providencia los cuide, que la Virgen de Guadalupe los cubra con su manta"—"may the divine providence take care of you and may the Virgin of Guadalupe protect you with her mantle."

* * *

ON THE IMPORTANCE OF MUTUALITY DURING SYSTEMIC COLLAPSE

Echoing Ricoeur (1992), the idea that a child's growth might be dependent upon helping another child also to grow—or *complementarity*—seems especially timely when a country needs to undergo great internal healing. In times of mounting systemic stress, as now, we hold it exceedingly important to find new meaning by connecting with one's own past and with others—and then using those meanings to impart a spin on the future social structures—that is, to fully experience soul.

From this long journey we feel we have come a little closer to "operationalizing" the development of an interior self who can learn to connect with others and pattern what Ruti (2006) might call a "reinvention of soul." We did this through (a) storytelling, (b) dreaming and (c) concrete action to put our dreams into effect. In times of great systemic stress, we believe these same steps can and must be taught in schools as tools to prepare future citizens to rebuild the infrastructure of a traumatized society and renew the democracy. It is by dreaming of positive change and then taking steps—in collaboration with others—to effectuate that dreamed of change that the actor truly becomes "an agental subject." These youth will not only come of age as full citizens but also acquire the collective capacity to heal the soul of a nation.

So what would a civil society in a "democracy for the subject" look like? Once we saw what was possible in our recently completed projects, we find more hopes and dreams nudging at us like the gentle waves lapping the shore of a cool, clear mountain lake. We see in the offing a new Constitutional amendment reversing the usurpation of representative democracy by the Supreme Court case of *Citizens United*; a World Congress of Participatory Democracies embraced by the United States; a flipping of the current national education policy away from top down content control and lack of funding to the inverse funding of under-resourced school districts nationally while leaving to local districts the responsibility for control of content; a designation of 1% of the federal budget to support the arts, music and performativity for distribution and control by local communities; and the widespread adoption of intersubjective storytelling and music in schools nationwide.

Accordingly, we are convinced *it is toward complementarity and mutual immanence that U.S. public education must next direct its considerable resources* if the United States is to ever bind together an increasingly diverse public and renew the democracy. What this means is that the future prospects for soul creation and civil society are more intertwined than ever before: in a larger sense, this is the onset of a new imaginary.

So what had begun for us as a dual storytelling exercise ripened into a far broader wish for a wholly new democracy and a more formal treatment of the self as an agent not just of one's own meanings but also of positive social change. As a result of this autoethnographic demonstration project, we hope that other researchers will want to explore their own inclinations to construct, *as subjects in mutuality with each other*, the precursors to a truly democratic social infrastructure that will accommodate their own needs and dreams.

Out of our dual storytelling thus comes an uplifting possibility: that if two people from very different socioeconomic and cultural backgrounds can come to share their stories—walking together, or *caminando juntos* (Flores, 2008)—then perhaps future U.S. leaders might benefit from learning the techniques of storytelling and dreaming while they are still young and in school or college. Indeed, what if an entire society could learn to do this? Under a mutual coming into being of this magnitude, the words of the Tojolabal in Chiapas could well acquire special purchase in an increasingly diverse United States, where at least two individuals from different backgrounds and histories can now declare *Todos somos Ramona* ("We are all Ramona!").

REFERENCES

Arratia, M. I. (1997). Daring to change: The potential of intercultural education in Aymara communities in Chile. *Anthropology & Education Quarterly, 28*(2), 229–250.

Arroyo, L. (In press). Mutual immanence in a year-long kindergarten curriculum. In G. Tanaka & S. Koo, Eds. (In press). *How to end racism in America: Teaching mutual immanence.* New York, NY: Peter Lang Publishing.

Austin-Fitts, C. (2016). Pyramid of lies could implode. Interviewed by Greg Hunter, *USAWatchdog. com* (March 6, 2016).

Baiocchi, G. (2003). Participation, activism and politics: the Porto Alegre experiment. In A. Fung & E. O. Wright (Eds.). *Deepening democracy: Institutional innovations in empowered participatory governance.* London: Verso.

Bartlett, L., & Vavrus, F. (2014). Transversing the vertical cased study: A methodological approach to studies of educational policy as practice. *Anthropology & Education Quarterly, 45*(2), 231–247.

Beverly, J. (2004). *Testimonio: On the politics of truth.* Minneapolis, MN: University of Minnesota Press.

Booze, R. (2006). *Teaching Kujichagulia: Mentoring strategies for African American females in predominantly white colleges and universities.* Paper presented at the annual meeting of the National Conference on Race and Ethnicity.

Bremmer, I. (2009). State capitalism comes of age: The end of the free market? *Foreign Affairs*, May/ June 2009.

Celente, G. (2016). Gerald Celente just issued one of his most prescient trend alerts of 2016. In *KingWorldNews.com* (June 8, 2016).

Chagolla, S. (In press). Applying intersubjective methods to current frameworks in early childhood education. In G. Tanaka & S. Koo (Eds.), *How to end racism in America: Teaching mutual immanence.* New York, NY: Peter Lang Publishing.

Chang, H. (2008). *Autoethnography as method.* Walnut Creek, CA: Left Coast Press.

Cochran-Smith, M. (2005). No child left behind: 3 years and counting. *Journal of Teacher Education, 56*(2), 99–103.

Couldry, N. (2004). In place of a common culture, what? *The Review of Education, Pedagogy, and Cultural Studies, 26*, 3–21.

Cruz, C. (2006). *Testimonio narratives of queer street youth: Toward an epistemology of the brown body.* Dissertation in education filed at UCLA.

Cruz, C. (2001). Toward an epistemology of the brown body. *International Journal of Qualitative Studies in Education, 14*(5), 657–699.

Deantoni, N. (2004). *The Freirean approach to education and participatory democracy in Porto Alegre, Brazil.* Paper presented at the annual meeting of the American Educational Research Association, April 2004. San Diego, CA.

Diamond, J. (2005). *Collapse: How societies choose to fail or succeed.* New York, NY: V Liking.

Duran, E. (2006). *Healing the soul wound: Counseling with American Indians and other native peoples.* New York, NY: Teachers College Press.

D'Urso-Cunningham, G. (In press). Intersubjective storytelling at a teen pregnancy center. In G. Tanaka & S. Koo (Eds.), *How to end racism in America: Teaching mutual immanence.* New York, NY: Peter Lang Publishing.

Fabian, J. (2002). *Time and the other: How anthropology makes its object.* New York, NY: Columbia University Press.

Farrell, P. B. (2010). Doomsday capitalism. *MarketWatch*.com (October 19, 2010), 4 pp.

Ferguson, N. (2008). *The ascent of money: A financial history of the world.* New York, NY: Penguin Books.

Flores, R. (2008). *Chicano artists and Zapatistas walk together asking, listening, learning: The role of transnational informal learning networks in the creation of a better world.* Ph.D. Dissertation, Rossier School of Education, University of Southern California.

Foucault, M. (1976/1990). *The history of sexuality: An introduction, Vol. 1.* New York, NY: Vintage Books.

Fung, A. (2003). Deliberative democracy, Chicago style: Grass roots governance in policing and public education. In A. Fung & E.O. Wright (Eds.), *Deepening democracy: Institutional innovations in empowered participatory governance*. London: Verso.

Gailey, C. (1987). *Kinship to kinship: Gender hierarchy and state formation in the Tongan Islands*. Austin, TX: University of Texas Press.

Garcia, M. E. (2005). *Making indigenous citizens: Development and multicultural activism in Peru*. Stanford, CA: Stanford University Press.

Giroux, H. (2004). *The terror of neoliberalism: Authoritarianism and the eclipse of democracy*. Boulder, CO: Paradigm Publishers.

von Greyerz, E. (2016). Global chaos and the road to $1,000 silver. KingWorldNews.com (December 11, 2016).

Grubb, N. (2005). Everything I really need to know I learned in Helsinki. *Los Angeles Times*, June 5, 2005.

Guano, E. (2002). Spectacles of modernity: Transnational immigration and local hegemonies in neo-liberal Buenos Aires. *Cultural Anthropology*, *17*(2), 181–209.

Guston, D. H. (1999). Evaluating the first U.S. consensus conference: The impact of the citizens'panel on telecommunications and the future of democracy. *Science, Technology & Human Values, 24*(4), 451–482.

Hornberger, N. (2000). Bilingual education policy and practice in the Andes: Ideological paradox and intercultural possibility. *Anthropology & Education Quarterly, 31*(2), 173–201.

Isaac, T.M & Heller, P. (2003). Democracy and development: Decentralized planning in Kerala. In A. Fung & E.O. Wright (Eds.), *Deepening democracy: Institutional innovations in empowered participatory governance*. London: Verso.

Johnson, C. (2008). The end of the black American narrative. *The American Scholar, 77*(3), 32–42.

Kim, J. S. & Sunderman, G. L. (2005). Measuring academic proficiency under the No Child Left Behind Act: Implications for educational equity. *Educational Researcher*, 34(8) 3–13.

Krieger, M. (2016). What's starting now will overturn the entire system: Complete collapse of everything. Interviewed by Greg Hunter, *USAWatchdog.com*, July 3, 2016.

Lancy, D. F. (2006). Book review of Eva Poluha (2004). *The Power of Continuity. Anthropology & Education Quarterly*, June 9, 2006.

Lenkersdorf, C. (1996). *Los hombres verdaderos: voces y testimonionos Tojolabales*. Mexico: Siglo Ventiuno Editores.

Lipman, P. (2004). *High stakes education: Inequality, globalization, and urban school reform*. New York, NY: Routledge.

Manarino, G. (2016). Collapse of empires is upon us. Interviewed by Greg Hunter, *USAWatchdog. com* (July 6, 2016).

Marcos, S. (2007). In E. K. Galactico (Eds.), *Beyond resistance: Everything*. An interview with sub-comanadante insurgente. Marcos: Paper Boat Press.

Menchu, R. (1983). *I, Rigoberta Menchu: An Indian woman in Guatemala*. London: Verso.

Ortner, S. B. (1995). Resistance and the problem of ethnographic refusal. *Comparative Studies in Society and History, 37*(1), 17–193.

Pateman, C. (1970). *Participation and democratic theory*. Cambridge: Cambridge University Press.

Poluha, E. (2004). *The power of continuity: Ethiopia through the eyes of its children*. Stockholm, Sweden: Norkiska Afrikasinstitutet.

Popkewitz, T. (1998). *Struggling for the soul: The politics of schooling and the construction of the teacher*. New York, NY: Teachers College Press.

Reed-Danahay, D. E. (1997). Introduction. In D. E. Reed-Danahay (Ed.), *Auto/Ethnography: Rewriting the self and the social*. Oxford: Berg.

Ricoeur, P. (1992). *Oneself as another*. Chicago: University of Chicago Press.

Roberts, P. C. (2016). Massive social instability, warns of economic collapse. Interviewed on *KingWorldNews.com* (July 8, 2016).

Roubini, N., & Mihm, S. (2011). *Crisis economics: A crash course in the future of finance*. New York, NY: Penguin Press.

Ruti, M. (2006). *Reinventing the soul: Posthumanist theory and psychic life*. New York, NY: Other Press.

Smith, L. T. (1999). *Decolonizing methodologies: Research and indigenous peoples*. London: Zed Books.

Solnit, R. (2010). *A paradise built in hell: Extraordinary communities that arise in disaster*. New York, NY: Penguin Books.

Taleb, N. N. (2007). *The black swan: The impact of the highly improbable*. New York, NY: Random House.

Tanaka, G. (2002). Higher education's self-reflexive turn: Toward an intercultural theory of student development. *Journal of Higher Education, 73*(2), 263–296.

Tanaka, G. (2003). *The intercultural campus: Transcending culture and power in American higher education* (231pp). New York, NY: Peter Lang Publishing.

Tanaka, G. (2007). U.S. education in a post-9/11 world: The deeper implications of the current systemic collapse of the Neoliberal regime. In K. Saltman (Ed.), *Schooling and the Politics of Disaster*. New York, NY: Routledge.

Tanaka, G. (2009). The elephant in the living room that no one wants to talk about: Why U.S. anthropologists are unable to acknowledge the end of culture. Reflection From the Field. *Anthropology & Education Quarterly, 40*(1), 82–95.

Tanaka, G. (2015). On collapse and the next U.S. democracy: Elements of applied systemic research. *Anthropology & Education Quarterly, 46*(4) 319–338.

Tanaka, G., Johnson, P., & Hu, N. B. (2001). Creating an intercultural campus: A new approach to diversity. *Diversity Digest, Winter, 2001*, 6–7.

Thompson, M (In press). Intersubjective "digital storytelling" as a vehicle for social change: Late elementary and early junior high age students. In G. Tanaka & S. Koo (Eds.), *How to end racism in America: Teaching mutual immanence*. New York, NY: Peter Lang Publishing.

Toscano, T. (In press). Everybody has a story: Teaching intersubjectivity in the second and third grades. In G. Tanaka & S. Koo (In Press). *How to end racism in America: Teaching mutual immanence*. New York, NY: Peter Lang Publishing.

Touraine, A. (2000). *Can we live together? Equality and difference*. Stanford, CA: Stanford University Press.

Viego, A (2007). *Dead subjects: Toward a politics of loss in Latino studies*. Durham, NC: Duke University Press.

White, M., & Epston, D. (1990). *Narrative means to therapeutic ends*. New York: W.W. Norton.

Wood, D. R. (2000). Narrating professional development: Teachers' stories as texts for improving practice. *Anthropology & Education Quarterly, 31*(4), 426–448.

Epilogue

(U)ltimately, if we want to see change, we must force it through. If we want to have a better world, we can't hope for an Obama, and we should not fear a Donald Trump. Rather, we should build it ourselves.

Edward Snowden on *Zero Hedge*, November 10, 2016[1]

1 Snowden, E. (2016). Addresses the U.S. election result in public webcast. Zero Hedge, November 10, 2016.

In Any Infrastructure Rebuilding, the Step That Comes Before Action Is Dreaming

GREGORY K. TANAKA

In a full blown "systemic collapse"—the breakdown of a human society's largest social institutions—those of us who do work in education and anthropology are presented with a challenge for which we as a subfield are richly suited. We tend to do *applied* work and as such, *are predisposed to building something new*. But in making contributions that match up against the magnitude of human need today, *how would we take that first step?*

A preliminary question, then, is whether we as applied researchers in the public interest will be caught in this propitious moment worshipping old research epistemologies and methodological registers—or instead be willing to alter the reach and aim of our work to match the size and scale of the task before us. The overall approach urged at the end of this book is therefore one of "bottom-up model building"—performed first in local communities and then directed ultimately to being replicated nationwide at the macro or systemic level. Twelve such models are presented in this section as potential exemplars for this inviting new era of experimentation in bottom-up democratic renewal. While all are promising models, they each began as a "dream," as an idea that today remains brilliant, inchoate and still "unformed," utopian and pure in its aim to be democratic, and thus pregnant with possibility. Readers are invited to join in the uplifting and exciting project of reclaiming America's democracy by offering dreams of your own.

—December 28, 2018

"The Eden Project"

SHANE MALDONADO

As an urban cyclist, I am usually the first to begrudgingly "down talk" cyclists and shake a very literal fist at their lack of courtesy, inability to observe basic traffic laws, and overall sense of entitlement over drivers. As a result, I don't feel a sense of camaraderie or community towards cyclists even though I have been actively shifting my life towards self-sustainability on a bike for over seven years. This journey has allowed me to cover 100 miles a day for weeks at a time and haul 150 pounds of supplies up and over 8,000 foot mountains at a 25% grade.

I think my feeling of alienation within the cycling community is a perfect example of the very real degradation of community and shared meaning—culture—within the United States today. While we may share the same morning commute or even live on the same block, we would much rather lock ourselves in our modern bunkers, turn on our internet capable electronics, and wash it all down with genetically modified convenience food.

What I refer to as The EDEN Project is in essence not a reclaiming of the "original" capitalistic promise of social responsibility, but *the conscious deconstruction of capitalism through capitalist practices*. Under the current capitalist system, new norms and values are established by way of domination—in which "original" shared norms and values are destroyed. What results is a ravaging, hate-filled dogmatic form of establishing cultural values (Bridges, 2001, p. 71). But a new model of capitalism would call for socially responsible businesses to utilize excess profits to purchase neighborhoods from banks and private businesses that have been exploiting and exacerbating the marginality of the working poor.

This model of buying back land—and re-instituting productivity of those lands via farming, permaculture and other productive uses—encourages community building and alleviates two major issues that challenge economic stability in high need communities: *(1) stable housing and (2) access to healthy and affordable food.* "Instead of focusing our efforts on bringing in tomatoes year-round…we should focus on making (citizens in all local communities) able to feed (themselves) now and in the future" (Lionette, 2007, p. 117).

Cutting and eliminating the cost of housing and food opens up the little in economic resources that these families do have to reinvest in the community—and overall national spending—without the utilization of the credit/debt-based model which now represents 90% of the GDP. Through community building, another implicit goal of The EDEN Project is to deconstruct the current animosities toward others harbored in neighborhoods nationwide and *encourage the reclaiming of community spaces for the sake of communities.* The EDEN Project seeks to dismantle notions of "othering" and internalized oppression and, instead, like the Aborigine, encourage communities to spend the 40 plus hours (otherwise wasted at work) in dreaming and culture building activities.

Where once elders, in story and ritualistic form, laid down the basic rules and beliefs of a given society, today's "institutionalized education" via No Child Left Behind and Common Core Standards, for example—and globalization of the economy—aims to rid the world of this ancient past-time and its rich local knowledge system. In fact, my view is that *the absence of cultural meaning and community*—which I also register on the road in biking—has led to the very real societal decay we face today. The already apparent decay of meaning is then exacerbated by the forced duality of "the have's and have-not's" which marks the have-not's as deficient and losers.

Renegotiating the roles of individuals in the "post-financial capitalist" society will be central to the sustainability of communities. Where currently individuals and family units are dependent on wages earned through work, the "necessities based society" will redirect the work force to trades, culture building, and food production activities. *The essence of my utopian ideal is a digressionist model where society is systematically returned to the once dominant agrarian, hunter-gatherer style community, albeit with a modern twist.* With the elimination of the financial capitalist system, specialist groups will work together to bring materials and manufacturing to fruition because they possess the passions, drives and skill sets to work on projects that enhance the community—and not for personal gain. In this way, the EDEN Project proposes to realign consumerism to match up directly with human need.

My beliefs are inspired by real life communities that instill the importance of cross-generational and cross-culture building. My first exposure to one way that America can begin to engineer such a shift occurred during my first trip to Barcelona, Spain in 2007. Coming from an extremely low-income Puerto Rican family, I had never dreamed of being able to travel to Europe. But I did and when I arrived in Barcelona in late August, the Festival de Gracias was in full swing. For one whole week, each block decorated their street with a previously chosen theme. I saw "California Dreaming" complete with *papier mache* "Surfer Dudes," surfboards, and a stage for a "Battle of the Bands."

But the most striking feature of this celebration was when the clock struck 10 PM. The stages were cleared away, the Surfer Dudes pushed to the side, and road tables were set up the length of the block. Each family brought out food—traditional dishes of their own choosing—to share with others and ate together every night of that festival week. As an American, my first thought was "That will NEVER happen in America!" I recalled the words of a thinker who wrote "Once we recognize how hegemonic cultural values have warped our own consciousness, we can actively resist these damaging influences by adopting an alternative episte-mology" (Zhang, 2011, p. 90). And so my next thought was "How can I make this happen in America?"

While I may never bond with every cyclist in the world, I now know that community begins with an individual's choice to be more receptive to the greater needs of the community, actively contribute to a renewal of the manifestation of culture, and as noted by Lorenz (2001, p. 497), rupture those naturalizing forces that push difference into the margins.

REFERENCES

Bridges, F. W. (2001). *Resurrection song: African-American spirituality*. Maryknoll, New York: Orbis Books.

Lionette, J. (2007). A view from behind the counter. In V. Shiva (Ed.), *Manifestos on the future of food and seed*. Cambridge, MA: South End Press.

Lorenz, H. S. (2001). Thawing the hearts, opening a path in the woods, founding a new lineage. In G. E. Anzaldua & A. L. Keating (Eds.) *This bridge we call home: Radical visions of transformation*. New York, NY: Routledge.

Zhang, L. (2011). Breaking our chains: Achieving NOS/OTRAS consciousness. In A. L. Keating & G. Gonzalez-Lopez (Eds.), *Bridging: How Gloria Anzaldua's life and work transformed our own*. Austin, TX: University of Texas Press.

SunUp and the Educators' Renewal Consortium (ERC)

MERRITT RICHMOND

With drastic cuts across the board in our country's education spending, as well as specific cuts to the arts, I would like to reconsider how to bring critical educational experiences to our children. As we see our schools teeter on the brink of an even more definitive failure than in years past, it is time begin "a work around." This project, the *Educators' Renewal Collaborative (ERC), explores the possibility of designing an alternative source of educational experiences for children—a hybrid between an interactive classroom, a field trip, an after-school enrichment program, and camp.*

It is a hybrid organization that at once borrows successful models for working with children and igniting their passion for learning, yet recombines and rebuilds them in such a way that the word "school" hardly applies. We will be rebranding the process of educating our children, calling into question many of the orthodoxies that plague our public schools and so often hold our educators (and our children!) hostage to outdated, unsuccessful, spirit-sapping experiences.

The heart of this project is an umbrella organization that will research and compile successful models of education from here and abroad. "Successful models" are those that:

*Develop in our children critical thinking skills, creativity and the capacity to work both independently and collaboratively;

*Engage our young people in the vital activities of human society—especially the arts;

*Explore the various approaches in education to achieving peace including mindfulness, cultural studies, community engagement, and interpersonal problem solving.

Examples of potential educational philosophies to support this include Montessori, Reggio Emilia, Quaker (Society of Friends), Summerhill, and current arts-based curricula. The functions of the ERC will include *curating a virtual library for use by participating school staff, hosting educator workshops, webinars and conferences to disseminate new approaches, the forging of partnerships with schools and districts to pilot innovative programs, and testing models that offer refreshing, empowering and relevant experiences in a lab setting* for school staff to observe and try out the new methodologies themselves.

SUNUP

One of our first projects I would like to personally launch is an innovative program-delivery and teacher-renewal project called "SunUp." The SunUp project begins with a partnership between ERC and a specific school. The partnership members work collaboratively to identify an area for needed staff development. The ERC could provide support as minimal as facilitating the conversation among administrators about what should be the focus of staff development or providing resource materials for it. Or, the ERC could develop and implement the entire professional development piece for the school. Drawing from its resources, ERC will be a full-service professional development "shop" for school administrators and provide both traditional resources like workshops and written materials and also mentorship, demonstration lessons, movies, visits to other schools, and whatever other innovative tools for reflection and renewal the team members can dream up.

The other critical component of SunUp is the direct delivery of educational services to students at the partner site. These classes will have three purposes. First, they will offer innovative, fun, creative and challenging educational experiences to the children served. Second, SunUp classes will help to carve out time for professional development for the regular staff at the partner school. *While SunUp teachers engage with the students, the staff at the partner school will be free from classroom responsibilities and able to focus on meaningful professional development* towards a renewal of their teaching practice. This brings us to the third purpose: teachers at the school can observe class to learn from the SunUp curriculum, meet with SunUp educators or their colleagues at the school in professional development contexts, or visit other schools off-site to observe examples of innovative curricula and/or delivery of services.

Imagine a group of mixed-age students spread out on the yard doing Tai Chi with a SunUp teacher and ERC member, while next door in the cafeteria a smaller group of K-3rd graders are making pancakes to serve to the whole school for breakfast. Down the hall in a third grade classroom, an older group of students from 4th through 6th grade is rehearsing for a debate on the potential for change that the Occupy Wall Street movement represents. Their SunUp teacher is a local judge who volunteers his time two mornings a week before he is due to appear in court. Meanwhile, staff members at this little school are busy collaborating on the day's lesson, planning how they will differentiate the lesson for their wide array of students, and reflecting upon the success of their new "learning commons" space created in the school's former computer lab.

The SunUp concept infuses needed energy into our classrooms first thing in the morning, offering our teachers and staff an immediate cure to any malaise or negativity in their current environment. It can also be designed to create a longer school day. For instance, schools with late start times that have some form of morning care for their students would be able to implement SunUp classes before the official beginning of the school day. Because many of our most marginalized and underserved students end up in morning care, there is a small window of opportunity for innovative and inspiring curricula to meet their needs right now.

Drawing upon interested members of the larger community, and fitting in these classes first thing in the morning before many citizens are required to be at their desks, we can imagine—and construct—a portal into a creative and collaborative world of education.

Education—Funding and Systems

EMILY KAPLOWITZ

In 2012 the public school system in Maryland was ranked #1 for the fourth straight year (marylandpublicshools.org). Throughout the 1990's, Maryland had received substantial funding for specific purposes (teacher professional development, low-income students, special education students, etc.). These funds were set to run out in 2001. Recognizing that this funding was crucial to the survival of the schools and that testing was about to become a graduation requirement, *the Maryland school system took it upon itself to make substantial changes in how it allocated money to schools* (mlis.state.md.us). The Commission of Education Finance, Equity and Excellence (Thornton Commission) was established to (1) review the current school finance system and accountability measures and (2) make recommendations regarding adequate school funding in public schools. *The Thornton Commission concluded that the state needed to establish performance standards for students and schools and provide adequate funding to meet these standards*, and that school systems and students needed to be held accountable if they did not meet the standards.

A study was conducted to determine how much money was required to support each student. The study found that *certain student populations required more funding*: e.g., low income, special education, English language learners, etc. This year's Kirwan Preliminary Report (Jan 2018) urges increases in per pupil (K–12) spending of:

K–12 enrollment × base per pupil cost × 1.58
Special education enrollment × base per pupil cost × 1.91
Free and reduced price meal enrollment × base per pupil cost × 1.35
Limited English proficiency enrollment × base per pupil cost × 1.35
Full-day pre-K × base per pupil cost × 1.29

Another issue that came to light was that of equity (see, e.g., Mosteller, 1997). At the time of this commission, schools were receiving money from the federal, state and local governments. This meant that wealthier counties were receiving more money per capita. *In 2002, a wealth equalization formula was put into place, which took into account how much money local governments were providing and equalized that amount through the amount that the state provided.* What emerged was the "Bridge to Excellence in Public Schools Act of 2002" (mlis.state.md.us).

UTOPIA

In my utopian society, every school in the United States will benefit from an approach to financing education similar to Maryland's. Equality will be key when deciding how much money to give to schools. Once the issue of school funding is settled, schools will examine curricula. K-5 programs will have an emphasis on reading, math, science, history and foreign language. Art, music and PE will be scheduled into the school week. Storytelling will also be a part of the curriculum. Elementary and middle school students will work on storytelling projects that provide them multiple opportunities for students to share their stories, culminating in a publication of the students' stories (see, e.g., Guajardo, Guajardo & Casaperalta, 2008).

The elementary school will act as a community center as well as an education center. Parents and family members will also have access to programs such as GED classes, time management workshops, financial literacy and other support services they feel necessary. The middle school curriculum will be similar but there will be an increased emphasis on career and college. Once students enter high school they will continue to learn what they had been learning but will be encouraged to narrow and deepen their scope of learning in areas that interest them. College will be free for students who agree to work in public service (government, teaching, non-profits, etc.) for at least two years after graduation.

TIMELINE

In Maryland, the commission took two years to study the public school budgets and determine the formula for spending per student. *The legislation also called for the State to increase funding to public schools by 75% over six years.* My proposal is to give states three years to conduct financial analyses of their school systems and have outside panels review the studies. Each state will receive funding to do this from the Race to the Top budget. At the close of three years, states will each have a proposal of how much they need per child including the multiplier indices for factors like a child being on free or reduced lunch requiring more funding than a student who is not.

The commissions will also suggest a way to raise the money necessary to provide this funding. (For instance, in Maryland the government added a 37 cents tax to cigarettes in order to raise a portion of the money.) States will need to propose and enact this new budget within three years of receiving the money for research from the federal government.

This model provides a sustainable, universal and affordable alternative to our current and unequal system for funding schools linked to the community real estate tax base. It also provides a working alternative to charter schools, while providing many of the local and community-based benefits that the smaller charter schools extend to their students.

BIBLIOGRAPHY

Class size matters (n.d.). http://classsizematters.org/wp-content/uploads/2012/11/STAR.pdf

Guajardo, M., Guajardo, F., & Casaperalta, E. D. C. (2008). Transformative education: Chronicling a pedagogy for social change. *Anthropology & Education Quarterly, 39*(1), 3–22.

Maryland public schools (n.d.). www.marylandpublicschools.org

Mosteller, F. (1997). The Tennessee study of class size in the early school grades. *The Future of Children,* 5(2), 113–127.

Public schools facilities (n.d.). http://mlis.state.md.us/other/education/public schools facilities/ Presentation 091802.pdf

Rethinking Education: A Moral Imperative

JAGUANANA LATHAN

I was born and raised in the Bay Area with a tight knit immediate and extended family. I attended public and Catholic elementary and middle schools and graduated from a public high school. I have experienced both poor and high quality education. The difference in experience, in my opinion, was the teachers' belief in the community and children they served.

Fast forward to high school...On September 21, 1992 I became a teenage mother (eleventh grade). I had a healthy baby boy. On my first day back to school after giving birth I was told by my white male counselor that attending a traditional high school would be a waste of time and that I should pursue my education at the local continuation school, and maybe, just maybe would then be able to attend community college. I did not accept the fate he proposed and chose to continue attending the high school. I am glad that I did not give up or fall into the stereotype that society and the school system had tried to force on to my life.

Being a single parent is rough. Being a single parent of an African American boy I would argue is even tougher. It's not that African American males somehow come out of the womb different from any other male child; it's the societal factors that make an impact on the lives of the children and families. When growing up, my son had academic challenges that made it difficult for him to grasp written complex information. He was also diagnosed with ADHD and ADD. Over the years I watched as he struggled with school, dropped out, and then went back. I advocated for him and I struggled with him. The education system simply did not allow him to make developmentally appropriate mistakes (social or academic), nor did the school system aspire to understand him or his learning style. Ultimately, like with many other African American males, regardless of the socio-economic status, the educational system was inequitable and intolerant. As a result of these experiences, *my passion is to eliminate inequitable systems and replace them with systems that are supportive of children of color and all children that are educated in urban areas.*

But how can we change these inequitable practices and create an ideal society that is intentional in its practices toward equity for all? In my dream of a better world, there is a "moral sentiment" (e.g., Smith, 1759/2009) that stems from a place of spirituality about the American vision. What this means today is that there must be the birth of a radical new ideology, the rise of a movement bent on transforming society based on that ideology—and the confirmation and perhaps even deification of that new kind of leadership (see, e.g., Burns, 1978). According to Burns, there are three stages to a transforming revolution: (1) the birth of a vision, (2) a demonstrated commitment to the vision by the leaders, and (3) a powerful sense of mission of end-values (id at 202).

The problem, in my view, is that the U.S. education system has merely attempted reform and always fallen short of the full "transformative revolution" required. No Child Left Behind was, for example, intended to hold educators accountable for the education of all students. However, the policy did not lead to wide-spread successful practice but instead perpetuated a failing education system. In my view, the vision we need for societal transformation is a kind of "cultural shift," both in the way we think about the quality of life and in the belief that each person in a democracy deserves the highest possible quality of education regardless of life experiences s/he brings to the education process.

The new leader will demonstrate her/his commitment to a more just U.S. society by shifting our current paradigm (Kuhn, 1962) to one where leaders truly wish to humbly serve others and act on behalf of the public moral sentiment. So this is both a cultural shift and a moral shift to a belief system in which power is shared and the decision-making practice is one of "participatory governance" where value is placed on advocating for local community needs and youth are educated in how to navigate and become leaders in their local political system. There will be some conflict during this "paradigm shift" as many people will not understand why this surge in new leadership forms is occurring (e.g., Kuhn, 1962).

There will be groups of people who have historically taken ownership of resources, education, and financial wealth who will not eagerly share what they believe they are entitled to. However, the truly bold and responsible leader will commit and press on for the benefit of all the people. These leaders will be found in all sectors of the current job force—teachers, administrators, police officers, doctors, prosecutors, gang members, politicians, bankers and CEOs—and begin to articulate what positive social change looks like: even doing so under ridicule and persecution. Participatory governance will thus require those in all walks of life to help shape and "operationalize" this new public sentiment. It will require people to think about more than just themselves. That's the American dream that I believed in the day I decided to finish my public high school education and commit my life to helping others to do the same.

REFERENCES

Burns, J. M. (1978). *Leadership*. New York, NY: Harper & Row.

Smith, A. (1759/2009). *The theory of moral sentiments*. London: A. Strahan.

Kuhn, T. (1962). *The structure of scientific revolutions*. Chicago: University of Chicago Press.

Morality in Public Education: Evoking the Common Good

JACQUE ROBY

In my view, morality and ethics are the foundational principles that people need to make personal and professional decisions. Without a moral and ethical code, people can instead make decisions that only advance their singular personal interests rather than making decisions that will ultimately advance the common good. I contend that leaders in both the private and public sectors have an obligation to the society in which they operate to look out for those around them (see, e.g., Smith, 1759/2009). The kinds of values that I would hope to see in a morally grounded society will include (1) the importance of teaching creativity to all students, (2) room for variation among individuals at the *"micro"* level of the self, (3) a *"macro"* system that allows for feedback and public initiated reform, (4) the great importance of community organizations at the *"meso"* level that enable each citizen to have a "desire to matter, to be seen, to have someone believe in us" (Zacharias, 2011), and (5) the fundamental interconnectedness of humanity. When we see this…"clearly, when we feel it deeply, suddenly we're all the same" (*ibid.*).

Like Zacharias, I believe we are not all that different, regardless of the uniqueness of the individual, and the variety of cultures in a given society. The human spirit, desires, needs, and feelings are constant factors that separate all humanity from other living things, and allow us to dream and create an environment that makes cohabitation more perfect for us all. But this takes an awareness of each individual in relation to herself, the community and the environment. It is this person—of both personal *and* social agency—who can then participate in the governing decisions and communal interactions of everyday life, taking into consideration the role of personal responsibility, others' needs, and the functions of the private and public sectors.

Today we place so much emphasis on core subjects such as Math, Science, and English. But in a society where we are moving away from having one uniform set of religious values, *schools will need to assume the role of supplementing their emphasis on core subjects with the teaching of values that can fill this void in morality.* Individual states or school districts could work with parents and community members to decide which values to place in the curriculum—and these values could include ones that emphasize community, care of "the other," a strong work ethic, a better sense of identity, etc. By teaching a core curriculum in conjunction with values like these, *we give our children the gift of being able to perform (and act on) both interpretation and judgment—and thus reproduce within themselves their own "moral compass."*

While having our children cement the application of morality through project based and service learning—which I will not develop here—it is also likely that the final component to moral based teaching will need to include assessment. How do we do this? One way is to deploy a "Moral Based Teaching and Implementation Pyramid:"

Collaboration between state, teachers, students, and community members

Moral based curriculum creation

Collaborative identification and implementation of morality and values in core subjects

Project based and service learning

Essay/presentation of experiences

Assessment here is not performed "by administering a test" but rather by having students engage not only in their own learning but in reflective journaling they perform in combination with work to provide service to create real change in their local communities. Once students complete the project they have worked on throughout the year, there should be an opportunity for students to share their work with one another. The idea is for students to learn how to reflect upon their practices, and secondly, to be inspired by one another.

Morality plays a large role in the functioning of community and is the catalyst to motivation, reaction and interaction, which are ultimately components that drive community. Thus, it would behoove members to not only identify what moral beliefs they hold to be true, but then to challenge their beliefs in relation to the common good; that is, the key concept is that the self should always be aware of, and at the appropriate times yield to, what is collectively known to be the common good. Only socially and morally responsible citizens—and arising from that, a critically and politically active body—can ensure the democratic survival of this government.

REFERENCES

Smith, A. (1759/2009). *The theory of moral sentiments*. London: A. Strahan.

Zacharias, N. (2011). *The scent of water: Grace for every kind of broken*. Grand Rapids, MI: Zondervan.

Why a New Leadership Model Is So Important in This Time of Systemic Collapse: Adding "Initiator Training" to the Basic Curriculum

LARS HENRICH

A breakdown is the act or process of failing to function or continue; it becomes "systemic" when it is pertaining to or affecting a particular system. Further, one part of a system can create collapse in the entire system. In our case, the part that creates the collapse is the global capitalist economy and the leaders of this economy who bring down the whole of human society.

The failure of leadership models today is not a problem that arises from capitalistic doctrine itself, but rather from the absence of human morality. At the same time, capitalism makes it easy for this problem with morality to occur: capitalism cannot by itself evoke and maintain that semblance of morality. One result of this lack of morality in capitalism is that the financial and social consequences can be much more extreme than in any other economic system. *The problem I'm talking about is the missing moral core of leaders today.* It is this inability of leaders to learn or follow a moral compass that has created the greedy manner of business that undermines the idea of a free market and ruins the whole of human society. If you trace this thesis, you can instantly discern why existing leadership models fail at least as to the question of morality. To work, a new leadership model is required that addresses the micro level of individual morality and in a way that leads to change on the macro level of that society.

I want to focus here on a practical leadership theory that will be closely linked to what I am calling "Initiator Training." The goal will be to alter the future of both democracy and capitalism by changing the thinking of students who will be tomorrow's leaders. To begin this process I want to add one class to the curriculum of the public school system, which is accessible to everyone (rich or poor) and is ideally independent of corporation propaganda or manipulation. *The scheme is to create "Initiators"—those who will help to transform both their own lives and human society.* As intended here, the semantic difference between the words "Leader" (one person acting in solo) and "Initiator" (a person who can initiate change and do so in collaboration with others) is *to show that everyone has to work on the kind of change needed during post-collapse renewal—and that we have to do this work of initiating together.*

In this class, a good student will be someone who advocates both for her or himself and others; who takes initiative and accepts responsibility for loss; who believes the community is more important than the individual. *If practiced broadly, this resurgence of shared meaning or culture will become a global culture, a "culture of mankind."* No longer will humanity follow the path of seeking the benefit of one group to the exclusion of others.

I link this practice to the theorizing about leadership presented by Bass (see Bass & Avolio, 1994). Departing from the notion of the "leader" who directs an enterprise or organization from the top down, Bass extends the work of Burns (1978) by emphasizing the development of the "transformational leader" who more nearly "influences" the organization and in this way, occupies the position of a moral leader. In the eyes of Bass, the transformational leader or influencer has to be a moral compass for the rest of society. He or she must behave selflessly, provide meaning, stimulate creativity, and be a good listener, mentor and coach. What this means, in my view, is that utopia is not a change of system or resources or government so much as it is a change in individual attitude and thinking.

The intention of my "Initiator Training"—and possibly a breakthrough of sorts—is to launch this work via workshops or trainings in the K-12 school system. In other words, starting with the top leaders in the wealthy class may not bring about the change we need. In my view *we have to start the new leadership model from the bottom up.* Instead of "leaders and followers," everyone must become a part of the process that requires every individual's effort and creativity.

To launch this training, I want to add one or more classes to the curriculum of public schools. The idea will be to transform students into creators/initiators/influencers in their own lives and for the interests of larger society. In this class a good student will advocate for him or herself and others; be someone who takes initiative and accepts personal responsibility for loss; and be a person who believes community is more important than the individual.

To change the current problems facing human society will take a long time—probably a generation at least. But while this will not be a quick solution, the idea of creating transformational leaders through bottom-up "Initiator Trainings" is positioned to help humanity to collectively identify and address the massive, systemic problems of today and into the future.

REFERENCES

Bass, B. M., & Avolio, B. J. (Eds.) (1994). *Improving organizational effectiveness through transformational leadership*. Thousand Oaks, CA: Sage Publications.

Burns, J. M. (1978). *Leadership*. New York, NY: Harper & Row.

A Humanities-Based Approach to Education Reform

BENITA M. BAINES

In "Going Back to the Source," Greg Tanaka and Roberto Flores shared their perspective of a mutuality-based approach to human development and the heightened significance of that work during systemic distress. They argue the capacity to dream and share stories about a better world would be what is needed for a truly "deep" democracy (Fung & Wright, 2003). In sharing their stories of family upbringing and of their own research experiences, they put in motion and operationalize the counter-authoritarian ideas of such thinkers as Alain Touraine (2000) and Nicolas Couldry (2004) who have called for the construction of a new and more egalitarian public sphere. Through their sharing of stories and dreams, they also urge the democratic value of transition from "Lack" to self-worth through mutual reliance in soul creation (Ruti, 2006). What I propose is the use of "storytelling and agency-based pedagogies" as catalysts by which to prepare for the onset of that deep democracy.

The problem is that current pedagogic reform practices tend to focus more on the failures of our education system through increased external regulation (Nussbaum, 2010). In my way of thinking, that formula operates more like acts of "surveillance" that only promise a future with punitive outcomes. The better approach, in my opinion, would be to focus on what is working well locally and design new pedagogies, based on this, that address local community need. More specifically, our nation needs to reinvest in the kind of education reform that will cultivate the local expression of self, meaning and agency as foundations for participation in a truly "deep democracy" (Fung & Wright, 2003)—where all citizens can have input.

So *I will argue here for a "cultural and human development paradigm" that will operate in place of the current U.S. growth-oriented, capitalist model of wealth accumulation and unequal distribution.* Under a cultural and human development paradigm of pedagogic and curricular reform, education is not about the passive assimilation of facts but about challenging the mind to become active, competent, and thoughtfully critical in a complex world where students are informed by the humanities and not by the rush to produce for an overarching capitalist regime (Nussbaum, 2010).

In order for effective reform to occur then, we will need to go beyond just knowing and measuring outcomes. Instead, we will need to be able to see ourselves in the problem through a collective process that considers the person as a "soul" who can enjoy the groundedness that comes from telling one's personal story and in this way enjoy a connection with "other souls." In this way, a "storytelling pedagogy and curriculum" will serve as the antidote to atomizing effects of the New World Order scripted learning model. So rather than seeing people as instruments or objects of this capitalist project, *this way of knowing enacts a "culture of interconnectedness" that I believe will be the necessary prerequisite to a participatory and deep democracy.*

Once we begin as a society to share our stories, we can then launch a new model for democratic leadership that is "bottom-up" and produces meaning that is shared among the people. Such new and exciting democratic vehicles as "participatory public budgeting" (Baiocchi, 2003) and other forms of participatory governance require first having a population that acquires and appreciates a storytelling and vision sharing skill set. It is to this requirement of sharing of meaning that makes for a level of trust to work together and learn from each other.

To be sure, our Federal Reserve system has been out of control of late with a free-for-all kind of money printing policy that seems to lead only to greater public debt and greater wealth inequality in the United States and around the world. A lack of transparency about this is what has led to a great deal of public distrust of the political and financial system, to be sure. And that distrust has reached a point where it presages a global social and economic collapse. But it is not enough to criticize this irresponsible and undemocratic U.S. model of asymmetrical financialization. *This profound and ugly transformation of our* United States *and global economy is neither inevitable nor irreversible.* According to Gatto (2002/1992) who writes in "Dumbing Down: The Hidden Curriculum of Compulsory Schooling," change can occur within our education system that will teach U.S. citizens that a new alternative is possible for our democracy that derives from self-sufficiency—beginning with families and communities.

Following the leads from data in Chapter 3 in this book—where it was revealed in a study of 157 U.S. colleges and universities that a strong humanities emphasis strengthens the sense of community on a diverse campus—I propose a humanities driven approach to U.S. pedagogic and curricular reform that teaches students: (1) how to perform storytelling and dream of a better world (Tanaka & Flores, 1999),

(2) how in this way to reinvent the self/the soul, and (3) how this learned approach can be part of part of a larger process of remaking the democracy itself. In this way, pedagogic and curricular model building becomes a way to test the feasibility of new vehicles for a democratic renewal that is based on community building and intercultural.

REFERENCES

Baiocchi, G. (2003). Participation, activism and politics: the Porto Alegre experiment. In A. Fung & E. O. Wright (Eds.). *Deepening democracy: Institutional innovations in empowered participatory governance*. London: Verso.

Couldry, N. (2004). In the place of a common culture, what? *The Review of Education., Pedagogy and Cultural Studies*, 26(1), 3–22.

Fung, A. & Wright, E. O., eds (2003). *Deepening democracy: Institutional innovations in empowered participatory governance*. London: Verso.

Gatto, J. T. (2002/1992). *Dumbing us down: The hidden curriculum of compulsory schooling*. Gabriola Island, B.C., Canada: New Society Publishers.

Nussbaum, M. C. (2010). *Not for profit: Why democracy needs the humanities*. Princeton, NJ: Princeton University Press.

Ruti, M. (2006). *Reinventing the soul: Posthumanist theory and psychic life*. New York, NY: Other Press.

Tanaka, G., & Flores, R. (1999, May). *Caminando juntos*. Presented as paper entitled "Intersubjective Storytelling" at the annual meeting of the California American Studies Association, Santa Cruz, CA.

Touraine, A. (2000). *Can we live together? Equality and difference*. Stanford: Stanford University Press.

"Gamification" and Its Untapped Potential in U.S. Public Education

ANDREW URATA

While participating in a multiplayer online role-playing game called "Final Fantasy XI," it occurred to me, as a person who was learning to become a school teacher, that gaming is a fun and even riveting way to learn new things—even though it has not yet been formally added or annointed as a pedagogical tool for U.S. public schools. As this "light bulb" went on in my head, I realized there were many high-level terms and concepts I was learning through this particular game that I had never had the opportunity to learn from my own formal education. Could public schooling benefit from adding gamification as one of its many tools for the formal classroom?

WHAT IS GAMIFICATION?

"Gamification"—a term coined by Nick Pelling in 2002 (Marczewski, 2012)—refers to the use of theories from the video gaming industry to motivate people to be continually interested in the system and accomplish tasks *in the context of an action based video game*. In Final Fantasy XI, for example, it was possible for me to learn words like "enfeebling magic" which, based on my authentic learning in the game context, meant magic that weakens the enemy. Typically, gamification involves the use of specific motivational techniques such as "leveling up," acquiring "new skills," and earning "achievements"—which tap into an immediate kind of student motivation and sense of accomplishment that are characteristic benefits of gamification and can be overlooked by more traditional learning approaches.

WHY IS GAMIFICATION IMPORTANT AND TIMELY TODAY?

In today's society, we are attempting to close the achievement gap through the Common Core State Standards. What I now believe is that we should also be researching and considering the already existing high level of interest that children have today in video games. This is not to say that Common Core or any other type of state standards are the problem, but the implementation of them can be limited and confining—and even come to treat all children as all the same.

INDIVIDUALLY CUSTOMIZED MOTIVATION

In much of formal U.S. schooling, the students in each class are given the same mo-tivators at the same time and without consideration of what actually motivates them individually. Students rarely internalize what their objectives are and seldom even know the daily objectives. Furthermore, they are never able to choose their path of objectives. However, when students are given multiple ways to be motivated, there is a higher likelihood that they will be motivated in accomplishing tasks, because they will choose the motivating force that best appeals to them. In role-playing games that are part of the gamification experience, people identify and select all of their objectives and can accomplish them on their *own* terms and at their *own* pace. They can fail as many times as they need to complete their tasks, in effect, diminishing negative effects in their affective filter about the potential for failure.

HOW CAN IT BE IMPLEMENTED IN THE CLASSROOM?

Here are a few motivators obtained through video games that I know from expe-rience can be adapted for the classroom:

Skill-Tree—The "skill-tree" is a component in a game where the player can choose abilities or skills, and s/he is aware of what skills and abilities that can be learned further down the tree. This can be readily ap-plicable to education where students are traditionally often taught lessons without an understanding of the importance or context of what they learn.

Levels and leveling—The "leveling" component of a game is where the player is able to have a general idea of how strong s/he is and has become by moving up to a higher level in the game. The player is also given "experience points" for overcoming adversity. If applied in schools, students can take ownership of and acknowledge the growth they have made through the experience points they will have earned and levels they will have gained. One particular example of how they can earn experience points is by completing a "formative assessment" (wherein the student can decide *when* to be tested) via homework, a quiz, or an exit ticket.

Questing or Missions—"Questing" is when players are given tasks that are rewarded after completion. Teachers, parents, and peers, for example, can give academic or social tasks to students. One idea might be where students are invited to help at least five other students in a skill that you have already mastered; those students may then earn the title of "Peer Mentor" for completing the task.

A PROPOSED PROGRAM FOR SUCCESSFUL IMPLEMENTATION OF GAMIFICATION

There are three main aspects for this program that are necessary for success. The first aspect is *video instruction*. This allows for students to learn at their own pace and choose from whom and what they wish to learn. That being said, the videos need to have high production value to be engaging and intrinsically motivating to watch. The second aspect is *software production*. In order for the gamification and the personalized learning to occur, the software needs to be elegantly designed (efficient and free from software bugs) and the user-interface (UI) needs to be aesthetically pleasing and intuitive. The third aspect is *the physical learning environment*. Students need to have multiple modalities of learning available to them. This can be solved through kits designed to be used in conjunction with particular video lessons.

For optimal success, students will need to have 1-to-1 access to computers during academic learning. Major computer companies may wish to help fund the testing and roll-out of this new type of learning system as this would bring desirability to their brand name and instill future brand loyalty. While work has begun in one state with support from the MacArthur Foundation and the Bill and Melinda Gates Foundation (Corbett, 2010), further research is needed. To complement computer based learning, students would also need to continue to have opportunities for social and emotional development as well as physical education.

THE NEED FOR EMPIRICAL STUDIES

These are the steps that I foresee being needed to develop and test each model gamification program for use in public schools. Ideally, there will be two classrooms at each site (one being the "experimental" classroom where gamification is applied and the other being a "control" classroom where gamification is not employed).

1. Obtain development grant.
2. Pilot testing.
3. Followed up by implementation at multiple sites with different demographics.
4. Comparative data must be collected and will ideally show positive impacts from a gamification approach.
5. Obtain additional funding for the operation of an entire school using gamification once these ideas and implementation approaches have been fully tested and realized.

OTHER APPLICATIONS AND BENEFITS FROM GAMIFICATION

The high level of motivation associated with gamification can also make for *positive applications in homes, businesses, and communities*. At home, parents, spouses, and roommates can use similar ideas to promote health, organization, and a sense of community. In businesses, managers can reinforce good practice from employees—and businesses can increase client motivation for their product. In fact, many businesses have already applied such strategies: in a similar application, many have already introduced frequent buyer cards where clients gain points to win prizes or rewards. In communities, gamification sites can become a place in which people can meet with and learn from each other, perhaps in combination with learning the skills for direct participation in one's local, state, or national democracy.

In addition, it is my firm belief that once we get computers into classrooms, the addition of gamification as one tool among many will have the benefit of *"leveling the playing field"* and reducing any negative effects from the so-called "achievement gap" and other deficit-based interpretations of asymmetrical learning across economic and race-based demographic differences. The process of learning gamification will also expose to children the sophisticated application of computers when they might not normally have that opportunity at home. The availability of a gamification model like this—where children can in effect "scale up" their own learning at their own chosen speeds, no matter their demographic background—would make for a wonderful empirical study in its own right. Further, success in one area or function of learning is likely to have a "spillover effect" in that the confidence gained there can positively impact learning from other modalities in the curriculum. This too can be researched.

There is another potential benefit to using gamification in classrooms—and that is the great potential for this sequential and choice-based medium to teach children *how to develop both tactics and long-term strategies*. This skill set—which is really about exercising agency in decision-making—is one they can build upon and further develop for the rest of their lives. This is also a skill set that is not always taught formally in public schools.

POTENTIAL CHALLENGES

One of the greatest barriers to the broad use of gamification in schools is the amount of money, time, and effort that will be needed to fully research and successfully test the elements and features of the best possible gamification learning programs. Before rolling out a program on a large scale, researchers will want to identify and perfect the best possible approaches to video instruction, software production, and physical learning environment construction. While a gamification-based pedagogy may offer high promise as a concept, it will likely also require at least five years of successful implementation and testing at one site to prove its long term (and ideally cumulative) benefits. But this does not mean the effort should not be made as I feel the same deep and long-lasting motivation that I experienced as a "gamer" would translate well to the kind of classrooms that I have just begun to teach in and master myself as a new elementary school teacher.

In addition, my belief is that by simply beginning to use this program themselves, any teachers who were not already gamers will very quickly come to enjoy its benefits and this will help them to be better instructors as they use this approach in their own classrooms.

As I reflect further on this, I also realize I was motivated to continue playing Final Fantasy XI, because I found there were lasting benefits from playing this game. I *enjoyed* the learning process involved with that game and wanted to come back and learn more. The hope would be that children in U.S. schools will one day encounter the same positive feelings that I have and become "hooked" not just on gamification as a tool but on the rich possibilities that come from making one's own choices both now and for the rest of their lives.

REFERENCES

Corbett, S. (2010). Learning by playing: Video games in the classroom. *New York Times* (September 15, 2010).

Marczewski, A. (2012). *Gamification: A simple introduction*. Amazon Digital Services LLC.

Utopia

ADRIENNE D. OLIVER

Ricardo Emmanuel Rodriguez was never "good" at school. At home, with his family, he was a hero. His *abuelita* adored him. His younger *hermanas* worshipped him. His padre would depend on him to continue the family's construction business long after he was gone. When he was at home, Ricardo felt like a superhero. He had never understood why he didn't feel the same way in the classroom at school. His family had immigrated to America from Mexico when he was a toddler. He had learned to speak English in his first year in kindergarten. Now, at 16 he found himself often translating difficult conversations for his parents and *abuelita*.

"I just don't fit in here," Ricardo thought to himself silently as he stared at the teacher explaining the day's history lesson. It was Black History Month. He sat watching Mrs. Anderson move her long, black dreadlocks from one shoulder to the other. She was the first teacher to go beyond the normal line-up of Martine Luther King, Malcolm X, and Rosa Parks. But as engaging as the petite, caramel-complexioned teacher was with his class, he still felt uneasy.

WHY AGENCY?

Agency is not a foreign concept to students. Many assume agental roles in their families, serving as leaders and contributors to the household. As Freirean educators, it is important for us to illuminate how similar roles can be made available to students in the classroom. Studies have shown that minority students function better in the classroom when care is infused into teacher-student interactions (Noddings, 2012).

Yet the social norms of the classroom can stand in stark contrast to those students find at home, and without the metacognitive faculties to think critically about this, students can feel ill at ease in the classroom environment. What this means is that the teacher's role as an interpretive guide in such circumstances is paramount.

This paper presents a framework that will help teachers to incorporate this important role into their classroom work. Under this approach, teachers will adopt the position of "agency enablers"—by facilitating learning in a way that encourages students to assume ownership of their own learning and become agents of their own lives and social spheres. But in order to teach educational agency to students, teachers will need to learn how to do this in their pre- or in-service training. Toward that aim, this paper will outline *a three-part model for fostering agency in the classroom.*

Mrs. Anderson called Ricardo to her desk when the bell rang.

"Ricardo, do you have a minute?"

"I don't want to be late for chemistry class."

"How is that class going?"

"It's okay," Ricardo said. He didn't understand why his History teacher would be worried about how he was doing in Chemistry.

"Well, I notice that you did extremely well on your last essay."

"I did?"

"Yes, you did," Mrs. Anderson assured him. "I sure could use some of your thoughts contributing to class discussion."

Ricardo's essay had been a reflection on how the Japanese American experience related to his own history. He concluded that both Japanese American and Mexican American histories had been overlooked in traditional history books. But he was also conflicted. He wanted to show that Japanese Americans were proud of their history in the United States but it seemed like they didn't want to remember the part about the internment camps during World War II.

"Mrs. Anderson?"

"Yes, Ricardo?" The class had ended and he was the only student left in the classroom with Mrs. Anderson.

"Why do you think Japanese-American history isn't really taught that much?"

"That's a great question, Ricardo," Mrs. Anderson replied. "What do you think?"

He looked at her but did not have an answer.

"You know, you made some important connections in class between the way both Japanese-American and Latino-American histories had been overlooked in school," she began. "Why don't you think about writing an editorial for the school newspaper?"

"An editorial?"

"Yes," Mrs. Anderson nodded. "It's a section in the newspaper where anybody can have voice and say what they want. What you noticed about is something that everyone should think about."

"Really?"

"Really."

AGENCY REVISITED

While Freire (1970) had described oppression as a state of being in which a subject is subordinated to the will or force of an external agent, he also indicated that each subject can at some point become an agent in her own right. How might this occur? It was Ruti (2006, p. 69) who noted that a subject can build a "special kind of relationship" with the discourses and social structures in which she operates and "forge agency within constraint" (*ibid.*, p. 66). My contention is that the teacher step into the role of helping this to happen—to be agency enablers—by establishing the conditions that lead students to help each other to become subjects/agents who can make their own meanings and begin to take action on those meanings.

> *Dear America,*
> *Is there a reason why I am left out of your book?*
> *O say to you sing your song…no hook?*
> *Needle stuck on one word of eternal verse*
> *Merry-go-round lyrics*
> *In star-spangled hearse*
> *We tailgate you to our ancestor's grave*
> *Silenced tombstones where spirits parade*
> *We become clouds floating above your*
> *Blue earth*
> *Whether or not you see us*
> *We still have worth*
>   *By Ricardo Emanuel Rodriguez*

REFERENCES

Freire, P. (1970). *Pedagogy of the oppressed*. New York, NY: Continuum.

Noddings, N. (2012). The caring relation in teaching. *Oxford Review of Education, 38*(6), 771–781.

Ruti, M. (2006). *Reinventing the soul: Posthumanist theory and psychic life*. New York, NY: Other Press.

"A City of Villages"

JASON COOK-HARVEY

Through the lens of "Food Justice," my life-long vision is to organize people to establish cooperatively owned food businesses and related "eco-friendly" systems that utilize the local environment and economy to create and sustain a food system that produces healthy food at a fair cost and economic benefits for all peoples. At its core, Food Justice is an approach that aims to dismantle racism by empowering low-income communities and communities of color to increase their voice and participation in co-creating an equitable, sustainable, local food system that is linked directly to their neighborhood's needs. Depending on the geographic region, this food system consists of an interwoven network of businesses, community institutions, backyard and community gardens, community-supported kitchens, and processing centers along with other needed production facilities. This network will attack unemployment levels by creating green jobs, employment skills development opportunities and broader education for residents who participate, benefitting, in particular, low-income urban communities where job and educational opportunities are few. By starting up such projects in underutilized public and private spaces, these jobs can be easily scaled up to city or regional models because the skills required for these jobs will only require a high school education.

For over four decades, Food Justice movements have taken root across the country and around the world. Local and national food justice communities, which now consist of hundreds of individuals and organizations of various sizes, rely on comprehensive, diverse networks that consider dismantling racism as a core principal of the collective work. In bringing together community voices and social change agents from diverse sectors of the economy to work with local governments, change comes from "the bottom" and in this way brings about true sustainability within the community.

Overall, Food Justice advocates that all people, despite their race, class or income, have a human right to access healthy, sustainable food that nourishes bodies, communities and the local ecosystems on which they depend. From the soil where we plant the seeds, to the workers who harvest the produce, to the way we treat the livestock, to the corner store where people shop—we must radically rethink our current collective mindsets and take into account every element of our local food system and design it to meet each community's basic human needs. The best way to do this would be to intentionally empower city residents, at the neighborhood level, through local initiatives, to become the leaders in setting up businesses, education models and mechanisms that allow them to apply Food Justice principles to work together cooperatively to meet their community's need for food and other eco-friendly resources.

A vehicle for creating a more sustainable world and helping residents to organize will be what I call "A City of Villages" model, which will connect people with common interests to support long-term food production projects in their neighborhoods, and other related eco-friendly projects based on prioritized community needs. Importantly, the "City of Villages" model will be positioned to be an immediate, people-driven response matched to the social and cultural contours of each community (Watson, 2011). Moreover, a "City of Villages" works in collaboration with local businesses and institutions functioning in a coordinated effort in response to the rapid increase in preventable health disparities, the collapse of the modern industrial food system, impending economic recessions and climate change. By having people work together cooperatively on these projects, over time, neighborhoods can be formed into vibrant regions that emphasize ecological sustainability. To this end, in order to fulfill the vision of "A City of Villages" model, there must be an established and committed group, existing as a powerful network of individuals, organizations, businesses and community based entities, to support a collective region-wide vision where all are working toward achieving a shared goal over time.

In the end, the foundation for "A City of Villages" model relies on effective, transparent democratic governance led by the people where neighborhoods will ethically select their own leaders who will learn to shift their awareness and mindset to see cities as living ecosystems; a model that will ultimately lead to further community participation and a broader sense of democratic decision-making based on the living environment. The necessary changes needed for ecological sustainability are ultimately based on informed community participants who are joined together in a mutually dependent partnership to ensure that humanity and all planetary life can co-exist and thrive together. Using the "City of Villages" approach, people become activated and empowered to work within their local environment, with their neighbors, to cooperatively build vibrant hubs of business and social enterprises that emphasize ecological sustainability. In the long-term, in achieving this vision, people will not only become powerful in their commitment to one another, the environment, and their collective persistence (and sustenance), but this "City of Villages" model will also prepare its community members for the ensuing transformation that will come with the approaching collapse of the modern industrial food system, growing social inequalities, lasting economic recessions and global climate change.

REFERENCE

Watson, J. (2011, January 26). 11 for 11: Jason Harvey dreams big at Oakland Food Connection. *Oakland Local*.

Final Thought for the Evening Sky

STEPHEN GAWRYLEWSKI

What I am calling for is a greater presence of reflection in the actions we take as agents of change. Themes larger in scope such as individualism, entrepreneurship, power, fear, greed, and so forth are and have been given consideration by philosophers, politicians, social agents, and academics alike as problematic and often the source of our problems. But *are social and educational change agents—when using tools like philanthropy, startups, new education models and nonprofits—recognizing some of the larger social mechanisms at work behind the problems they are trying to address?*

CONTRA-DICTION

In my view, philanthropy and nonprofits are not solutions to a cause, but are ways of ameliorating the symptoms of the greater issues. What compounds the issue, for me at least, is that these social mechanisms operate under the same norms of the system they operate in, some of which are the same social mechanisms that created the very social woes they are trying to fight. Let me develop these two main criticisms a little further.

1. By lessening the effects of the social inequities in this system, or at least by trying mitigate them, they are, in my opinion, *allowing that which caused these social inequities to surface in the first place to perpetuate.* In essence, these social movements, though seen as an appropriate response to the unhealthy balance of power within this system, are in effect allowing that system of power to perpetuate itself. As the gap grows, so do the mechanisms that attempt to fill that gap. But, since they are

not geared towards eradiating the cause of their need, they allow that which caused it to also grow. It is, in a way, a symbiotic relationship. For example, philanthropy from foundations alone reached an approximate amount of $51 billion in 2012. In constant U.S. dollars, this is about a 30% increase since 2001 (Foundation Center, 2013). Yet, what has happened to the income gap during that time? It has increased by far more than that.

2. Based off of what I have witnessed, at least in the Bay Area, *there are norms at work behind these efforts and these are the same norms that have brought us here, namely entrepreneurships and the celebration of the individual.* Many people are trying to find their own creative solutions to problems. I applaud them in their efforts, their desire to help others, and their ingenuity. However, using the financial tools and social constructs of the system in which they are operating will severely hinder their ability to effect change on that system. Questioning the merits of a system is a good beginning, as is taking action to try and correct the disparities caused by a system. But, critical reflection upon methods used in these fields is essential and, in my opinion, lacking. Many efforts that fuel new education models, the financing of not for profit social change models, etc. are driven by capitalistic structures that, again, are motivated by that individualistic, entrepreneur spirit. Most ironic are those education initiatives that are trying to better prepare underprivileged youth to become successful in the system that is responsible for their disenfranchisement in the first place.

What we are seeing is a burgeoning crop of education startups and nonprofits, all trying to effect change on a limited scale, often suffering from myopia in their direction and potential. But, are we reversing the trend of disparity? Delaying it? Or perpetuating it? In my opinion, we are simply delaying the inevitable, unsettling, growing experience that this country must undergo in order to advance from this greedy individualistic adolescence to a more mature form of social structure.

POWER

Power can be simplistically defined as the ability or aptitude for influencing or manipulating other human beings. More sophisticated approaches analyze power from specific or contextualized frameworks, such as gender or colonialism. However, there has been little in-depth reflection since the 19th century regarding how power is at work within Being and how it ontologically operates in our reality. Schopenhauer and Nietzsche, the latter greatly influenced by the former, would describe the *progenies of power*, as described in post-colonialism and feminist theory, for instance, as having sprung from deeper forces at work; the Will to Life and the Will to Power, respectively. Yet power, in the simplistic understanding of it, is generally problematic because it is often aligned with the interests of an individual or the interests of a specific group of people, such as a religious body or a nation state. Even though power can be directed towards positive ends, it is difficult to conceive of a power that will not necessitate the oppression of that which gives it power.

So how do philanthropy and nonprofits fit into this picture I am painting? Could they possibly be seen as mechanisms of a greater power that allow for continual oppression? If we were to continue the line of thought explored above, where philanthropy and nonprofits are seen as cushions that soften the blows of the social inequities derived from our current social system of power, then we must view the two as integral components of those systems of power.

NARRATIVE AND LACK OF SOCIAL PERSPECTIVE

However, contraposition, as we see occurring in many religious belief systems, does have the effect of entrenchment and resistance and, in turn, strengthens the resolve of those that adhere to the narrative to cling all the tighter to it. Capitalism v. communism, Christianity v. Islam, conservative v. liberal, etc. In other words, these dichotomous relationships are the ways by which systems legitimate themselves. The problem is how narratives in contraposition are the strongest forces of division within humanity. *What is missing is a metanarrative.*

There are many grand narratives at work today. I would include in this theological narratives. These narratives are quite pervasive and are powerful influences in the lives of billions. The problem is these types of narratives are often seen as incompatible by those within them. So, *is there room for a secular grand narrative that is independent of a theological belief system?* To build such a narrative, it would have to operate as a metanarrative; one would have to start with simple truths regarding existence, such as basic human rights and the desire for healthy society, and build with historical perspective in mind.

Without a metanarrative we are and will continue to be a global society with no clear purpose or mission and with no binding sense of unity. And thus, those who obtain power and influence have been the predominant source of mission and purpose behind the use of social resources and the formation of many societal ideologies. We are a fairly trusting society and we do readily buy in to the messages delegated by both the media and the government, though there do exist enclaves of resistance and, with the most recent issues surrounding surveillance, trust in the government has severely waned.

We have yet to understand our grand narrative, but in order for others to be born into the womb of global peace nothing will be more imperative. For human race to unite at some point a metanarrative that does not conflict with existing theological narratives will have to be established and adopted.

A QUICKENING PACE FOR A DYING RACE

What I write here is a reflection upon an elusive, underlying force at work in U.S. society. How we view reality and how we interpret and interact with our surroundings is largely based on social constructs that we inherit during early childhood. There is a specific construct that I find disquieting, which is the pace at which we live our lives. Both technology and population growth have advanced far faster than our oral and social maturity. And capitalism is fueled through the unreflective and unhampered desire for material objects and the more you want the faster and harder you have to work to get it.

Do we equate, subconsciously, slowing down with retreat or giving in to the pull of death? Is it The Nothing that drives us as fast as we can run in the opposite direction, while ironically coming full circle at the end of our lives?

But with life spans increasing, what if we were to *slow down the education process*? The pace at which we are living is much to blame for why we are now teaching algebra to 5th graders. A roadblock to slowing down society and the pace of education is that we do not have the necessary social support structures in place to allow that, like universal childcare.

FINAL THOUGHT FOR THE EVENING SKY

The point is this: we are here together, flotsam in space, comprised of the same atomic particles, the same particles that stars are made of, self-aware, conscious beings that can share meaning and love. What is more astounding than the little knowledge we have about the universe and what could be more *humbling*? I just hope (would pray if it were in my nature) that on this small planet we are big enough to one day unite in a common aspiration for the living. If we are to weather the explosion of population and the resulting ideological conflicts spurred by the need for survival, *we must join together*.

REFERENCE

Foundation Center. (2013). *Key Facts on U.S. Foundations: 2013 Edition*.

Figure E.1: Liberty Bell Sketch by Tina Urata.

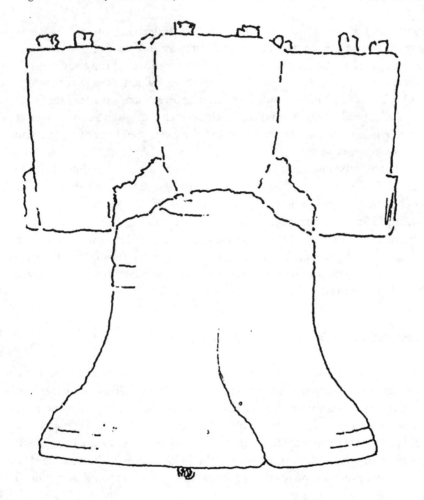

Afterword

LAURENCE BRAHM

The Caligula politics of Washington D.C. has stymied our nation domestically and internationally. Ivory tower think tanks on the payroll of Wall Street, and the military industrial complex, have concocted financial alchemy serving the ultra rich, quashing and impoverishing the middle class, and binding generations into debt. Frustration widens with income gaps. Meanwhile our mainstream media portrays a Disneyesque "Main Street USA," a façade of prosperity glossing over ever-incubating anger and increasing violence in the street.

In the 2016 U.S. election, our democratic system demonstratively reached the abyss of dysfunctionality. The American people were faced with an election in which there was no choice. This election was not about "the lesser of two evils," because whichever presidential candidate won would still be evil. This past 2016 election has been one built on racial fears and inflamed hatred, cementing a caste as opposed to a class system. We may have the privilege of witnessing one of those unusual moments in history—the disintegration of the American empire, which has increasingly looked like empires that have risen and fallen before it. That is, unless we can save it. And that is what Dr. Gregory Tanaka has proposed in this book, a way to save it.

I remember since my childhood, Americans always voted for the candidate of their choice. They argued and campaigned for the person they felt would be best qualified to lead the country. In recent decades, however, the whole voting process has turned meaningless and a waste of time, an embarrassment the rest of the world has come to take note of and pity.

It was not always like that: the American democracy had before been about giving the people a real choice. In fact, it was this positive ideal and dream that America had given the world—the ability to have a choice and act on that choice. However, as the world observed the 2016 presidential election, the American democracy has left its people living with the feeling of forlorn hopelessness, because this time the American people had no choice.

Dr. Gregory Tanaka has unveiled several of the underlying sources of this breakdown of democracy. And our system today is clearly one that needs reform. We cannot talk about "structural reform" of other nations before we undertake it ourselves. Our constitution is not working. Our electoral college is a sham. The structure of our senate ensures corruption with six-year terms and our House of Representatives is all about corruption to keep them elected with only two-year terms. Maybe we no longer need two houses. Maybe we need to abolish the electoral college. Maybe we need to get rid of primaries and presidential election campaigns that last for nearly two or three years. We have to reform our system. And this is the hope that Dr. Tanaka gives us, a template for bottom-up democratic reform that I believe many Americans silently wish for and need. But how to get there?

In terms of change, the status quo promises none. Dr. Tanaka points this out clearly. Our government has become a byzantine bureaucracy that has assured a continued "through train" of policies from Bill Clinton to George Bush Jr. to Barack Obama. The policies of three presidents are almost unchanged, regardless of whoever is elected. About 70% of Americans are disillusioned with both parties. Most of them hate Washington D.C., and see it as the ogre and source of America's own national dysfunctional disorder and local community disempowerment today.

Removal of the Glass-Steagall Act by Bill Clinton led our nation to economic dependency on capital markets in such a way as to create an unregulated and unfettered market fundamentalism that ultimately led to the 2008 financial crisis that brought the house down and served as the precursor to today's massive economic collapse. And ironically, it was this economic asymmetry later that brought the protesters out to "Occupy Wall Street" during Democrat president Obama's administration. Even more ironically, that was when Bush neoliberal policies were solidified and fully came home to roost.

Quantitative easing that began in Bush's era accelerated in Obama's. From Greenspan to Bernanke to Yellen, it's also been a continuing through train of monetary policy in America. Nothing went into the promised infrastructure, renewable energy systems that could make America compete again, or the communities of diversity and color, which have been marginalized outside of the system. What is happening is a perpetuation and expansion of wealth within a very thin band of elites.

In America, with cheap money flooding into the so-called tech stocks a mirage of prosperity that has been created with celebrity tech CEOs, admired by all the rich white millennial generation playing with computers in incubators awash with debt dollars. In San Francisco, right outside Twitter's swash headquarters, poor and destitute line the streets in the way that they have not since the Great Depression, streets awash with drugs and violence. You do not see scenes like that in New Delhi anymore, nor in Dar es Salaam or Kigali.

George W. Bush's war of terror against the world witnessed in its aftermath a spending spree, and the ultimate collapse of America's capital markets due to the entirely leveraged artificial economy created on the back of trading derivatives and using so-called technologies that are in fact social media NSA traps for collecting data and information about our own people. Quantitative easing reinforced the wealth of these elites within the banking and financial systems.

Our financial system perpetuation has mirrored, paralleled and benefited from the endless wars: in Afghanistan, Iraq, Libya and now Syria on the horizon—one more through train of accumulated military interventions and destabilizations that ultimately gave rise to ISIS who we now claim to be the enemy. In fact ISIS, like Al-Qaeda, is our own creation. It all came from the failed, narrow and ideological policies of Washington, funding the wrong people, not understanding what we were doing or the long term implications of ideologically or academically made decisions.

Dr. Tanaka has shown us how these policies of perpetuating what John Kenneth Galbraith once called the "new industrial state" have assured continued empowerment of the elite, disempowerment of most Americans, and along division of caste rather than class lines. In short, a select group of people made money from these wars. But this should not be our national ideology and certainly not our principles. It is not how a democracy behaves.

Unfortunately that false and schizophrenic national identity is built on racial thinking. Nostalgia is embedded in the genocide of Native Americans, which became the foundation of America's national ideology of global expansion and "exceptionalism" for over a century and a half. Have you ever thought about why we celebrate Thanksgiving? It was a victory feast after the white pilgrims massacred Native Americans for their land. Has anything really changed?

The Boston marathon bombing, San Bernadino, Dallas. All such events further disempower Americans and serve as a smokescreen while wealth is further concentrated among only a few.

So revolt is now stirring just as our American revolution did against the British authority and dictatorship of the crown, the imposition of unreasonable taxes and the intervention into our daily lives. As the first American revolution was about identity—for those Americans born on this land rather than those coming from England—those New Americans stood up to fight against an imperial British government that was disconnected and irrelevant to their future. And it is the very same feeling that is beginning to spread quickly across America today.

In America, the nation that preaches human rights to the world, there is one brutal outright racially based killing of an ethnic minority by police every 28 hours. People of color are locked in an income trap dictated more by their race than by their class. Educational systems in neighborhoods of color are under-financed and those neighborhoods are fast slipping into in "economic free fall." These same communities have not benefitted from the great quantitative easing that has re-financed and enriched Wall Street.

Dr. Tanaka has revealed these racial and greed-capital based discrepancies and violent juxtapositions to be somewhat interdependent functions. Indeed, racism lies at the core of a system that ensures disempowering youth of color and multiple forms of diversity, while securitizing white economic and political supremacy for those attached to specific religious cult associations.

Young teenagers are easy prey to drug dealers and in turn, prey to police brutality and police random searches in outright violation of constitutional rights. Once labeled with a felony, one cannot get a job. It is a brand, like the brands put on slaves. Our recent so-called "increase" in employment rates is achieved by putting people into privatized prisons or sending them off to die in desert wars.

Yes, in America our prison system itself has been privatized. How could any country privatize its prison system? This is one of the most grotesque violations of human rights in the history of mankind. Of course, by privatizing prisons, this creates and sustains a business that must of course seek growth: the more prisoners, the more profitable. So we have created a situation where unemployment is being solved, by putting people into prison.

Dr. Tanaka has highlighted so clearly the dichotomy that racism still perpetuates itself in American society, and at the same time taking on the challenge of overcoming racism to achieve full realization of our national dream of an America for Americans that is accepting of other cultures, and moreover embracing of each American for her or his individual identity.

However, America was historically the last society in the world to keep slaves as a component of national policy. For over a hundred years it maintained a national policy of genocide toward Native Americans, and even after the Civil War and civil rights movement a hundred years later, America still functions as a neo-apartheid state. Are African-Hispanic-Arab-Asian-Native Americans equal today to whites?

America preaches democracy and human rights to the world, which now looks at the American democracy no longer as a beacon of freedom, but rather as the largest hypocrisy in the world. As an American living abroad and on the outside looking in, the cities of Dallas and Orlando ring like Peshawar and Mogadishu. Gun violence seems to reign in the United States, at least in the eyes of the rest of the world.

Now could those Hollywood movies that depict a grim future for America with only a rich elite controlling everything serve as bad entertainment, or a projection of the reality that this cabal wishes to have Americans begin to accept? But what happened in Dallas could now spread across America. This is not about the approach of Malcolm X versus Martin Luther King. It is about people who do not accept the distribution of wealth of today and are standing up against a flawed economic system that is in the process of deterioration if not self-cannibalization.

Yet in the past 12 months alone, I have been fortunate to meet with leaders and thinkers abroad who have all given me a fresh sense of hope—and an unshakable belief that it is still possible to have and work toward a democracy in its purest and best form, that serves the interests of the people and requires in the long term protecting the environment in the interest of human health, and survivability of mankind.

In the Royal Kingdom of Bhutan, its elected Prime Minister Tshering Tobgay has talked with me concerning the fragility of environment and as a state leader, the importance of prioritizing environment in the interest of people, their heritage, and health.

Iceland's President Olafar Grimsson reflected on how he pulled his country through the 2008 financial crisis that decimated the nation, by ignoring the IMF advice and instead seeking policies that could build real economics owned by the people themselves.

In Senegal, founders of the African Consensus movement, activist Alioune Tine and rapper Didier Awadi, reflected on how they went to the streets to lead protests in 2011 that ended attempts by then President Wade to change the constitution and extend his term indefinitely, reviving free elections with multi-parties and multi-media organizations covering the politics. In their mind, America has no right to lecture Africa about democracy. When Obama spoke before the African Union in the last year of his term, the leaders were infuriated listening to him lecturing them about transparency and the need to end money politics. Because in the minds of Africans, this is exactly what America's is now lacking.

Just this week in Austria, in my meeting with author of the classic *Megatrends*, John Naisbit, pondered the question of how a nation like America that once gave us leaders like John F. Kennedy (whom Naisbit served as advisor to) is now reduced to delivering candidates like Hilary Clinton and Donald Trump.

In Nepal, at the most recent convention of the Himalayan Consensus dedicated to environmental protection and community empowerment, leaders reflected on how Nepal has come to re-write its constitution embracing multi-parties, including Marxist, Communist, and business elite, within the broader framework of participatory democracy, after a decade long Maoist insurgency. They looked to many models for a solution, but not ours.

All around the world, people are clamoring for democracy and yet the greatest irony I have encountered in my life is that the democracy that I grew up in—and had once served as the model for this wide world to follow—has lost its own way. What Gregory Tanaka is calling for is a return to that spirit of democracy, and this time in an even better form. With this thought we receive a fresh injection of inspiration: the belief that democracy is still possible and that the country that gave the world its first working model of a citizen-led democracy can once again find its way.

So yes, what is erupting on the surface of America are the mind-numbing expressions and extensions of a racializing, fear-mongering media and an elitist federal government that are both under the direction and control of the same neo-liberal system and its "quantitative easing," "clamor for war," and "bank bailouts" that have done nothing but enrich the white and "uber wealthy"—while impoverishing the middle class and fragmenting the communities of diversity and color.

In 2016, it turned out not to matter who became president of the United States; the dysfunctional politics was bound to continue. Further deterioration of our system and our global credibility is the predictable outcome. Hope lies in neither political party and certainly not with our politicians who claim to represent us. In fact, they do not. America's only hope lies in its own people and communities solving our own problems locally. From the knowledge that arises with their experience, new approaches and models will arise, and with them new values. Collectively, the alternative will become the new mainstream.

But now, in the midst of this democratic unraveling, Dr. Gregory Tanaka's book speaks on behalf of the alternative movement that will become our new mainstream. He provides more than an analysis of our current self-created imbroglio. This book constitutes a call to specific, concrete action, urging all of us to rise up, go out there, and work together to bring back both the spirit and function of democracy, this time to a nation that had once ably served as its cradle.

Proposed Legislation for a New Division Within the United States Department of Education

D'ANDREA ROBINSON

To help establish, enhance, and increase agency and communication between local education professionals and communities and the U.S. Congress and U.S. Department of Education for the purpose of creating and promoting new education policy.

Be it enacted by the Senate and House of Representatives of the United States of America in Congress assembled,

SECTION 1. SHORT TITLE

This Act may be cited as the "Democratic Engagement for Education Act."

SECTION 2. PURPOSE

The purposes of this Act are:

(1) to involve local educational professionals through the creation of professional development think tanks in the national education discussion for creating education-based policy; (2) to establish relationships between national officials and local school educators and administrators by forming regional centers where local school communities can communicate with and have access to national policymakers; and (3) to enhance the implementation

of education-based legislation because local educational professionals will have an opportunity to provide input.

SECTION 3. DEFINITION

[For the purpose of the assignment, this section is omitted. This section will be completed for the purpose of the actual legislation.]

SECTION 4. DEMOCRATIC ENGAGEMENT FOR EDUCATION PROGRAM

PROGRAM AUTHORIZED

(a) IN GENERAL. A new division within the US Department of Education would be created in order to reach out and support the creation of educational delivery models and approaches at the local community and school district level then forwarding them on to policy makers in Washington, D.C. The Democratic Engagement for Education program allows education professionals from school districts around the country to collaborate through professional development with national policymakers on solutions for issues in the teaching practice and school community. The data collected is synthesized through each state's Democratic Engagement for Education office and is channeled through to Washington, D.C. in order to inform education-related policy.

SECTION 5. APPLICATIONS

(a) IN GENERAL. The new division, known as DEE [Democratic Engagement for Education] is implemented on a state level as an extension of each state's Education Department and includes five members. Directors of DEE convene on a biannual basis to prioritize issues and solutions facing national public education which are then sent to Washington, D.C. policymakers.

(b) CONTENTS. The following are the objectives of DEE: 1) Learn school culture within communities across the country, 2) Develop relationships with local education professionals, 3) Promote professional development in the teaching practice, and 4) Create effective education-based policy.

Department Structure: 5 people

1. *Department Director*
   a. *Paid elected official who represents the face of DEE for the state*
   b. *National liaison to USDOE*
   c. *Meet semi-annually with all 50 Directors to share data and draft legislation*
   d. *Manages entire state Department*
2. *Data Analyst*
   a. *Paid state employee who collects and aggregates information collected from school sites during professional development meetings*
   b. *Evaluates qualitative and quantitative data received to inform director of region's education climate*
   c. *Creates reports on top priorities facing Kindergarten through 12th grade public education within the state*
3. *K-12 Public Education Administrator*
   a. *Paid state employee who organizes and facilitates school site professional development meetings and supports the region administrators*
   b. *Researches newest information on teaching practices in order to assist and provide suggestions to education professionals on resolutions to problems that arise*
   c. *Meets regularly with Department Director, Department Data Analyst, and School District Superintendents to remain knowledgeable of education practices within the state*
4. *K-12 Public Education Liaisons (two positions)*
   a. *Paid state employee who schedules professional development meetings with school sites, assists with facilitating professional development meetings, gathers data from the meetings, and supports school site administrators*
   b. *Visit school sites: classroom walk-throughs, evaluations with school site administrators and faculty meeting participation*

As mentioned in the breakdown of the department, DEE Administrators hold meetings at school sites during staff professional development time in order to 1) dialogue about issues affecting education in the community, 2) discuss newly researched model schools and teaching practices that have been acknowledged as having local and/or national success, and 3) create solutions for education community problems. The information gathered from the meetings is synthesized by the data analyst to generate a state education climate report, which delineates the educational needs and solutions of the school site. These specific meetings are known as a School Community Assembly (SCA).

The SCA is the school community collective which includes but is not limited to:

- *K–12 Teachers*
- *Elementary, Middle School, and/or High School Counselors (at least one from the High School level)*

- *Elementary, Middle School, and High School Principals (at least one from each education level)*
- *Elementary, Middle School, and High School Vice Principals or Deans (at least one from each education level)*
- *School District Administrator (i.e., Educational Services Superintendent)*

The School Community Assembly is closed to specifically the above mentioned school community members.

SECTION 6. STATE USE OF FUNDS

This Act would be funded through federal education grants and can be defined as a TRIO program. State grants would also be used to fund the Department's 5 employee salaries initially at the amount of $405,000 plus benefits: Department Director, $110,000; Data Analyst, $85,000; Operations Manager ($80,000), and two Liaisons (at $65,000 each).

SECTION 7. SUBGRANTS

[For the purpose of the assignment, this section is omitted. This section will be completed for the purpose of the actual legislation.]

SECTION 8. RESEARCH, EVALUATION, AND DISSENATION

(a) IN GENERAL. The Secretaries shall enter into an agreement with the National Academy of Sciences, under which the National Academy of Sciences shall conduct a study and evaluation, including a report, on best practices that support the purposes of this Act, including best practices— for gathering data across the state and country with the purpose of informing education-based legislation.

(b) SPECIFC ACTIVITIES. The evaluation described in subsection (a) shall carry out all of the following:

1. Assess the impact of each state's department using evidence of the program's outcomes, including—increased engagement at staff professional development meetings because of the opportunity relay information that will be enacted into policy.

2. Identify factors that foster or hinder the successful implementation of each state's department program.

3. Utilize the data on best practices, as described in subsection (a) to provide information to each state department that can be used to drive improvement.
4. Generate and disseminate information about best practices as described in subsection (a) that are associated with increased data being shared with policymakers that will inform educational policy.

(c) REPORTING SCHEDULE AND PLAN. The Secretaries shall work with the National Academy of Sciences to establish and approve a reporting schedule and a research, evaluation, and dissemination plan for the evaluation described in subsection (a).

(d) REPORT TO CONGRESS. The Secretaries shall submit an annual report on the lessons learned through the program funded under this Act.

SECTION 9. GENERAL PROVISIONS

[For the purpose of the assignment, this section is omitted. This section will be completed for the purpose of the actual legislation.]

SECTION 10. AUTHORIZATION OF APPROPRIATIONS

[TBD]

Be it enacted by the Senate and House of Representatives of the United States of America in Congress assembled,

SECTION 1. SHORT TITLE

This Act may be cited as the "Democratic Engagement for Education Act."

SECTION 2. PURPOSE

The purposes of this Act are:

(1) to involve local educational professionals in the national discussion to create new education-based policy through the creation of professional development think tanks; (2) to establish relationships between federal officials and local public school educators and administrators by forming regional centers where local school communities can communicate with and have access to federal policymakers; and (3) to enhance the implementation of

education-based legislation through input, ideas and/or evidence received from local educational professionals who now have the opportunity to contribute early and directly to education policy formation and improvement.

SECTION 3. DEFINITIONS

(TBD)

SECTION 4. DEMOCRATIC ENGAGEMENT FOR PUBLIC EDUCATION PROGRAMS

(TBD)

Contributors

Benita M. Baines, the Governor's Appointee for the California Employment Development Department, Workforce Services Branch, received her masters in public administration at California State University Stanislaus and a masters and a doctorate in educational administration from Mills College.

Laurence Brahm, lawyer, economist, and international statesman, is chair of the Himalayan Consensus and believes that conflicts are not driven by clashes of culture and religion but by economic disempowerment and marginalization of cultural identity. The solution is economic and people to people connectivity by mobilizing shared resources and harnessing technological opportunities that are smart, green, and blue.

Ruth Cotton currently works with clients to foster sustainable and healthy business growth, and marketing initiatives, and performs creative storytelling through graphic design, photography, and short film. She has a BA degree in English literature from UC Berkeley, a master's in educational leadership and master's in business administration from Mills College.

Derek Fenner is an artist, educator, and researcher living in Oakland, California. He earned his MFA from the Jack Kerouac School of Disembodied Poetics at Naropa University and a MA and an EdD in educational leadership from Mills College. Formerly an arts educator and administrator in the Massachusetts juvenile justice system, he is the arts learning program manager at the Alameda County Office of Education in California.

Roberto Flores obtained a BA in anthropology in 1971 from UCLA, a master's in bilingual education in 2000 from Loyola Marymount University, and a doctorate in international and intercultural education from the University of Southern California. His dissertation explored the informal mutual learning relationship between Chicanxs and Zapatistac Communities. Roberto's current work on autonomy is inspired by a life-long search, study and activism for non-statist horizontal democracy.

Stephen Gawrylewski (BA, history; MA cultural studies of religion; MBA/MA, business and education) is currently working as an information systems and operations consultant with clients in the energy sector.

Jason A. Cook-Harvey is currently an arts and social sciences teacher. A veteran of the U.S. Air Force, Mr. Cook holds a BA in American history with an emphasis in holistic health from San Francisco State University and a MA in educational leadership from Mills College. He is also a certified nutrition educator and master gardener and is pursuing a Credential in Special Education.

Lars Henrich works for Technische Universitat, Kaiserslautern, and holds a MBA/MA in educational leadership from Mills College and a master's in pedagogy, political science and philosophy from Johannes Gutenberg University Mainz.

Emily Kaplowitz (MBA/MA in educational leadership) is currently following her passion at a charter school in Newark, New Jersey, where she is working with high school graduates and supporting them through college.

Jaguanana Lathan, who earned her EdD in educational leadership from Mills College, is Principal in Residence at the San Diego County Office of Education.

Shane Maldonado currently holds a joint MBA/MA in educational leadership and works as an education consultant in the San Francisco Bay Area.

Peter L. McLaren, PhD, whose work has been translated into 30 languages and praised by Paolo Freire, Noam Chomsky and Henry Giroux, is Distinguished Professor in Critical Studies at Chapman University and Honorary Director of the Center for Critical Studies in Education at Northeast Normal University, China.

Adrienne D. Oliver (MFA, EdD) is Professor of English at Laney College in Oakland, California, where she is a hip hop scholar and curriculum catalyst.

David Reed (MS, EdD) currently serves as Interim Dean of Academic Support and Learning Technologies at Canada College in Redwood City, California. His work is focused on deconstructing barriers to access and success for students and building learning-centered programs and services.

Merritt Richmond has a master's degree in educational leadership from Mills College and a BA in art history from Duke University. Merritt currently works with school leadership teams and teachers to think strategically about their values and to bring joy, creativity, and natural curiosity into the lives of their students as they work collaboratively towards those values.

Jacque Roby is a project management and communications professional who holds a BA degree in English language and literature from the University of California at Berkeley and an MBA from Mills College. She is currently Assistant Project Manager for PG&E.

D'Andrea Robinson, MEd, and currently a doctoral student at San Francisco State University, has been an educator for over a decade in San Francisco Bay Area classrooms. She is dedicated to championing equitable public education to students of color.

Gregory K. Tanaka, a former acting law school dean and bank president, is Co-Director of the Center for the Study of Democracy and Social Change and Executive Director of Anamatangi Polynesian Voices in East Palo Alto, CA.

Andrew Urata is a fifth-grade teacher at Rocketship Mateo Sheedy Elementary School in San Jose, California, and is a gamification designer.

Tina Urata (BA, Japanese Studies) works as an intercultural trainer for Brookfield Global Relocation Services. Formerly the course director for the Boy Scouts of America in Santa Clara and Monterey Counties in California, she also edited *The Crucible of Trials and Tribulations: Memories of a Meiji Missionary, Gi'ichi Tanaka* (2005).

Evangelia Ward-Jackson is Academic Dean at Making Waves Academy Middle School in Richmond, California. She holds three master's degrees from UC Berkeley, an EdD from Mills College, and a PhD from Forrest Fire College of Theology. Evangelia is a family-oriented person who enjoys singing, writing, and cultivating others toward success.

Index

F

G